Japanese Studies
in Shakespeare
and His Contemporaries

International Studies in Shakespeare and His Contemporaries

Jay L. Halio, General Editor

Central and Eastern European Studies, ed. J. Limon and J. L. Halio
French Studies, ed. J.-M. Maguin and Michèle Willems
Russian Essays, ed. A. Parfenov and Joseph G. Price
(In preparation)

Israeli Studies, ed. Avraham Oz
Italian Studies, ed. M. Marrapodi

Editorial Advisory Committee

Japanese Studies
in Shakespeare
and His Contemporaries

Edited by
Yoshiko Kawachi

DELAWARE

Newark: University of Delaware Press
London: Associated University Presses

PR
653
.J37
1998

Associated University Presses
440 Forsgate Drive
Cranbury, NJ 08512

Associated University Presses
16 Barter Street
London WC1A 2AH, England

Associated University Presses
P.O. Box 338, Port Credit
Mississauga, Ontario
Canada L5G 4L8

The paper used in this publication meets the requirements
of the American National Standard for Permanence of Paper
for Printed Library Materials Z39.48-1984.

Library of Congress Cataloging-in-Publication Data

Japanese studies in Shakespeare and his contemporaries / edited by Yoshiko Kawachi.
    p.   cm. — (International studies in Shakespeare and his contemporaries)
    Includes bibliographical references and index.
    ISBN 0-87413-673-3
    1. English drama—Early modern and Elizabethan, 1500–1600—History and criticism.   2. Shakespeare, William, 1564–1616—Criticism and interpretation.   3. English drama—17th century—History and criticism.   4. Shakespeare, William, 1564–1616—Contemporaries. 5. Criticism—Japan.   I. Kawachi, Yoshiko, 1936– .   II. Series.
PR653.J37   1998
822'.309—dc21   98-15801
                                                                              CIP

03499

Contents

Preface

SINCE Shakespeare was introduced in Japan in the middle of the nineteenth century, he has been not only a symbol of Western culture but also a target of scholarship and criticism. His works have been translated into Japanese, read and performed, and sometimes adapted for the Japanese stage and film. Lovingly called "Sao," Shakespeare has been a general favorite in Japan.

The present collection is devoted to the work of Japanese scholars. It presents some fresh thoughts on various aspects of Shakespeare and other English Renaissance dramatists. Some of these essays were originally written in Japanese or have been previously published in journals and books circulated in Japan only. But all of the essays translated into English or written in English are worth reading because they present recent scholarship and criticism by Japanese scholars.

Arata Ide analyzes the internal and external forces evoking the devil's appearance during the performance of Marlowe's *Doctor Faustus* and discusses this topic in a theatrical and a social context. Mariko Ichikawa attempts to estimate the length of time needed by exiting actors in Shakespearean plays, considering the features of the Elizabethan stage. Yoshiko Kawachi discusses the relationships between Japan's reception of Shakespeare and the concurrent cultural development of Japan, referring to the first Japanese adaptation of *The Merchant of Venice*. Yukari Yoshihara considers the problem of money and sexuality in *Measure for Measure,* focusing on substitution, exchange, replacement, and sexual reproduction, with which the play is concerned. Soji Iwasaki discusses the first performances of *Macbeth*, considering the architectural background, the stage *tableau,* and the iconography of the play. Miki Suehiro discusses the relationship between the representation of the female body and the economic principle in *The Winter's Tale*. Ted Motohashi analyzes *The Tempest* in a colonial context, focusing on the discourse of cannibalism and considering the plural representations of selves and others. Akiko Kusunoki examines the construction of female subjectivity in early modern England, centering on two plays, *The Tragedy of Mariam*

7

by Lady Elizabeth Cary and *Love's Victory* by Lady Mary Wroth. Shoichiro Kawai evaluates Fletcher's dramaturgy and tries to solve the mystery of Fletcher's tremendous popularity in the seventeenth and the early eighteenth century. Manabu Noda investigates the perception of Shakespeare's characters in Garrick's period, emphasizing the psychology of the body or the physical discourse. Noriyuki Harada asserts that Johnson cares about the individuality of Shakespeare's characters and that the difference between Johnson and his antagonists should be reexamined. These essays will be interesting to a wider and more varied audience who otherwise might not have easy access to Shakespearean studies in Japan.

The editor wishes to express her thanks to the Editorial Advisory Committee of *International Studies in Shakespeare and His Contemporaries,* chaired by Professor Jay L. Halio, and to Professor Ted Motohashi who assisted her in collecting and editing the essays for publication. In addition, it is a distinct pleasure that this book is published with close and friendly cooperation between European, American, and Japanese scholars. The editor feels keenly that Shakespeare is indeed worldwide and that Shakespearean studies should be more international. The editor also appreciates the warm support of the International Shakespeare Association for this project, as well as the kindness of the University of Delaware Press and Associated University Presses.

Japanese Studies
in Shakespeare
and His Contemporaries

Doctor Faustus and the Appearance of the Devil

ARATA IDE

1

SOME interesting episodes regarding the performance of *Doctor Faustus* (hereafter *DF*) are classified as legendary. This is due to the common report that, during the performance, a real devil appeared and threw the audience into consternation. For instance:

> The visible apparition of the Devill on the stage at the Belsavage Play-house, in Queen Elizabeths dayes (to the great amazement both of the actors and spectators) while they were there prophanely playing the History of Faustus (the truth of which I have heard from many now alive, who well remember it) there being some distracted with that feareful sight.[1]

It is difficult to believe that the devil really appeared or even that this episode itself holds any historical reliability. Fortunately, however, the storyteller can be identified, and it is possible to understand the nuances of this legend. The episode cited above appears in *Histrio-Mastix* (1633) where William Prynne presents the event as an example of God's judgment on profane actors and playgoers. His intention is quite clear; he exploits the devil's appearance to justify and strengthen his denunciation of the theater.

Here is another report in which a similar critical attitude can be observed:

> Certaine Players at Exeter, acting upon the stage the tragical storie of Dr. Faustus the Conjurer; as a certain number of Devels kept everie one his circle there, and as Faustus was busie in his magicall invocations, on a sudden they were all dasht, every one harkning other in the eare, for they were all perswaded, there was one devell too many amongst them; and so after a little pause desired the people to pardon them, they could go no further with this matter; the people also understanding the thing as it was, every man hastened to be first out of

dores. The players (as I heard it) contrarye to their custome spending the night in reading and in prayer got them out of the town the next morning.[2]

The man who described this episode cannot be identified, but as seen through his sarcastic remarks about the actors' haste, he is obviously inviting the readers to draw a lesson from God's judgment, as Prynne does.

It is worth paying attention, not to the credibility of the story, but to the writer's purpose in attaching a moral to the devil's appearance. Devils can be seen not only in the theater, but also in the church, as we find in *The Wonders of This Windie Winter* (1613). One may ask, why did the devil make his appearance in the church? The reason is clear: "the parishioners haue an evil custome among them, for continually, be it either in seruice or sermon time, they wil stand in troupes of foure or fiue in a company in diuers parts of the Church, conferring and talking of worldly affaiers, not regarding at all the words of the Minister, but rather behaue themselves, as it were in a faier or market."[3] In this moral, we find the explanation that the devil necessarily appears wherever the profane flock together and God inflicts a terrifying punishment upon them.

It can be said, therefore, that there is an important meaning in the stories of the devil's appearance. The devil was considered to be "God's hangman" who executed God's punishment against the reprobates, so it is no wonder that he appeared in places which were morally degenerate and attracted impious people.[4] The person who pretended to have religious authority manipulated the devil for his/her own use. The devil could be an indispensable instrument in attacking or even rejecting a person or a group in society. By inventing a story that the devil had direct contact with the victim or even possessed him, and sometimes making this individual the cause of disasters, the authorities could stigmatize those whom they wanted to reject. At the same time, this attack against an opponent in league with the devil legitimatize their own divine order and authority.[5] Puritans frantically disseminated the formula <Theater = Devil> which we find in the statement, "Play-house is the Devils Chappell," their purpose being to eliminate the theater from society by linking the two closely.[6] In the episodes concerning the performance of *DF*, the Puritans' strategy can be discerned and, when considered in the context of Puritan criticism, these episodes suggest a desire to eliminate the theater.

Legendary episodes about *DF* are also seen in a text produced by John Aubrey the antiquary free from puritanical bias. He tells us that Edward Alleyn "played a Demon, with six others, and was in the midst of the play surpriz'd by an apparition of the Devil."[7]

The sequel to this story is that Alleyn's retirement from the stage was due to the incident. It is most likely, however, that Aubrey's account originated in the biased discourse (which can be obliquely perceived by his skeptical stance), and furthermore, that all the *DF* legends are merely baseless fiction fabricated by an antitheatrical prejudice. If this is the case, we have no grounds for believing in "the terrors" of the audience and the actors, or "the devil's appearance."

It is useful to ask why the devil had to appear during the performance of *DF*. The devil in *DF* cannot have been novel enough to be the object of terror or criticism. According to John Melton, dramatic presentation of the devil was common, for "a man may behold shagge—hayr'd Deuills runne roaring ouer the Stage with Squibs in their mouthes."[8] His comment reminds us of Titivillus or Satan in the morality plays, and this kind of character was also quite familiar to the Elizabethan audience. Then, what prompted these legendary episodes of *DF?*

A necromancer who conjures up a spirit in Latin and makes a contract had certainly never been staged before Faustus.[9] Considering the novelty of this, it is possible to discern the audience's shock at the realism. The invocation scene probably had such great verisimilitude and was so impressive that it stimulated the audience's imagination and "work'd on their fancy."[10] Consequently, they mistook the actor playing the devil for a real one. For the Puritan, the sensation the play caused became a target for criticism.

Is this the most convincing explanation for *DF* legend? Partly so. But when we consider the significance of the devil to the audience, as well as for the strategy of the critical Puritan, the legend ceases to be a report merely telling us of the dramatic effects of a scene some 20 lines long and the cunningness of the Puritan. Rather, it turns out to be the key to understanding *DF* within the creative tension between the theater and its social context, and to examining the dynamism *DF* had for the audience and society.

2

Surely the loude grones of rauing sicke men: the strugling panges of soules departing: In euery house griefe striking vp an Allarum: Seruants crying out for maisters: wiues for husbands, parents for children, children for their mothers. . . .[11]

This quotation from Dekker shows that London was a hell on earth. Early in September 1592, the plague had already "greatly increased with in the City" and was rampant until the end of the next year. The plague burials registered in the cities and liberties totaled 10,775 in 1593.[12] England had not experienced such a large scale and prolonged disaster since the prevalence of the bubonic plague in 1563. Thomas Lodge noted the plague's principle symptoms: high fever, rigidity of the body, mental derangement and "blewnesse and blacknesse appearing about the sores and carbuncles."[13] Not until the nineteenth century was it known that the bacterium *Pasteurella pestis* caused these symptoms. Physicians in the Elizabethan age tried to discover efficacious treatments for the disease in vain, and medical charlatans drove a prosperous trade by taking advantage of people's fears. An angry Dekker accused physicians of their inability: "Their drugs turned to durt, their simples were simple things: *Galen* could do no more good than Sir Giles Goosecap: *Hipocrates, Auicen, Paracelsus, Rasis, Fernelius*, with all their succeeding rabble of Doctors and Water-casters, were at their wits end."[14]

Elizabethans could not cure the disease, but they thought they knew its major cause. They had only to look in the Bible and take note of Jehovah's plague on the children of Israel. Simon Forman, in "A Discourse of the Plague," classifies the cause of the pestilence into three categories ("natvrale," "dyvele," "god") and elucidates the cause in length by quoting the Scriptures.[15] Forman's attitude toward the disease implicitly suggests that he despaired of all human remedies, while believing that divine sovereignty would punish sinners and heal them of the disease with His miraculous grace. For people placed in an extreme situation, however, it probably did not matter whether the ultimate cause was natural or supernatural. To be freed from anxiety and horror must have been paramount to all else. Unfortunately, there were few physicians who could give the people any consolation. The total number of physicians, surgeons, apothecaries and practitioners in London, either licensed or unlicensed, is estimated at about 500. Since London had a population of approximately 200,000 in 1593, there was at most one practitioner for every 400 individuals.[16] Even if a patient was lucky enough to be able to consult a licensed doctor, he could not have obtained a positive promise of recovery from the plague at all. He only knew that he could not be saved without the miraculous intervention of a supernatural being, and that "yf the black spots be seen on one that hath the blacke plague then he dyeth *without* remedie."[17]

The people did not have to look very far for consolation. There is no doubt that not only taverns and recreational facilities, but also the church, the authority in matters of the supernatural, played an important role in offering them solace. The church was able to explain the tragic situation persuasively enough. And the church alone could assemble the people under license, while other meetings were regulated due to "dangerous infection."[18] The church saw the plague as a scourge of God to punish stiff-necked people, and promised relief through repentance and prayer. It may readily be imagined that, at the time of the plague, the people's devotion to a supernatural power was temporarily revived and that they gathered in church to seek a remedy. James Bamford says in the preface of *A Short Dialogve concerning the Plagves Infection* (1603) that "Ye frequent Friday Lecture as dilligently (euer since the Plague was kindled) as in winter nights: wheras many in & about London are winter hearers, attending the word when they haue nothing else to do."[19] Dekker had good reason to say "This was a rare worlde for the Church."

It is also quite natural to think that superstitious people, who had already declined religious commitment to the reformed church, would have sought moral support not from church, which was trying to "eliminate the protective ecclesiastical magic which had kept the threat of sorcery under control," but rather from sorcerers or witches able to offer magical relief.[20] This tendency must have been most conspicuous when the people were thrown into an extreme situation such as this plague. They could turn to the devil as a last resort for help, for he had been not only an executioner of God's judgment, but also a heroic figure who ruled the world and granted all requests in exchange for souls. At the sight of the Clown in dire poverty, Wagner says, "Alas, poore slaue, see how pouerty iesteth in his nakednesse, the vilaine is bare, and out of seruice, and so hungry, that I know he would giue his soule to the Diuel for a shoulder of mutton, though it were blood rawe." (A/366–69)[21] Undoubtedly, the Clown was not the only one who craved the devil's help when an inescapable hell unfolded itself before one's eyes. There must have been many who thought "if I be troubled with such a malady, what care I whether the devil himself, or any of his ministers by God's permission, redeem me?"[22] In *Spirituall Perseruatiues against the Pestilence* (1593), Henry Holland censures the people who ask the devil for help while being tested by God:

> In time of triall, wherein the wicked run to any of the creatures, rather then to God, yea sometimes to Sathan himselfe, before they seek any refuge or comfort in the Almighty. Such as rest in the ordinarie

creatures only, are meere Atheists: such as seeke to Sathan and his
artes, are bewitched Papists, idolaters and such like.[23]

3

Puritans took advantage of the disaster to denounce their enemies as being corrupt. It was inevitable that the theater became
the first victim of their attack. The plague inflicted such a great
loss of lives by God's permission that the theater seemed to be a
hotbed of disease and vice. "To play in plagetime is to encreasce
the plage by infection: to play out of plagetime is to draw the plage
by offendinges of God vpon occasion of such playes."[24] Holland
praises the Mayor of London for his endeavour to "cast downe the
deuillish theaters, the nurceries of whoredome and vncleannesse"
and requests him to exterminate "the spiritual causes" as well as
"the naturall causes" of the plague, for "they are *Cupids* and *Venus*
temples, they are Bacchus and Sathans pallaces, they corrupt the
youth of your citie intollerablie: all eies can see, and all chast eares
can witnes & some of the masters of these euils are driuen to
confesse (when the Lord hath humbled them by some great terrors)
in extreame passions and pangs of death."[25] The theater, on the
other hand, had no persuasive counterargument and could not
prove its innocence against their attack. Hence, it was more dia-
bolically represented as "deuillish theatres" or "Sathans pallaces"
than would have been normal.

In the winter of 1593–94, the plague abated, allowing a short
term of performances, but on 2 February, the Privy Council cautiously ordered restraint on the ground that "the dangerous infection of the plague, by Gods great mercy and goodnes well slaked,
may again very dangerously encrease and break foorth."[26] In April
and May, theaters were open, but the authorities kept a constant
vigilance over them until October, for "infected people, after theire
longe keepinge in, and before they be clered of theire disease and
infection, beinge desirous of recreacion, vse to resort to suche
assemblies, where throughe heate and thronge, they infecte manie
sound personnes."[27] *DF* was performed and enthusiastically wel-
comed by the audience at a time when people were still haunted
by the plague, and when the theater was closely associated with
the devil on an imaginary level.[28] As if intending to offend Puritan
susceptibilities, the Admiral's Men staged a play in which the devil
took an active part, and the people, for their part, willingly went

to the "deuillish" theater to see the devil and "seeke to Sathan and his artes."

What exactly did *DF* offer to the audience "desirous of recreacion"?

4

Faustus' skepticism, no doubt, had a great impact upon the audience, particularly upon intellectuals like Nashe.[29] We should take into consideration, however, that the groundlings under great stress "after theire longe keeping in" were probably there, not for theological arguments, but for "sports." The Clown, who "runnes vp and downe crying" at the appearance of two devils, has conjured them up after learning that the devil can offer him some entertainment: "Would you teach me to raise vp *Banios* and *Belcheos?*" (A/419–20) It is no wonder that disastrous circumstances such as disease, poverty, and starvation aroused the same desire within the audience. They would probably have given their souls to the devil for temporary pleasures, if not for a shoulder of mutton.

> O this is admirable! here I ha stolne one of doctor Faustus coniuring books, and ifaith I meane to search some circles for my owne vse: now wil I make al the maidens in our parish dance at my pleasure starke naked before me, and so by that meanes I shal see more then ere I felt, or saw yet. (A/949–53)

Through the devil's assistance, the audience obtained in the imaginary space of the theater what they could not in the actual world, and that space was an escapist realm which magically endowed them with a wide range of possibilities. The devil had such a great hold over both worlds of fantasy and actuality that he could easily mix one with the other, and the audience craved the devil's assistance to see the dangereous illusions which might be realized by his power.

What the audience asked for was to be "cloy'd with all things that delight the heart of man." Mephostophiles complains, "How am I vexed with these vilaines charmes? From *Constantinople* am I hither come, / Onely for pleasure of these damned slaues." (A/ 1026–28) Certainly, since he has to appear for the mere pleasure of the vulgar fellows, there is a good case for his saying so. But Faustus, in employing the devil for pleasure's sake, also does the same thing as "these damned slaues." For instance, immediately after the decision to discard his theological study and deliver the lofty manifesto to be a demi-god in power, honour and omnipotence, he substitutes his intellectual will for material appetite.

> Ile haue them flye to *India* for gold,
> Ransacke the Ocean for orient pearle,
> And search all corners of the new found world
> For pleasant fruites and princely delicates.
>
> (A/114–17)

Here, Faustus is dominated by the same materialism as the Clown's.[30] He cannot free himself from an intense desire to escape, and gives himself up to ephemeral delights. The only difference between Faustus and the Clown is that Faustus is privileged to taste what the devil offers as much as he likes.

Almost all the pleasures in *DF* are offered in a spectacle. The play is interspersed with entertainments like the dance of the devils, or the pageant of the Seven Deadly Sins, aiding the viewer to momentarily evade the dilemma arising from his consciousness of terminability and religious melancholy. The devil is the director of these entertainments and entices Faustus to indulge himself in fleeting pleasures: "*Faustus* we are come from hell in person to shew thee some pastime: sit downe and thou shalt behold the seuen deadly sinnes appeare to thee in their owne proper shapes and likenesse." Faustus welcomes his offer and becomes addicted to these narcotic pleasures, which the audience shares with him at the same time as spectators of the play-within-the-play.

But Faustus cannot be satisfied with his role as a spectator. Travelling around the world with Mephostophiles, he comes to Rome to see St. Peter's feast. He askes that "There did we view the Kingdomes of the world, / And what might please mine eye, I there beheld. / Then in this shew let me an Actor be." (B/875–77) In order to get more pleasure out of the devil's entertainment, Faustus himself participates in it as an actor.[31] What is more interesting, however, is that later in the play, Faustus transforms himself into the entertainer who acts as intermediary between the devil and the audience and who entertains them with demonic magic. After this transformation, it is quite natural for the audience to feel a stronger affinity to Faustus, for he acquires the position not of a profane magician, but rather of an entertaining hero. The Duke of Vanholt, who is one of the spectators on stage, voices the audience's feeling toward Faustus:

> *Lady.* My Lord,
> We are much beholding to this learned man.
> *Duke.* So are we Madam, which we will recompence
> With all the loue and kindnesse that we may.
> His Artfull sport, driues all sad thoughts away.
>
> (B/1769–73)

Critics who attach great importance to the theological conflict and morality in *DF* are embarrassed with the slap-stick and vain spectacles which predominate the play as well as Faustus' enthusiasm for them. They explain these scenes as a series of diversions, by attributing them to Faustus' gradual degradation.[32] His intimacy with a succubus in the guise of Helen is, therefore, interpreted as the climax of this degradation, making his perdition decisive. Certainly, theological logic demands this kind of reading, and it is one-sided to ignore this aspect of the play, but the dramatic current runs in a different way. The spectators, watching these magical entertainments, probably could not have condemned him from a theological or ethical viewpoint, for in the play they are urged to take part in the devil's performance with Faustus as the entertainer, and they must have been more than willing to do so. The son of a London merchant described by Francis Kirkman makes an interesting comment on *DF*, in which we may trace their willingness: "One of my Schoolfellows lent me *Doctor Faustus*, which also pleased me, especially when he travelled in the Air, saw all the World, and did what he listed."[33]

5

Faustus, as the entertainer, generously shares the pleasurable wonders and adventures which he has obtained with the audience, that they are able to enjoy them to the full with him. But he is often seized with religious melancholy and forced to face reality, where "all our pleasure" is "turned to melancholy." For instance, at the scene of the contract with Lucifer, Faustus' joyful intoxication due to his hope of omnipotence suddenly turns to horror:

> *Consummatum est,* this Bill is ended,
> And Faustus hath bequeath'd his soule to *Lucifer.*
> But what is this inscription on mine arme?
> *Homo fuge,* whither should I flie?
> If vnto god hee'le throwe thee downe to hell,
> My sences are deceiu'd, here's nothing writ,

I see it plaine, here in this place is writ,
Home fuge, yet shall not *Faustus* flye.

(A/515–21)

When he has completed the contract, his association with Christ
on the cross is strenthened as he "becomes a kind of perverted
Christ."[34] In the biblical context "Consummatum est" is Christ's
proclamation of victory over death and hell, uttered in committing
his soul to God; in *DF* it is used as a symbolic speech which
suggests Faustus' submission to death and hell in committing his
soul to Lucifer. "*Homo fuge,* whither should I flie?" also ironically
echoes Psalms 139 which praises God's omnipresence, while suggesting the ubiquity of hell.

Faustus' illusion of hell as Elysium is suddenly shattered by
the inscription on his arms. He and the audience find themselves
surrounded with hell: inner hell, as in Faustus' conflict of conscience, and the plague still vivid in their memory, a hell on earth
from which there is no escape when the "inscription" from God
or "gods markes" appear on their arms and bodies. Thus, when
Faustus becomes disillusioned, the audience is also forced to recognize ephemerality of this escapist realm in the theater. But Faustus, as well as the audience, is never compelled to face up to hell
long, for the devil's entertainments suspend the pangs of hell. Faustus' conscience is benumbed by demonic powers: "Ile fetch him
somewhat to delight his minde." (A/523) When the devil presents
a spectacle, they willingly run to it to momentarily evade the
dilemma.

Thus, through the tragic conflict of Faustus, the inevitable realities of hell are sporadically inserted throughout the play. They
neither spoil the entertaining quality of the escapist realm, nor
dampen the audience's enthusiasm. The juxtaposition of the imaginative space providing escape and the disastrous realities waiting
for Faustus as well as the audience have reciprocal effect; this
forms a striking contrast between entertainment and tragedy.
Hence, although this fleeting pleasure is restricted by time (24
years—actually 2–3 hours of performance) and Faustus and the
audience are conscious that the entertainment is fictitious, they
are not disillusioned and do not disregard the "fun," but rather
crave more. The dynamism of *DF* depends on this exquisite balance and lively tension.

It is worth noting that Faustus, who has been a good entertainer,
is enslaved by his illusion at the end of the play and hopes for its
realization so earnestly that he begins to confuse illusion with real-

ity. Just before the expiration of the term, he seriously wishes "That I may haue vnto my paramour, / That heauenly *Hellen*, which I saw of late." Faustus is well aware that characters in the spectacle "are but shadows, not substantiall." He requests the spectators' silence and advises them to enjoy the entertainment as fiction, ironically while blindly seeking his *raison d'être* in what is "not substantiall":

> Sweete *Helen*, make me immortal with a kisse:
> Her lips suckes forth my soule, see where it flies:
> Come *Helen*, come giue mee my soule againe.
> Here wil I dwel, for heauen be in these lips,
> And all is drosse that is not *Helena*.
>
> (A/1359–63)

Although he knows that Helen is but a shadow to entertain the spectators, he fanatically comes to believe that she *is* substantial and that her "sweete embraces may extinguish cleare, / Those thoughts that do disswade me from my vow." The audience, which has enjoyed participating in the spectacles of the play-within-the-play as well as *DF* itself, see that the entertainer and hero has become caught up in the self-made illusion. But they could not have been able to laugh and dismiss his absurd behaviour with the same detachment as the Old Man, for they had become close to Faustus and he became attractive in their eyes. They must have become "so rauished with the sight" of characters on the stage, almost to the extent of Charles the German Emperor who "would haue compast" them. The audience cannot help being enthralled by these shadows and earnestly believing in their substantiality, even while being aware that the devil invents only shadows. And the moment comes when this belief makes the audience, as well as Faustus, confound shadow and substance. When *DF* aroused such a confused sense of reality in the audience, the devil made his appearance.

The heavenly bliss found in Helen's beauty and the frightfulness of hell circumventing it; vehement desire for the escapist realm and acute cognition of its fictitiousness—the voltage of the tension between polarities in *DF* reaches its peak in the scene with Helen. Here, when Faustus confounds illusion with reality, the well-balanced tension is finally lost. After the culmination of his hope, there is nothing left but his fall to the bottom: Faustus is thrust down into Hell and the audience into hell on earth. This is repeated in the line, "But mine must liue still to be plagde in hel" (A/1495).

6

Fanatical belief makes the appearance of the devil possible, especially under extraordinary conditions where both the accuser and the victim need his assistance. When *DF* held the stage just after the decimation of the people by the plague, Puritans made the most of the devil as an instrument to eliminate the theater, the hotbed of moral degeneration, disseminating the formula <Theater = Devil>. The devil's appearance in the theater was quite favorable to them. It was not only the Puritans, however, but also the audience who fervently wished for it. In the midst of the upsurge of anti-theatrical sentiment caused by the social crisis of the plague, the devil was invoked in "the deuillish theatre." The theater took advantage of these attacks, and gave the audience access to a kind of Elizabethan dream. The audience was so fascinated that it confused shadow with substance. When the devil, the object of worship under extreme conditions, came on the stage as an director, the imaginative space magically dominated by him became highly entertaining and verisimilar. The devilish theater became a rare place which enabled the audience to enjoy dangerous sports.

Thus, the internal as well external forces desiring the devil's appearance are focused on the stage, and the devil appears as a result. To be more precise, the "internal" force is the audience's belief in the substantiality of things found in the escapist realm of imagination, and the "external" force refers to Puritan attacks against the theater. When these two forces were focused on the stage with the contemporary social crisis as a backdrop, they created social phenomena which recognized the appearance of the devil as being desirable. Under such circumstances the legendary episodes originated. The scene of Faustus' conjuring up the devil in Latin probably contributed to the creation of these episodes to some extent, because it made a great sensation. What the *DF* legend essentially suggests, however, is not the shocking realism of the scene, but rather the audience's enthusiastic desire for self–emancipation which could result from the reciprocity of the theater and its social context.

Notes

1. William Prynne, *Histrio-Mastix: The Player's Scourge, or Actor's Tragedy,* intro. Peter Davison (New York: Johnson Reprint, 1972), 1: fol. 556ʳ.

2. E. K. Chambers, *The Elizabethan Stage* (1923; reprint, Oxford: The Clarendon Press, 1974), 3: 424.

3. Cited by K. M. Briggs, *Pale Hecate's Team* (London: Routledge & Kegan Paul, 1962), 161.

4. George Gifford, *Discourse of the Subtill Practises of Devilles* (London, 1587), sig. I₂ʳ. Also cf. Keith Thomas, *Religion and the Decline of Magic* (London: Weidenfeld & Nicolson, 1971), 472–73.

5. Cf. Thomas, 469–77; Stuart Clark, "King James's *Daemonology*. Witchcraft and Kingship," in *The Damned Art: Essays in the Literature of Witchcraft*, ed. Sydney Anglo (London: Routledge & Kegan Paul, 1977), 175; Barbara Rosen, ed. *Witchcraft*, The Stratford-upon-Avon Library 6 (London: Edward Arnold, 1969), 8.

6. Prynne, 1: fol. 555ᵛ.

7. Chambers, 3:424.

8. John Melton, *The Astrologaster, or, The Figure-caster* (London, 1620), 31, cited by John Bakeless, *The Tragicall History of Christopher Marlowe* (1942; reprint, Westport, Connecticut: Greenwood Press, 1970), 1:298.

9. Robert R. Reed, Jr., *The Occult on the Tudor and Stuart Stage* (Boston: The Christopher Publishing House, 1965), 87.

10. For instance, see Briggs, 127.

11. Thomas Dekker, *The Wonderfull Yeare*, ed. Alexander B. Grosart, *The Non-Dramatic Works of Thomas Dekker* (1885; reprint, New York: Russell & Russell, 1963), 2:105.

12. John Stow, *Annales, or, A Generall Chronicle of England*, aug. Edmund Howes (1607; reprint, London, 1631), 766. On the mistake of Stow's calculation, cf. Samuel Schoenbaum, *William Shakespeare: A Compact Documentary Life* (1978; reprint, Oxford: Oxford University Press, 1987), 168, fn. On annual burials and other informations of the plague in 1592–93, also cf. Paul Slack, *The Impact of Plague in Tudor and Stuart England* (London: Routledge & Kegan Paul, 1985), chapter 6 and J. F. D. Shrewsbury, *A History of Bubonic Plague in the British Isles* (1970; reprint, Cambridge: Cambridge Univ. Press, 1971), chapter 6.

13. Thomas Lodge, *A Treatise of the Plague*, in *The Complete Works of Thomas Lodge* (1883; reprint, New York: Russell & Russell, 1963), 3, sig. C₃ʳ.

14. Dekker, 2:116–17.

15. Simon Forman, "A Discourse of the Plague," Bodleian Library Ashmole MSS 208: fol. 110–34.

16. Margaret Pelling and Charles Webster, "Medical Practitioners," in *Health, Medicine and Mortality in the Sixteenth Century*, ed. Charles Webster (Cambridge: Cambridge Univ. Press, 1979), 188.

17. Ashmole MSS. 208: fol. 113ʳ.

18. Chambers, 4:313.

19. James Bamford, *A Short Dialogve Concerning the Plagves Infection* (London, 1603), sig. A₄ʳ.

20. Thomas, 498; also cf. Michael MacDonald, "Religion, Social Change, and Psychological Healing in England, 1600–1800," in *The Church and Healing, Studies in Church History* 19, ed. W. J. Sheils (Oxford: Basil Blackwell, 1982), 101–25.

21. Recently, the A–text has come to be accepted as being closer to the original work of Marlowe and his collaborator, and no longer can be neglected as a "Bad Quarto." I have focused upon A–text as the text with primary authority, but quoted some passages from the B–text to understand the entertaining mood of the earlier play. Quotations are from W. W. Greg, *Marlowe's Doctor Faustus 1604–1616* (Oxford: Clarendon Press, 1950), and I have specified the versions. As

for the text of *DF*, see Eric Rasmussen, *A Textual Companion to Doctor Faustus* (Manchester: Manchester University Press, 1993).

22. Robert Burton, *The Anatomy of Melancholy*, ed. Holbrook Jackson (1932; reprint, 3 vols. in 1 (Totowa: Rowman and Littlefield, 1978), 2nd Print, 7.

23. Henry Holland, *Spirituall Perseruatiues against the Pestilence* (London, 1593), fol. 5ʳ. Also cf. William Cupper, *Certaine Sermons concerning Gods Late Visitation in the Citie of London* (London, 1592), 43–44.

24. Chambers, 4:301.

25. Holland, sig. [A₅ᵛ]–[A₆ʳ].

26. Chambers, 4:314.

27. Ibid., 315.

28. For the influence of the plague upon *DF*, I am deeply indebted to Christopher Ricks, "*Doctor Faustus* and Hell on Earth," *Essays in Criticism* 35 (1985): 101–20.

29. Charles Nicholl, *A Cup of News: The Life of Thomas Nashe* (London: Routledge & Kegan Paul, 1984), 97.

30. On Faustus' materialism, see Michael Hattaway, "The Theology of Marlowe's *Doctor Faustus*," *Renaissance Drama*, n.s. 3 (1970): 60.

31. Judith Weil has rightly pointed out this tendency of Faustus: cf. *Christopher Marlowe: Merlin's Prophet* (Cambridge: Cambridge University Press, 1977), 64–65.

32. For instance, see W. W. Greg, "The Damnation of Faustus," *Modern Language Review*, 41 (1946): 97–107; Gerald H. Cox, III, "Marlowe's *Doctor Faustus* and 'Sin against the Holy Ghost'," *Huntington Library Quarterly* 36 (1973): 119–37.

33. Francis Kirkman, *The Unlucky Citizen*, cited by Louis B. Wright, *Middle-Class Culture in Elizabethan England* (1935; reprint, New York: Octagon, 1980), 86–87.

34. James H. Sims, *Dramatic Uses of Biblical Allusion in Marlowe and Shakespeare*, in *University of Florida Monographs in the Humanities* 24 (Gainesville: University of Florida Press, 1966), 25.

Time Allowed for Exits in Shakespeare's Plays

MARIKO ICHIKAWA

1

(1) *Bass.* I pray thee good *Leonardo* thinke on this,
  These things being bought and orderly bestowed
  Returne in hast, for I doe feast to night
  My best esteemed acquaintance, hie thee goe.
    Leon. My best endeuours shall be done heerein. *Exit Leonardo.*
                        Enter Gratiano.
    Grati. Where's your Maister.
    Leonar. Yonder sir he walkes.
    Grati. Signior *Bassanio.*
              (*The Merchant of Venice* Q1, C3v; 2.2.163–69)[1]

(2) *Ham.* Why looke you there, looke how it steales away,
  My father in his habit as he liued,
  Looke where he goes, euen now out at the portall. *Exit Ghost.*
    Ger. This is the very coynage of your braine,
              (*Hamlet* Q2, I4r; 3.4.125–28)

Rᴇᴀᴅɪɴɢ these passages, one can easily visualize the moves of the exiters, Leonardo and the Ghost.[2] In passage (1), Leonardo begins to leave just after replying to the order of his master Bassanio, meets with the newcomer Gratiano when he is in the process of making his exit, and goes out of a stage door, probably shortly after answering Gratiano's question. In passage (2), the Ghost begins to leave shortly before Hamlet says, "looke how it steales away," continues walking, and disappears through a doorway of the tiring-house facade soon after Hamlet says, "Looke where he goes, euen now out at the portall."[3] In these instances, the moves of the exiters, or the time it takes for the exiters to complete their moves, is obviously incorporated into the accompanying dialogue.

25

It seems reasonable to believe that *The Merchant of Venice* Q1 was printed either from a fair copy in Shakespeare's own hand or from a very accurate transcript of such a document, and it is generally agreed that *Hamlet* Q2 was printed from Shakespeare's foul papers.[4] Both texts were set up by the same two compositors, X and Y, at James Roberts's printing house, and the sheets on which passages (1) and (2) are found were both set by X.[5] In either case, judging from the fact that there is enough space for the exit stage direction to the right of the lines preceding and succeeding the line at the end of which the exit stage direction is printed, compositor X probably set the exit stage direction in the same position where it had stood in his copy. Therefore, we may be reasonably sure that both exit stage directions were originally written by Shakespeare himself, but that one was placed at the point where the exiter should begin his move while the other was placed at the point where the exiter should complete his move. (However, this does not mean that Shakespeare marked each exit stage direction to ensure the precise timing of the beginning or completion of the exit. It is most likely that Shakespeare almost automatically wrote each stage direction to the right of the last line referring to the exit.)

Scholars once thought that the dimensions of the Elizabethan public playhouse stage were very great. The stage at the Globe, for example, was often estimated to be 43 feet wide by 27 feet 6 inches deep, the size deduced from the building contract for the Fortune. However, this estimate has been seriously questioned, particularly since the Rose excavations revealed that the stage of at least one public playhouse of Shakespeare's time was rather small and tapered. John Orrell, who has been reexamining old assumptions about Elizabethan playhouses, argues that both stages and tiring-houses were commonly built within the yards of arena playhouses, and insists on the likelihood that the Globe stage was wide but comparatively shallow. On the hypothesis that the Globe was a twenty-sided polygon about 100 feet across, which he believes to be the likeliest interpretation of recent Globe discoveries, he suggests 53 feet 9 inches wide and 37 feet 5 inches deep at the center for the stage and tiring-house area.[6]

In Elizabethan public playhouses the action usually took place downstage to allow the audience positioned on three (or four) sides of the stage to see and hear better.[7] Therefore, whether the stage was very deep or comparatively shallow, actors clearly needed some length of time to return to the tiring-house. Shakespeare, an actor as well as a playwright, a man of the theater in all senses, was no doubt fully aware of this fact. It is reasonable to suppose that, even in those instances where the moves of exiters are not clearly built into the accompanying dialogue, a certain amount of time would have been allowed for the actors to complete their exits. The main purpose of this paper is to estimate the supposed length of time allowed to exiters in Shakespeare's plays in terms of the number of lines delivered by other characters while the exiters are walking to one of the two (or three) doors of the tiring-house facade.

2

Certain mid-scene exits and mid-scene entrances are correlated in the sense that completion of the former is required for the latter to be made. Presumably, the number of lines delivered between the beginning of an exit and the making of an entrance related to the exit includes at least the number of lines delivered between the beginning and the completion of the exit. The number of lines delivered between the beginning of an exit and the making of its related entrance shall be hereafter referred to as "NL." Examining instances in which NL is small may help to determine how many lines are usually allowed to exiters in Shakespeare's plays.

The exits and entrances mentioned above are divided into the following patterns:

A   =   A character exits and reenters.
A^+ =   A character exits to fetch something and reenters with it.[8]
B   =   A character exits to summon another character, and the summoned character enters either alone or with the summoner.

I have restricted myself to those instances in which the exit and its related entrance are both made on the main stage, leaving aside those in which an ascent to the upper stage by the exiter himself is involved, and those in which the exit is made from the upper stage. That is to say, pattern A does not include those instances in which (Ca) a character exits below (from the main stage) and reenters above (on the upper stage); (Cb) a character exits above and reenters below; or (Cc) a character exits above and reenters there. (see Appendix 2).[9] Although pattern A^+ is a variant of pattern A, it could be combined with pattern B, for these patterns share a very important feature: the exit itself presages its related entrance.

Using Quarto and Folio texts, I have searched all of Shakespeare's plays for instances of each pattern. Needless to say, it would be unreasonable to rely very much upon stage directions to determine when characters begin to exit or when they enter, that is, appear through one of the stage doors. I have therefore sought to find the primary basis for deciding on the moments of the beginnings of exits and the makings of entrances from speeches themselves.

In Shakespeare's plays, an exit is usually denoted in the dialogue—through an intention to depart spoken by the exiter himself, an instruction or request from another character telling or asking the exiter to depart, or the like. Such lines serve primarily as cues for the actor to begin an exit. As a rule, therefore, I have placed the beginnings of exits just after these "exit cues." However, where there is a stage direction indicating a different point of exit, I have accepted that point as an alternative possibility, unless it is unreasonable to assume that the exiter begins to leave at the point. (Thus I have tried to guard against ignoring correctly placed stage directions. I am inclined to believe that a number of exit stage directions which modern editors assume to be placed too early are in fact placed at the point where the characters begin to exit.[10] It is true that in some cases a character's exit is not indicated either by an "exit cue" or by an exit stage direction, but is implied only by the fact that the character reenters later. However, in such cases we usually find something that can serve as a cue for his exit, no matter how vague a cue it may be, such as a noise made within or a speech delivered by, or spoken to, the character. (According to this view, I have placed the beginning of Bardolph's exit and that of Seyton's at *2 Henry IV,* 2.4.371 and at *Macbeth,* 5.5.8 respectively.)[11]

In Shakespeare's plays, an entrance is usually announced through a speech spoken by, or to, the enterer or a speech referring to his approach. I have placed entrances just before such "entry announcements." In the majority of cases, entry stage directions are placed just before such speeches, not only in texts based upon Shakespeare's copies or scribal transcripts of them, but also in texts based upon promptbooks or scribal transcripts of them. (For example, in *Macbeth* F1, which is based upon a promptbook, there are forty-four mid-scene entry stage directions, of which thirty-seven are placed just before "entry announcements.") Some extant non-Shakespearean promptbooks do show that bookkeepers occasionally marked entry stage directions some lines before such points. Here it is assumed that their intention was to allow enterers time to join onstage characters just before they first speak or are addressed.[12] Furthermore, in Fredson Bowers's view, in any printed (or manuscript) text, it is a convention that a character's entrance is marked just before he speaks, whereas in performance his entrance must have been made slightly earlier.[13] There must, therefore, be a considerable number of instances in which we should place the entrance some lines before the enterer first speaks or is addressed in spite of the position of the entry stage direction. But, in practical terms, it is impossible to judge how many lines earlier we should place the entrance in each particular case. Accordingly, I have generally followed the aforesaid principle, and where there is an entry stage direction indicating an earlier point, I have accepted that point as an alternative possibility, unless it is clear that the stage direction is absolutely misplaced.[14]

The following is an important instance:

(3) *Hor.* Sirra *Biondella,* goe and intreate my wife to
come to me forthwith.   *Exit. Bion.*
Pet. Oh ho, intreate her, nay then shee must needes
come.
Hor. I am affraid sir, doe what you can
                    Enter Biondello.
Yours will not be entreated: Now, where's my wife?
Bion. Shee saies you haue some goodly Iest in hand,
She will not come: she bids you come to her.
                    (*The Taming of the Shrew* F1, TLN 2636–44; 5.2.91–97)

The Taming of the Shrew F1 was printed either from Shakespeare's foul papers or from a transcript which had undergone some minor theatrical adaptation. It is certain that Biondello begins to exit in response to Hortensio's instruction at the end of 5.2.92, where the stage direction for his exit is placed. On the other hand, although he is first addressed in the middle of 5.2.95 ("Now, where's my wife?"), the stage direction for his entrance is placed at 5.2.94 (just after "I am affraid sir, doe what you can"). That is to say, the entry stage direction seems to be marked half a line too early. Does the half line allow Biondello to approach Hortensio? If the entry stage direction was originally Shakespeare's, it was probably placed at the end of line 94 in his foul papers. We can suppose that, either just after he wrote line 94 and the first half of line 95, which make up a sentence, or more probably just after he wrote lines 94–95, which are prefixed by a single speaker's name, Shakespeare marked the entry stage direction to the right of line 94 at least partly because sufficient space was left for it. However, if the entry stage direction was originally the bookkeeper's, rather than Shakespeare's, its F1 placement may have resulted from the usual practice whereby the bookkeeper marked annotations beside speeches in the left margin of the copy received from the author. In this case, he would have had no choice but to place the entry stage direction to the left of line 95, even if he thought that the middle of line 95 was the proper moment for Biondello's entrance. In short, it seems that the entry stage direction does not necessarily mark the point at which Biondello enters. I have therefore tentatively concluded that Biondello reenters with a message from the Widow in the middle of 5.2.95, while conceding the possibility that he reenters at 5.2.94. Thus, in Appendix 2 this instance is referred to as "*SHR* 5.2.92–95m[94]" and counted as an instance of pattern A^+ in which NL is 2.5 or 2 ("$A^+ = 2.5[2]$").

3

The Quarto and Folio texts of Shakespeare's plays are of various kinds. To what extent do the examples of the three patterns mentioned above reflect the nature of the particular text which provides them? For several plays there are two or three authoritative or substantive texts. For example, there are three substantive texts of *Hamlet:* the text printed from Shakespeare's foul papers (Q2); the text printed from a transcript of the promptbook reflecting Shakespeare's revised version (F1); and the reported text which reflects performances based upon the promptbook from which F1 descends (Q1). For the variation in data which these three texts provide, see Appendix 1.

Since the plot of the F1 version is somewhat simpler than the Q2 version, F1 lacks certain examples found in Q2. Fortunately, the three or four omitted instances (Appendix 1, numbers 7, 19, 24, and 25) do not seem to be very important, for in these instances NL is at least above ten, which is not small enough to be crucial to our argument. In the instances found in Q2 and F1, both texts give substantially the same readings for "exit cues" and "entry announcements," though in several instances these texts do not agree concerning the positions of stage directions (Appendix 1, numbers 2, 14, 16, 17, 21, and 22). Consequently, I have placed all the beginnings of exits and entrances at the same points in both texts. In no fewer than seven instances (Appendix 1, numbers 1, 2, 5, 8, 14, 22, and 26), Q2 and F1 have differences in NL because of F1's omissions and additions of lines (due to authorial or theatrical revision) and Q2's omissions of lines (due to compositorial negligence) between the beginnings of the exits and the entrances.

However, the fact to emphasize is that in all these instances the variation of NL occurs in quite high numbers. The fact that the F1 omissions and additions (and the Q2 compositorial errors) can be seen either just before the entrances or a considerable number of lines (at least eleven) after the beginnings of the exits, never just after the beginnings of the exits is also significant. None of the differences between the data provided by Q2 and those provided by F1 is vital to our argument.

Besides *Hamlet,* there are several plays which exist in two kinds of text: (1) texts based upon Shakespeare's copies or scribal transcripts of them and (2) texts based upon promptbooks or scribal transcripts of them, or at least influenced by theatrical manuscripts such as promptbooks. For these plays, I have made comparisons between the two kinds. (In those cases where a reprint edition comes between them, I have also consulted the intervening text.)[15] Only in the case of *King Lear,* has the comparison between Q1 and F1 revealed the same kinds of change and to the same extent as in *Hamlet.* However, in other plays, the two kinds of texts provide almost the same data for the plays.[16] Judging from these comparisons, I conclude that the influence of the nature of the text on the data concerning the play would not be crucial, whichever text we might use, whether it is a text based on Shakespeare's copy or a scribal transcript thereof or a text based on the promptbook or a scribal transcript thereof, and whether the text contains Shakespeare's revisions or not.[17] In the cases of multiple-text plays, I have chosen to use the text closer or closest to the promptbook of Shakespeare's company, while also consulting the other text(s).

Hamlet Q1 provides only half as many instances as F1. In the case of pattern B, three of the five instances are missing from Q1 (Appendix 1, numbers 4, 21, and 23), though a new instance has been added (Appendix 1, number 3). It may be that, even though the actor-reporter was well aware of the correlation between summoners' exits and summoned characters' entrances, it was very difficult to memorize each particular instance, for such a correlation has nothing to do with the story itself. In any event, three important examples, in which NL is very small, are missing from Q1. It is clear that reported texts, or "bad quartos" do not serve our purpose. With the exception of *Pericles,* however, we have no need to use such a text.

I have counted the examples found in all of Shakespeare's plays, including *Pericles.* However, I have excluded those instances in which a sound or an action fills the gap between the beginning of the exit and the entrance. Therefore, such instances as *LR* 5.2.4–4

(Edgar's exit and reentrance) and *HAM* 3.2.129–29 (Player Queen's exit and reentrance) are not among instances of A = 0. Where two or more instances share the same exit or entrance, I have counted only the one in which NL is smaller or the smallest. For example, the instance in which Charmian exits and returns with a Messenger (*ANT* 2.5.81–84m (B = 2.5)) has been included, but not the instance in which the Messenger exits and reenters with her (*ANT* 2.5.74–84m (A = 9.5)). Lastly, I have included those doubtful instances in which it is not certain whether the exit and entrance are really correlated, or whether the exit and entrance both actually occur.

Because, as mentioned above, those instances in which NL is small are important for our purpose, it will be sufficient for the present occasion to show the number of instances of each pattern in which NL is between 0 and 10. See Table 1. (For the instances themselves, see Appendix 2. However, for reasons of space, only the instances in which NL is between 0 and 4 are listed.)

Table 1
Number of Instances of Each Pattern

Pattern	NL*										
	0	1	2	3	4	5	6	7	8	9	10
A	0	0	0	4	8	2	7	5	8	3	4
A⁺	2	3	2	4	3	4	5	3	3	2	1
B	9	5	13	11	12	10	4	4	7	8	1
Total	11	8	15	19	23	16	16	12	18	13	6

*In this table, extra half lines are counted as full lines.

4

There is a total of eleven instances in which NL is 0, but, as can be seen in Appendix 2, the majority are doubtful or controversial examples. In total, there are only a few indisputable instances in which NL is 0 or 1, but there are many in which NL is 2. We can say safely that in Shakespeare's plays, characters are generally allowed at least two lines to complete their exits. (Incidentally, indisputable instances in which NL is 0 or 1 are found only in the Theater and Globe plays. In other words, the plays which were performed at the Rose or the Blackfriars, where the stages were small, unexpectedly provide no reliable instances in which NL is 0 or 1.)

In the case of pattern A, although there are no instances in which NL is 0 or 1 or 2, there are a few instances in which NL is 3 and several instances in which NL is 4. All the exiters in the instances where NL is 3, namely, Whitmore, First Murderer, (Catesby), and (Bardolph) are minor characters while some exiters in the instances where NL is 4, namely, Titus, (Mistress Ford), Othello, and Lear are major characters. However, the important thing to note is that Whitmore and First Murderer do not exit alone but with major characters, namely, Suffolk and Clarence respectively. There is no reason to assume that they begin their exits from upstage. From these observations, we can infer that exiters are usually allowed about four lines, and occasionally about three lines, to walk from the main acting area, i.e., downstage, to one of the two (or three) stage doors.

There is no important difference between the distribution of instances of pattern A⁺ and that of pattern B. As Appendix 2 shows, in the case of pattern A⁺, while there are no reliable instances in which NL is 0 and only one in which NL is 1, there are a few in which NL is 2; in the case of pattern B, there are several reliable instances in which NL is 0 or 1 and a considerable number in which NL is 2.[18] In those instances of both patterns where NL is between 0 and 2, almost all the exiters are minor characters, such as servants and attendants. The reason why such minor characters are usually allowed about two lines, and occasionally only one line or less, to complete their exits is that their acting area is ordinarily upstage, and they are usually expected to move very quickly.

We can suppose that exiters who are allowed only one line or less are expected to begin their exits from extreme upstage positions. Characters who neither speak nor are addressed until they are told to pursue offstage business, such as Knight (*LR* 1.4.46–47 (A⁺ = 1)) and Attendant (*2H6* 5.1.145–45 (B = 0)), are possibly standing near the stage doors while they are onstage. Those who enter only to announce that other characters are waiting offstage for their entrances and who exit to summon them immediately, such as Hostess (*1H4* 2.5.511–11 (B = 0)) and Dennis (*AYL* 1.1.89–90 (B = 1)), quite naturally would stand by the doors through which they have entered during their very short presence on the stage. I have examined each of the doubtful instances from this point of view. In the case of *AWW* 2.1.90–91 (B = 1), in particular, it is unlikely that Lafeu would begin his exit from an extreme upstage position, for

he exchanges speeches for some thirty lines with the King of
France, the central character in *All's Well That Ends Well*, 2.1,
before he begins to move.[19] It seems reasonable to conclude that
he does not really leave the stage, but only walks a few paces
toward a stage door and beckons offstage for the newcomer Helen
to enter.

To sum up, in Shakespeare's plays, major characters are usually
allowed about four lines to complete their exits, while minor characters are ordinarily allowed about two lines to do so. This suggests
that the major characters normally occupy a downstage position,
and so have further to walk to their exit doors than the minor
characters. While each exit should be discussed individually, I
hope that the conclusions we have reached will serve as a framework within which to do so.

5

The conclusions imply that the four or so lines or fewer following
the beginning of an exit can be related to the exit itself. Here are
examples of four-line speeches following the beginnings of major
characters' exits.

(4) *Cla.* I must perforce: Farewell.   *Exit Clar.*
     Rich. Go treade the path that thou shalt ne're return:
     Simple plaine *Clarence*, I do loue thee so,
     That I will shortly send thy Soule to Heauen,
     If Heauen will take the present at our hands.
     But who comes heere? the new deliuered *Hastings*?
                    (*Richard III* F1, TLN 123–28; 1.1.117–22)

(5) *Lear.* Then there's life in't. Come, and you get it,
     You shall get it by running: Sa, sa, sa, sa.   *Exit.*
     Gent. A sight most pittifull in the meanest wretch,
     Past speaking of in a King. Thou hast a Daughter
     Who redeemes Nature from the generall curse
     Which twaine haue brought her to.
     Edg. Haile gentle Sir.
                    (*King Lear* F1, 2644–50; 4.5198–204)

In both cases, the exit stage directions are placed at or around the
points where the exiters should begin to leave. In passage (4),
though Richard's speech consists of five lines, there is a clear break
between the fourth and fifth lines in terms of content. In passage

(5), the Gentleman's speech consists of just four lines, and is not followed by a speech which shares the same theme.

Let us assume that these four-line speeches are delivered while the exiters are leaving the stage. Richard's four lines give the meaning of "a walk to the other world" to Clarence's exit and by doing so these lines express more strongly and forcefully the overwhelming advantage which Richard holds over Clarence. On the other hand, it is obvious that the Gentleman's four lines serve as a comment on Lear's exit, telling the audience that however pitiful the appearance of his exit may be, this very exit will lead to the reunion scene in which Lear's broken heart will be healed by his loving daughter, Cordelia.

In passage (5), Lear probably completes his exit before the Gentleman finishes delivering the four lines, for he exits running. Moreover, in passage (4), Clarence may complete his exit either before or after Richard finishes delivering the four lines, because there is nothing in the text to indicate the precise timing of the completion of his exit. But the fact that there are such instances as passages (4) and (5), in which four-line speeches are clearly intended to add meaning to major characters' exits made roughly while the speeches are being spoken, confirms our conclusion that Shakespeare allowed about four lines for major characters to complete their exits. It indicates also that the approximately four lines or fewer following the beginning of an exit may have meaning which we cannot fully appreciate unless we hear or read them as we pay attention to the exit.

6

Bernard Beckerman points out that the extant Elizabethan theatrical plots indicate entrances without identifying which door is to be used, and conjectures that "entrances were made at one conventionally designated door and exits at the other unless the actor was specifically instructed otherwise."[20] If this principle is applicable to all cases, then whenever a character exits and reenters, the actor would have to walk through the tiring-house from the "exit door" to the "entrance door" between the completion of his exit and reentrance. This would apply to all instances of patterns A and A$^+$ and many instances of pattern B. The width of the Globe stage suggests that the two doors were at a considerable distance from each other. (Even the third central door would have been at some distance from either of the two side doors.) Therefore,

it is unreasonable to assume that two to four lines can provide
sufficient time for an actor to complete an exit and also walk to
the opposite (or another) door. Even in those instances of pattern
B where a character exits to summon another character who then
immediately enters alone, it is possible, but hardly natural, that
the moment the summoner goes out of one door, the summoned
character appears through the other (or another). To be fair to
Beckerman, his main purpose is to furnish a general principle concerning Elizabethan stage practice. I agree with him when he argues that there was some system for entrances and exits, and I do
not find the convention which he suggests entirely unacceptable.
However, or rather therefore, I presume to add that it does not
apply to certain entrances and exits, such as those instances in
which an exit is immediately followed by its related entrance.[21]
Entrances and exits in the plays of Shakespeare and his contemporaries leave much to be discussed.

Appendix 1: Instances in the Three Substantive Texts of *Hamlet*

	Q2 (1604–5)	
1	1.1.48m(49)–106* (106*)	A = 76.5
2	2.2.39(39)-220 *(218)*	A = 108[178]
(3)		
4	2.2.53–58m*(57)*	B = 4.5[4]
5	2.2.219–380(380)	A = 103
6	3.1.57–164(164)	A = 107
7	3.1.164(164)?–81m?	A = 16.5?
8	3.2.45–129(129)	A = 82
9	3.2.49–87(87)	A = 38
10	3.2.50(50)–87	A = 37
11	3.2.129(129)–29(129)	A = 0
12	3.2.129(129)–29(129)	A = 0
13	3.2.129–47(147)	A = 18
14	3.2.129–231(232)	A = 106
15	3.2.144–47(147)	B = 3
16	3.2.258(258)–78*(282)*	A = 20[24]
17	3.2.258(258)–331*(329)*	A = 73[71]
18	3.2.258(258)–360(361)	A = 102
19	4.1.3*–31(30)	A = 28
(20)		
21	4.5.16–20*(16)*	B = 4[0]

22	4.5.72–154(152)	A = 81.5
23	4.6.3–5(5)	B = 2
24	5.2.143–54(154)	B = 11
25	5.2.154*–70*(170*)	B = 16
26	5.2.143–70*(170*)	A = 40
27	5.2.301m[264]–1(301)	A$^+$ = 0.5[A = 37]

	F1 (1623)	
1	1.1.48m(49)–106(106)	A = 58.5
2	2.2.39(*39m*)–220(221)	A = 181[180.5]
(3)		
4	2.2.53–58m(*57*)	B = 4.5[4]
5	2.2.219–380(380)	A = 161
6	3.1.57(57)–164(164)	A = 107
7	†–†	
8	3.2.45(45)–129(129)	A = 84
9	3.2.49(49)–87(87)	A = 38
10	3.2.50(50)–87(87)	A = 37
11	3.2.129(129)–29(129)	A = 0
12	3.2.129(129)–29(129)	A = 0
13	3.2.129(129)–47(147)	A = 18
14	3.2.129(129)–231(231)	A = 102
15	3.2.144–47(147)	B = 3
16	3.2.258(258)–78(278)	A = 20
17	3.2.258(258)–331(331)	A = 73
18	3.2.258(258)–360(361)	A = 102
19	†–4.1.31(31m)	
(20)		
21	4.5.16–20(20)	B = 4
22	4.5.72(72)–154(153)	A = 82
23	4.6.3–5(5)	B = 2
24	5.2.143–†	
25	†–5.2.170(170)	
26	5.2.143–70(170)	B = 27
27	5.2.301m[264]–1(301)	A$^+$ = 0.5[A = 37]

	Q1 (1603)	
1	B1v26(26)–B2v6(6)	A = 50
2	D3r32≠E2v8(*5*)	A ≠ 224[221]
(3)	E2r12(12)–E2v8(*5*)	B = 31[28]
4	†–D3v9(9)	
5	E2v7(9)–E3r23(23)	A = 51
6	D4v25≠E2r5(6)	A ≠ 88

7	E2r5(5)–†	
8	F2v10(10)–F3r16(16)	A = 40
9	†–F2v32*(34)*	
10	†–F2v32*(34)*	
11	F3r17(17)–19(19)	A = 0
12	F3r19(19)–†	
13	F3r20(20)–35(35)	A = 14
14	F3r19(19)–F4r8m	A = 58.5
15	F3r31–35(35)	B = 3
16	F4v4(4)–13(13)	A = 8
17	F4r36(36); F4v4–22?	A = 17[20]?
18	F4v4(4)–G1r19m(21)	A = 47.5
19	†–†	
(20)	G3v21(21)–28*(30)*	A = 7[8]
21	†–G4v25*(27)*	
22	H1r23(23)–H1v17(17)	A = 28
23	†–†	
24	I2v29*(28)*–†	
25	†–I3r1m*(2)*	
26	*I2v29(28)–I3r1m(2)*	B = 7.5[9]
27	†–†	

Characters:

1 Ghost
2 Rosencrantz, Guildenstern
(3) King—Rosencrantz, Guildenstern
4 Polonius = Valtemand, Cornelius
5 Polonius (Corambis)
6 King, Polonius (Corambis)
7 Ophelia
8 Players
9 Polonius (Corambis)
10 Rosencrantz, Guildenstern
11 Player Queen
12 Player Lucianus
13 Player King, Player Queen
14 Player Lucianus
15 Prologue—Player King, Player Queen
16 Rosencrantz, Guildenstern
17 Players [Player]
18 Polonius (Corambis)
19 Rosencrantz, Guildenstern
(20) Rosencrantz, Guildenstern
21 Gentleman—Ophelia [Horatio = Ophelia]
22 Ophelia
23 Gentleman [Attendant]—Sailors [Sailor]

24 Osric (Braggart Gentleman)—Lord
25 Lord = King, Queen, etc.
26 Osric [Osric (Braggart Gentleman) = King, Queen, etc.]
27 Osric

Key:

Line numbers in parentheses show the positions of exit and entry stage directions. The printing of a line number in italics indicates that, although the position of the stage direction is different from the position at which I have placed the beginning of the exit or the making of the entrance, it can be accepted as an alternative possibility.

? indicates that it is doubtful whether the exit or entrance is really made or not.

* indicates that the Q2 line is not found in *The Complete Oxford Shakespeare.*

† indicates that the exit or entrance does not occur in the F1 or Q1 version

For Q1, references are to the signature of the page and the number of the printed line, exclusive of the running title. |⊬| and |≠| indicate that there is a scene break between the exit and entrance.

In the list of characters' names, the equals sign (=) between the name of a summoner and that of a summoned character indicates that the summoner reenters with the summoned character; a minus (−) between the name of a summoner and that of a summoned character indicates that the summoned character enters alone.

Appendix 2: Instances of Each Pattern in which NL is between 0 and 4

$A = 3$:

1. *2H6* 4.1.140–43	Whitmore	
2. *R3* 1.4.265–68	1.Murderer	
3. *R3* 3.7.91–94	Catesby	$A = 3[Ca = 3]$
4. *2H4* 2.4.385–88	Bardolph	?
i) *2H4* 2.4.371[369]–72	Bardolph	$A^+ = 1[A = 3]$*
ii) *TMP* 1.1.32–36[35m]	Seb., Ant., Gon.	$A = 4[2.5]$*

$A = 4$:

1. *TIT* 5.2.160–64	Titus	
2. *WIV* 1.4.33–37	Rugby	?
3. *WIV* 4.2.93[91]–97	Mrs. Ford	$A = 4[6]$
4. *2H4* 2.4.207–212	Bardolph	
5. *OTH* 1.2.49m–53m	Othello	
6. *LR* 1.4.269–73	Lear	
7. *COR* 4.5.2–6	1.Servingman	

8. *TMP* 1.1.32–36[35m]   Seb., Ant., Gon.   A = 4[2.5]*

A⁺ = 0:

  1. *TGV* 4.4.115–15   Attendant (Ursula)   ?
  2. *1H4* 2.5.486[328]–86   Bardolph   A⁺ = 0[A = 158]

A⁺ = 1:

  1. *2H4* 2.4.371[369]–72   Bardolph   A⁺ = 1[A = 3]
  2. *HAM* 5.2.301m[264]–1   Osric   A⁺ = 0.5[A = 37]
  3. *LR* 1.4.46–47   Knight

A⁺ = 2:

  1. *SHR* 0.1.72–74   Servingman
  2. *SHR* 5.2.83–85   Biondello
  i) *SHR* 5.2.92–95m[94]   Biondello   A⁺ = 2.5[2]

A⁺ = 3:

  1. *SHR* 4.1.125–28   Servants
  2. *SHR* 5.2.92–95m[94]   Biondello   A⁺ = 2.5[2]
  3. *TIM* 1.2.162–65   Flavius
  4. *H8* 1.4.51m–53   Servant   A⁺ = 2.5

A⁺ = 4:

  1. *1H4* 2.5.486[401]–90   Hostess   A⁺ = 4[A = 89]
  2. *TRO* 5.2.61–65   Cressida
  3. *MM* 4.2.86–90   Provost   *?
  i) *2H4* 4.1.318–23[322]   Westmorland   A⁺ = 5[4]

B = 0:

  1. *SHR* 5.1.84–84   Servant – Officer   ?
  2. *2H6* 5.1.145–45   Attendant – Salisbury, Warwick
  3. *R2* 4.1.1m–1m   Lord = Bagot   ?
  4. *1H4* 2.5.511–11   Hostess – Sheriff
  5. *TRO* 4.2.60–60   Pandarus – Troilus   ?
  6. *TIM* 1.2.118–18   Servant – Cupid   ?
  7. *PER* 21.8–8   Gentlemen = Lysimachus   ?
  8. *WT* 4.4.340–40   Servant – 12 Satyrs   ?
  9. *H8* 4.2.109m–9m   Griffith = Caputius   ?
  i) *TN* 3.4.14m–15[14m]   Maria = Malvolio   B = 1.5[0]?
  ii) *AWW* 5.3.154–56m[154]   Attendant = Bertram   B = 1.5[0]
  iii) *H8* 2.2.116[117]–17   Wolsey = Gardiner   B = 1[0]

B = 1:

  1. *AYL* 1.1.89–90   Dennis – Charles
  2. *OTH* 3.1.38[38m]–39   Iago – Emilia   B = 1[1.5]
  3. *AWW* 2.1.90–91   Lafeu = Helen   ?

4. *ANT* 4.2.9m–10m	One – Servitors	?
5. *H8* 2.2.116[117]–17	Wolsey = Gardiner	B = 1[0]

B = 2:

1. *SHR* 5.2.101–3	Grumio – Katherine	
2. *JN* 1.1.47–49m	Sheriff = Falcon., Bast.	B = 1.5
3. *HAM* 4.6.3–5	Attendant – Sailor	
4. *TN* 1.5.158–60	Malvolio – Viola	
5. *TN* 3.4.14m–15[14m]	Maria = Malvolio	B = 1.5[0]?
6. *TRO* 4.7.41m–42	Aeneas = Troilus	B = 1.5?
7. *MM* 4.2.58[57]–60	Pompey – Claudio	B = 2[3]
8. *AWW* 5.3.154–56m[154]	Attendant = Bertram	B = 1.5[0]
9. *TIM* 1.2.125–27	Cupid = Masque	*
10. *PER* 4.80–82	Lord = Pericles	
11. *WT* 2.2.2m–4m	Gentleman = Jailer	
12. *WT* 2.2.21–23m	Jailer = Emilia	B = 1.5
13. *H8* 5.1.83–85	Denny = Cranmer	
i) *WIV* 2.2.146m[147]–49	Bardolph = Ford	B = 3.5[2]
ii) *OTH* 3.1.38[38m]–39	Iago – Emilia	B = 1[1.5]

B = 3:

1. *R3* 3.7.214m–16	Catesby – Buckingham, etc.	B = 2.5
2. *LLL* 3.1.63–66[67]	Mote = Costard	B = 3[4]
3. *HAM* 3.2.144–47	Prologue – P. King, P. Queen	
4. *MM* 2.2.22–25m	Servant – Isabella	B = 2.5
5. *OTH* 4.2.109–12	Emilia = Iago	
6. *TIM* 1.1.246–49	Servants – Alcibiades	
7. *ANT* 2.5.81–84m	Charmian = Messenger	B = 2.5
8. *COR* 1.3.46–49	Gentlewomen = Valeria	
9. *WT* 4.4.215–18	Servant – Autolycus	
10. *TMP* 5.1.256m–58	Ariel = Cal., Ste., Trin.	B = 2.5
11. *H8* 1.4.61–64	Chamberlain = King, etc.	*
i) *MM* 4.2.58[57]–60	Pompey – Claudio	B = 2[3]

B = 4:

1. *1H6* 1.3.39m–42	Bastard = Joan	B = 3.5
2. *1H6* 5.1.24m–27	Attendant – Ambassadors	B = 3.5
3. *R2* 4.1.148–52	York = Richard	
4. *WIV* 2.2.146m[147]–49	Bardolph = Ford	B = 3.5[2]
5. *JC* 3.1.143–47	Servant – Antony	
6. *HAM* 4.5.16–20	Horatio = Ophelia	
7. *MM* 2.2.2m–6m	Servant – Angelo	B = 3.5
8. *OTH* 4.2.20–24	Emilia = Desdemona	
9. *LR* 3.7.22–26m	Servants = Gloucester	B = 3.5
10. *MAC* 3.2.5–9	Servant – Macbeth	
11. *ANT* 5.2.319–23	Guardsman – Dolabella	

12. *H8* 3.1.19m–23m   Griffith = Wolsey, Campeius
  i) *LLL* 3.1.63–66[67]   Mote = Costard   B = 3[4]
  ii) *HAM* 2.2.53–58m[57]   Polonius = Val., Cor.   B = 4.5[4]
  iii) *AWW* 5.3.27–32[31]   Attendant – Bertram   B = 5[4]

Ca = 2:

  1. *2H6* 1.4.52–54   Stafford   ?

Ca = 3:

  1. *2H6* 1.4.10–13   Hume   ?
  2. *JC* 3.2.8m–10   Brutus   Ca = 2.5?
  3. *JC* 5.3.22–25m   Pindarus   Ca = 2.5
  i) *R3* 3.7.91–94   Catesby   A = 3[Ca = 3]

Cb = 0:

  1. *ROM* 3.5.67–67   Juliet
  2. *TIM* 5.5.65–65[86m]   Senators   Cb = 0[20.5]

Cb = 2:

  1. *SHR* 5.1.53–55   Pedant
  2. *R2* 3.3.182–84   Richard, etc.
  3. *JC* 5.3.33–35   Pindarus

Cb = 3:

  1. *JC* 3.2.162m–64   Antony   Cb = 2.5?

Cc = 3:

  1. *ROM* 2.1.180–83   Juliet
  2. *ROM* 2.1.199–202   Juliet

Key:
   * in the third column indicates that a sound or an action occurs between the beginning of the exit and the entrance.
   ? in the third column indicates either that it is not certain whether the exit and entrance are really correlated or that it is doubtful whether the exit and entrance are both really made.
   In the listing of instances of pattern B, the equals sign (=) between the name of a summoner and that of a summoned character indicates that the summoner reenters with the summoned character; a minus sign (−) between the name of a summoner and that of a summoned character indicates that the summoned character enters alone.

Notes

This paper was first published in Japanese in *Studies in English Literature* (The English Literary Society of Japan) 68 (1992): 189–206.

1. Quarto and Folio readings are from *Shakespeare's Plays in Quarto: A Facsimile Edition of Copies Primarily from the Henry E. Huntington Library*, ed. Michael J. B. Allen and Kenneth Muir (Berkeley and Los Angeles: University of California Press, 1981) and *The First Folio of Shakespeare: The Norton Facsimile*, ed. Charlton Hinman (New York: W. W. Norton, 1968). Act-scene-line references are those of *William Shakespeare: The Complete Works*, eds. Stanley Wells and Gary Taylor (Oxford: Clarendon Press, 1986).

2. We need some economical and exact terms to describe those characters making entrances and those making exits. I should like to use 'enterers' and 'exiters' as the most economical denotations.

3. It seems possible that the Ghost departs through the central opening. According to Andrew Gurr's private suggestion to author, May 1992, the word "portall" means a grand doorway, larger than the ordinary side doors.

4. For the nature of the early texts of Shakespeare's plays, I have relied on Stanley Wells and Gary Taylor (with John Jowett and William Montgomery), *William Shakespeare: A Textual Companion* (Oxford: Clarendon Press, 1987).

5. See John Russell Brown, "The Compositors of *Hamlet* Q2 and *The Merchant of Venice*," *Studies in Bibliography* 7 (1955); 17–40.

6. John Orrell, "Beyond the Rose: Design Problems for the Globe Reconstruction," in *New Issues in the Reconstruction of Shakespeare's Theatre*, ed. Franklin J. Hildy (New York: Peter Lang, 1990), 111–16. See also Hildy, "Reconstructing Shakespeare's Theatre," in *New Issues*, 13–17.

7. See, *e.g.*, Fredson Bowers, "Authority, Copy, and Transmission in Shakespeare's Texts," in *Shakespeare Study Today*, ed. Georgianna Ziegler (New York: AMS Press, 1986), 19. However, Robert Weimann's theory about the distinction between the downstage *platea* and the upstage *locus* should not be ignored. See *Shakespeare and the Popular Tradition in the Theater: Studies in the Social Dimension of Dramatic Form and Function* (Baltimore: Johns Hopkins University Press, 1978), 73–85, 208–52.

8. Those instances in which a character exits to investigate a noise made within and those in which a character exits to obtain expected information are also classified under this type.

9. It is obvious that at least pattern Ca, which includes an exit from the main stage, is not irrelevant to our discussion. I have collected all the instances of patterns Ca, Cb, and Cc. (See Appendix 2.) The results are not inconsistent with the conclusions reached in this paper.

10. See, *e.g.*, the exit stage direction for Boyet at *Love's Labor's Lost*, 2.1.35 (Q1, B4v; F1, TLN 526), and the exit stage direction for Reynaldo at *Hamlet*, 2.1.74 (Q2, E2r; F1, TLN 967).

11. Alan C. Dessen's discussion of the possibility that Seyton does not leave the stage is interesting. See *Elizabethan Stage Conventions and Modern Interpreters* (Cambridge: Cambridge University Press, 1984), 5–7; *Recovering Shakespeare's Theatrical Vocabulary* (Cambridge: Cambridge University Press, 1995), 93–94. However, I have included likely and less likely examples of patterns A, A+, and B in my discussion.

12. See W. W. Greg, *Dramatic Documents from the Elizabethan Playhouses* (Oxford: Clarendon Press, 1931), 1: 216–17. However, we must take seriously William B. Long's warning about the danger of making generalizations about what playhouse bookkeepers would or would not do. See his "Stage-directions: A Misinterpreted Factor in Determining Textual Provenance," *TEXT* 2 (1985): 121–37.

In the manuscript of Philip Massinger's *Believe as You List,* for example, the bookkeeper marks at least twenty-eight stage directions for mid-scene entrances onto the main stage, of which twenty-one, or possibly twenty-two, are anticipatory directions. Nineteen of these twenty-one or twenty-two are placed about two or three lines before speeches spoken by, or to, enterers or speeches referring to their approaches. If the bookkeeper's intention was to allow the actors time to walk the distance between a stage door and the center or forward part of the stage, these observations can also support the conclusions reached in this paper. I have used the Tudor Facsimile Texts (ed. John S. Farmer, 1907; reprint, New York: AMS Press, 1970).

13. Fredson Bowers, "Authority, Copy, and Transmission in Shakespeare's Texts," 19–20.

14. Such speeches as "Here he comes," "Who comes here?" and the like can be classified under speeches referring to enterers' approaches. Even in texts based upon promptbooks or scribal transcripts, a considerable number of entry stage directions are preceded by such speeches and may possibly imply that entrances were not always made before the speeches referring to the enterers' approaches. (In *Macbeth* F1, for example, six entry stage directions are followed by such speeches and three are preceded by them.) But I have placed all entrances accompanied by "Here he comes" and its equivalents just before them, and where there are entry stage directions after these speeches, as well as where there are entry stage directions a few lines earlier, I have treated the positions of the stage directions as alternative possibilities. See Mariko Ichikawa, "A Note on Shakespeare's Stage Direction," *Shakespeare Studies* 22 (1985): 31–56.

15. I.e. *Titus Andronicus* (Q1–(Q3)–F1); *Love's Labor's Lost* (Q1–F1); *A Midsummer Night's Dream* (Q1–(Q2)–F1); *Romeo and Juliet* (Q2–(Q3)–F1); *Richard II* (Q1–(Q3)–F1); *The Merchant of Venice* (Q1–F1); *1 Henry IV* (Q2–(Q6)–F1); *2 Henry IV* (Q1–F1); *Much Ado About Nothing* (Q1–F1); *Troilus and Cressida* (Q1–F1); *King Lear* (Q1–(Q2)–F1).

16. In the case of *Richard II,* there are some important changes between Q1 and F1. The "abdication episode" (4.1.145–308) was expunged as an act of censorship from the three editions which were published in Queen Elizabeth's lifetime, i.e., Qq1–3. Owing to this special cause, an instance of $B = 4$ (4.1.148–52) and an instance of $A^+ = 7$ (4.1.258–65) are missing in Q1.

17. It is likely that the F1 texts of pre-Globe plays reflect the staging of their revivals at the Globe or the Blackfriars. The results of the Q–F comparisons concerning these plays seem to suggest that Shakespeare was able to have consistent expectations about his stages, whatever the planned venue. For the playhouses in which Shakespeare's plays were performed, I have relied on Andrew Gurr, *The Shakespearean Stage 1574–1642,* 3rd ed. (Cambridge: Cambridge University Press, 1992), 232–43.

18. There is no great difference between the distribution of instances in which summoners reenter with summoned characters and that of instances in which summoners do not reenter.

19. Because *All's Well,* 2.1 is a ceremonial scene, it is likely that the King sits on the chair of state. In Andrew Gurr's view, the chair must have occupied center stage. See his "The 'State' of Shakespeare's Audience," in *Shakespeare and the Sense of Performance,* eds. Marvin and Ruth Thomson (Newark: University of Delaware Press, 1989), 177.

20. Bernard Beckerman, "Theatrical Plots and Elizabethan Stage Practice," in *Shakespeare and Dramatic Tradition,* eds. W. R. Elton and William B. Long

(Newark, Del.: University of Delaware Press, 1989), 109–24. See also Long, "*John a Kent and John a Cumber:* An Elizabethan Playbook and Its Implications," in *Shakespeare and Dramatic Tradition,* 136–37.

21. Incidentally, in those cases where a character enters only to announce that another character is waiting offstage for his entrance and exits to summon him immediately, too, it seems sensible to assume that the character exits through the door from which he has just entered.

The Merchant of Venice and Japanese Culture

Yoshiko Kawachi

In the sixteenth century Venice became one of the most prosperous hubs of East-West trade. Trading and commercial activities in the city filled the city's coffers and stimulated a growth in moneylending. Consequently, a Shylock could find eager clients who needed to finance the cost of supplying and manning merchant ships. At that time, traders could reap huge fortunes or lose everything, and merchant ships commonly sailed from Venice to England, Lisbon, Mexico, the Barbary Coast, and India. Only a few ships sailed to Japan, perhaps because of the distance.

William Adams, a contemporary of Shakespeare's and a pilot of Dutch merchant ship, *de Liefde,* landed in Japan in 1600. Born in 1564, Adams was the first Englishman of note to arrive in Japan. He became a close adviser of Ieyasu Tokugawa, the lord who succeeded in pacifying the warring lords and establishing a close-knit, highly regulated feudal society. Adams provided Tokugawa with useful information about shipbuilding, European foreign and trade policies, and Western culture and civilization. In return, Tokugawa rewarded Adams by bestowing upon him the rank of a minor feudal lord.

Had trade continued between Japan and England, Shakespeare and his plays might have been introduced to the Japanese during the Tokugawa period (1603–1867). Iemitsu Tokugawa, however, had closed Japan to other countries, except Holland and China, and forbidden Japanese from trading with the "hairy barbarians."

During the Meiji period (1868–1912), Japan shook off the feudal system of the Tokugawa period and adopted vital aspects of Western culture and civilization. Significantly, Shakespeare and his plays gained currency among the literati of Japan during this period.

Mention of Shakespeare came as early as 1841 in a translation into Japanese of Lindley Murray's *English Grammar.* In 1871, a short biography of Shakespeare and the famous quotation from *Hamlet,* "Neither a borrower nor a lender be" (1.3.75), were introduced in the translation of Samuel Smiles' *Self-Help.* And in 1874, Charles Wirgman, an English correspondent who established the *Japan Punch* magazine in Yokohama, translated the "To be, or not to be" soliloquy into broken Japanese. This is regarded as the first translation of Shakespeare into the Japanese language.

As early as 1864, English language newspapers made their appearance in Yokohama. Soon after, Japanese language newspapers appeared and became part of the ongoing modernization process. Newspapers and periodicals helped spread the stories of Shakespeare to a reading public hungry for Western culture. In 1875, *Hamlet* was published in a newspaper. The first Japanese production of *Hamlet* took place in 1886 under the title of *Hamlet Yamato Nishikie (The Japanese Color Print of "Hamlet")*. In 1877, *Kyoniku no Kisho (A Strange Litigation about Flesh of the Chest)*, an adaptation of *The Merchant of Venice*, was published in two installments in the *Minken Zasshi (Popular Rights Magazine)*, by Keio Gijuku, a school founded by Yukichi Fukuzawa. The anonymous writer explained that the story was an adaptation of a novel written by Shakespeare of England. In those days, most translations were either loose adaptations of Shakespearean plots, or constructed from *Tales from Shakespeare* by Charles and Mary Lamb.

Kyoniku no Kisho, the first of Shakespeare's plays printed in book form, takes place in Sakai, a seaport near Osaka. The translator renamed the characters, giving them Japanese names for easier comprehension by Japanese readers. Portia, for example, became Kiyoka, meaning the Odor of Purity, and Shylock became Yokubari Ganpachi, or Stubborn Close-Fisted. Below is a summary of the plot.

> Once upon a time there lived near the seaport of Sakai a rich man named Setsunosuke Matsugae. He possessed a chivalrous spirit and was always willing to provide assistance to those less fortunate. His friend Umejiro Murano, whose father died while Umejiro was still a young boy, became the pupil of Gaunsai Shirane, an expert in military science. Umejiro studied hard and Gaunsai was pleased. He placed his future hopes on young Umejiro. Then misfortune struck. Umejiro's mother became seriously ill and in need of medicine. Umejiro, penniless, went to Setsunosuke to borrow money.
>
> Setsunosuke was sympathetic to Umejiro's request and decided to lend him the money. However, until his ship returned after having finished a trading expedition in the northern provinces, Setsunosuke himself had to borrow money. He went to Yokubari Ganpachi, a man

of great wealth, to seek a loan. Ganpachi agreed upon the condition that Setsunosuke repay with one *kin* of flesh cut from his heart should Setsunosuke fail to repay the debt on the date agreed.

The date for repaying came, but Setsunosuke learned that his ship would be delayed one day. He asked Ganpachi for a day's grace; Ganpachi refused. "The court will decide which of us has right on our side," Ganpachi said.

In the meantime Gaunsai heard about the situation. Known also for his civic wisdom, the Governor of Sakai often consulted him. The governor sent for him in order to discuss Setsunosuke's predicament. Now among Gaunsai's students was an intelligent woman named Kiyoka, the daughter of wealthy parents. She had recently become betrothed to Umejiro and was surprised at the painful situation Umejiro and Setsunosuke were in.

Gaunsai, feigning illness, sent Kiyoka to the governor instead. Kiyoka, disguised as a lawyer, pleaded the case for Setsunosuke, citing appropriate Buddhist teachings. Ganpachi argued that he cared for nothing but the law of the state. Then she offered to repay Ganpachi three times the amount borrowed. Ganpachi refused. Then Kiyoka said she was ready for a judgment. She asked Ganpachi if he brought with him scales to weigh the *kin* of flesh and a surgeon. Ganpachi had brought the scales but did not bring a surgeon, since it was not required by the contract. Kiyoka then told him that the *kin* of flesh was his by law, but that no drop of blood must be spilled. "If a drop of blood is spilled, you shall be put to death without mercy," Kiyoka said. Ganpachi became nervous and backed away from the contract. The governor then said: "I spare your life in mercy, but your wealth is forfeit by law."

Because the story shows both the swift turning of the heavenly wheel of retribution and the upholding of poetical justice, it appealed to large numbers of the reading public who were familiar with similar themes in Kabuki plays.

In 1883 Tsutomu Inoue translated *The Merchant of Venice* into Japanese and gave it a Japanese title, *Seiyo Chinsetsu Jinniku Shichiire Saiban (A Western Strange Story of the Trial of Pawned Flesh)*. This adaptation condensed and Japanized Lamb and was popular enough to warrant several reprintings after it was first published by Kinkodo. A brief outline of Inoue's translation follows. He used a Japanese name only for Shylock.

There was a moneylender named Sairoku (Shylock) in Venice. People hated him because he was a cruel and unmerciful Jew, a person likened to the hated *eta-hinin*, the humble people of the lowest class in Japan who lived in a limited area. Antonio was a rich merchant who had many steamships. He was kind enough to help Bassanio marry

Portia, he borrowed 300 dollars from Sairoku, and he gave it to Bassanio. Sairoku wanted to take a *kin* of Antonio's flesh as security for the loan.

Portia was a rich and beautiful lady who had black hair and red lips. She lived in Belmont together with her maid Nerissa. Bassanio took a train to Belmont together with Gratiano to propose to Portia. When Portia met Bassanio, she gave him a diamond ring, and they married. Gratiano and Nerissa also got married.

They received Antonio's letter saying that he was imprisoned because he could not pay back the borrowed money to Sairoku. Portia advised Bassanio to hurry to Venice, and she disguised herself as a lawyer and went to the court. Portia tried to persuade Sairoku, telling him the importance of mercy, but he refused to listen to her. Therefore, Portia ordered Sairoku not to shed blood while cutting Antonio's flesh. Thus Sairoku, a plaintiff, lost the suit and signed the bond in which his possessions should be given to his daughter after his death. Antonio's life was saved. Bassanio was very pleased and thanked Portia. She coaxed him to give her his diamond ring which she had given to him before. Unwillingly, he agreed to her request. Then Portia went back to Belmont by train. Antonio and Bassanio came to Belmont later, and the truth was revealed. After the quarrel between the couple, the ring was returned.

The translator, Inoue, concludes, "This is a moving story of Europe where virtue and goodness are admired."[1] In this translation, Inoue stressed the court scene and used three of his six chapters to describe the details of the trial. The translator omitted the casket scene, the story of Shylock's conversion to Christianity, and the plot of Jessica's elopement with Lorenzo, her Christian boyfriend. In other words, he made no mention of the religious opposition between Jews and Italian Christians.

Possibly Inoue omitted the story of Jessica's elopement because Japanese women were forbidden from marrying anyone their families did not approve. Cecil Roth writes that the Renaissance period in Italy was, from certain points of view, an age of feminine emancipation in life, if not in law.[2] If so, Jessica's elopement may be evaluated from the viewpoint of feminism. Therefore, the translator may have deleted this sub-plot because elopement was regarded as immoral in Japan due to the strong influence of Confucianism. Moreover, the translator describes Portia as an obedient and uneducated Japanese woman.

It is also interesting that Inoue's characters took a train—an invention which Shakespeare had never even imagined—from Venice Station to the fictitious town of Belmont.[3] In Inoue's translation, the characters travel this way because it was in keeping with

the process of modernization then occurring. In 1872 Japan's first
train line between Shinbashi and Yokohama opened. Two more
lines were built: between Osaka and Kobe in 1874, and between
Kyoto and Osaka in 1877. The opening of these train lines excited
the Japanese imagination.

The translator's use of *eta-hinin,* or outcasts, to make comparisons with the Jews of the fifteenth and sixteenth centuries, reflects
in part Inoue's cultural and social milieu. During the Tokugawa
period, the Japanese social order was divided into four classes: the
samurai class, the peasants, the artisans, and the merchants. At
the very bottom were the outcasts.

Forced to live in restricted areas, they engaged in the leather
industry and were hired to perform tasks looked down upon by
the other classes, such as executing criminals. In 1871, the Meiji
government passed a law emancipating these people. However,
they remained *de facto* outcasts.

Perhaps another reason Inoue makes the comparison between
the Jews in Venice and the outcasts in Japan comes from his interpretation of Shylock's words: "He hath disgraced me, and hindered
me half a million; laughed at my losses, mocked at my gains,
scorned my nation, thwarted my bargains, cooled my friends,
heated mine enemies, and what's his reason?——I am a Jew. Hath
not a Jew eyes? . . ." (3.1.50–4)

As minorities both the Jews and the outcasts in Japan suffered
the sting of discrimination. We know that the Jews were ordered
to live in Ghetto Nuovo in Venice in 1516. As Roth writes: "In the
Venice of the sixteenth and seventeenth centuries, which became
one of the luxury cities of Europe, Jews intermingled freely with
non-Jews."[4] In addition, the Jews engaged in business activities
and professions that the outcasts of Japan were forbidden from
entering. Thus the comparison breaks down. Outcasts were considered unclean and unworthy of living in general society and were
restricted to performing jobs and tasks considered unclean in a
predominantly Buddhist society. Jews, though forced to live in
ghettos, could work among gentiles as moneylenders, doctors, and
scholars. Undoubtedly, Inoue did not know these details of Jewish life.

In 1885 Bunkai Udagawa, a journalist, adapted *The Merchant of
Venice* for a newspaper entitled *Osaka Asahi Shinbun,* and Genzo
Katsu dramatized it for the Nakamura Sojuro Kabuki Company.
The title of this adaptation, performed at the Ebisu-za Theater in
Osaka on May 16, 1885, was *Sakuradoki Zeni no Yononaka (The
Season of Cherry Blossoms: The World of Money).* It was also

performed under the same title at two other theaters in Osaka in June 1885 and November 1893.

This adaptation, set in the Osaka of the Tokugawa period, was the first performance of Shakespeare in Japan. In fact, until the end of World War II it was the most frequently performed play of all of Shakespeare's plays; and sometimes the trial scene alone was performed as an independent production. (Since 1945, *Hamlet* has become the most frequently performed play of Shakespearean plays.)

Why was *The Merchant of Venice* chosen as the first staging of Shakespearean plays in Japan? Why was its adaptation so successful in Osaka? The summary below indicates the reasons.

In Osaka there was a woman whose name was Ume. Her father, a rich peasant, asked Denjiro Kinokuniya, a wealthy ship merchant, to take care of her when he died. After her father's sudden death, Ume came into a rich inheritance. Her uncle, Gohei, was a usurer like Shylock. He intended to rob her of her property. After the funeral he went to the crematorium to steal money and goods from her father's coffin. Then an old traveler came, and Gohei, robbing him of his money, put the old traveler into the fire.

Shotaro Aoki, a middle-class *samurai* and scholar, happened to come to the crematorium. He thought that the dead traveler must be his teacher, Dr. Kansai Nakagawa, a famous scholar of Japanese, Chinese, and Dutch studies, who was going to Nagasaki, the mecca of Dutch studies.

One year later, Gohei forced Ume into an apprenticeship at a *geisha* house. But Tamaei, Dr. Nakagawa's only daughter, saved Ume, and Ume became Tamaei's maid. Tamaei had been proposed to by two students of her father, Aoki and Ichinojo Kawashima. Aoki did not have money to buy the right to be adopted into the Nakagawa family and to succeed Tamaei's father as head of the family. Therefore, Aoki prepared himself for death, but his friend Kinokuniya offered his help, borrowed money from Gohei, using his own flesh as collateral, and gave it to Aoki.

Going on a trip to Nagasaki, Dr. Nakagawa willed his property to his daughter and ordered her to marry the man who would find his will in one of three caskets—the first made of gold, the second of silver and the third of iron. Tamaei and Aoki had loved each other. Aoki who had already gotten the money to defeat his rival chose the iron casket. Luckily, it was the right casket and he was able to marry Tamaei, while his rival Kawashima chose the gold one and was expelled. At night, just before the couple consummated their marriage, they received the news that Kinokuniya's ships had been wrecked. Aoki said to Tamaei, "Please pay back the money to Kinokuniya later," and left her immediately. Tamaei asked Ume to carry money to Kinokuniya, but on the way Ume was robbed of the money and was cast into the river.

In the trial scene, Kawashima, a judge, became angry when he learned that the money in question was the key money for the marriage of Aoki and Tamaei, and ordered Gohei to cut the flesh of Kinokuniya's chest according to the bond. Just as Gohei was going to cut it, a public servant named Heijiro Mizuki told him not to shed the defendant's blood. Gohei resigned himself to receiving the money, and he was subsequently arrested. He repented his misconduct. Aoki and Tamaei had a happy life because Dr. Nakagawa returned home safely from Nagasaki, and Kinokuniya married Ume.

As noted earlier, *Sakuradoki Zeni no Yononaka* was originally a novel published in serial form in an Osaka newspaper from April 10 to May 20, 1885. The novel was dramatized and performed on May 16, 1885, even before it was completed. In both the novel and the stagescript, Kinokuniya is equivalent to Antonio, Aoki to Bassanio, Tamaei to Portia, and Gohei to Shylock. Ume plays the role of Nerissa, though she is a typical old-fashioned woman in feudal Japan.

The full text of *Sakuradoki Zeni no Yononaka,* published by Bunpodo in 1886, consists of 190 pages and contains a series of illustrations. The title page says, "The idea is from Shakespeare's 'Flesh of the Chest' and the style is that of Kabuki script written by Tanehiko Ryutei, a dramatist of the Edo period. . . ."[5]

In the Preface, the young literary scholars meet by chance in the center of Osaka where the cherry blossoms are in full bloom. One has a Kabuki script by Ryutei while the other has the translation of *The Merchant of Venice* by Inoue. The latter young man says,

"I hear that recently the pupils of the primary schools learn the English language. English studies have become more and more popular, and there is a tendency for people to read English books. This is a shortcut to our Westernization, I think. By the way, the book you have now is, as you know, written by Shakespeare, a famous English dramatist. Its original title is 'Flesh of the Chest' and it is a novel written to let the people know the relationship between morality and law. It is a very good book for the public, but its idea is a little strange."[6]

The first young man says, "The spirit of European novel is noble, but the idea of Japanese and Chinese novels is much better." The second replies, "European novels appear to be simpler than Japanese novels because the Westerners, who are more scientific and intelligent, do not want to speak about strange or complicated things." Thus the two young men are remarkably influenced by European literature. Then the third boy says,

> "I have overheard your conversation. At a bookstore near here, I bought an old manuscript, a collection of the trial records of the Edo period, one of which is very interesting. I will be very grateful to you if you lend me your books tonight. I want to write a story and mix the spirit of European novels with the idea of Japanese novels, by referring to this trial record. I will follow the Kabuki style. I wish to ask you to criticize my story when it is completed."[7]

This is, in effect, how this adaptation was written. At the same time Japan was at the peak of Europeanization. We find in this adaptation the reflection of Japanese cultural and social development of that time. For instance, the adapter changed the gold, silver, and lead caskets of Shakespeare's original to gold, silver, and iron. Why? The reason may be explained by the following words in the adaptation:

> Iron is very important because it is used for guns, swords, spears, spades, hoes, scythes, axes, hammers, saws, pots and pans which the people of the four social ranks of Japanese feudal society (warriors, farmers, craftsmen and merchants) use everyday. Without iron, we Japanese can neither defend our country nor make our living. Iron is the most valuable treasure for us. We hear that the railroad has been built of iron recently in Europe and that they have made iron ships for wars.[8]

In this passage, the adapter stated the practical importance of iron for Japan's industrial development and showed the people's concern for technology. Thinking that iron was more important than lead in Japan's policy for enhancing wealth and military strength, he changed the casket from lead to iron. However, if the choice of the lead casket symbolizes wisdom and also allegorically represents the choice of Christ as Wisdom, as Joan Ozark Holmer suggests,[9] the Japanese adapter who changed the lead casket into an iron casket ignored the Christian background of the scene.

This adaptation gained in general popularity mainly because of the trial scene. The people of those days were very interested in law; they studied European law as a model for modernizing the legal system. In Japan, the criminal codes were promulgated in 1880, the constitution was established in 1889, and the civil codes were completed in 1896. The amazing frequency of the performances of the trial scene in this comedy indicated the Japanese people's growing interest in and awareness of their legal system.

The shocking episode depicting Gohei's attempt to cut Kinokuniya's flesh must have both horrified and thrilled audiences. When Gohei demands Kinokuniya's flesh, Tamaei—in the disguise of a boy, Yoneda—says to him, "Gohei, you were born in Japan, a country of gods. I'm sure that you believe in gods. The gods always tell us to have mercy. You know that a human being should show mercy to the poor and the weak."[10] The gods mentioned here refer to the gods of Shintoism and Buddhism. Shintoism and Buddhism were mixed in those days, and people prayed to both at home. In addition, the cruel episode must have reminded audiences of the Kabuki play, *Shakanyorai Tanjoe (The Picture of the Birth of Buddha)* written by Monzaemon Chikamatsu in 1695. In act 3, a foolish man named Handoku kills a dove, and the servant of Davedatta, a disciple of Buddha, is going to cut the flesh of Handoku.[11] This episode found in Buddhist scripture seems to have been based on an historical event. Audiences were probably accustomed to this kind of story and were surprised to find a similar episode in a different cultural context.

The second reason this adaptation gained in popularity may be found in the title, *Zeni no Yononaka (The World of Money)*. People of the Meiji era believed that Western civilization had a close relationship with economics and that finance was most important for Japanese modernization. Therefore, this Japanese title must have appealed to audiences who were gradually becoming aware of capitalism.

Shylock performs the function of a banker in a capitalist society: he lends money and charges interest. That explains in part why Shylock dislikes Antonio: Antonio "lends out money gratis" (1.3.42). Many Christians considered usury to be sinful. They cited Deuteronomy, where it is written: "Thou shalt not lend upon usury to thy brother. . . . Unto a stranger thou mayest lend upon usury" (23:19–20). For Christians, lending freely is a way to show wise love, but lending at interest violates the love of friendship.[12] But Shylock, a Jew, is an alien in Venice. Therefore, he lends money at high interest to Christians without feeling any guilt.[13]

Note that the adapter changed the setting from Venice to Osaka, an old commercial city. Many wealthy merchants lived there, and the citizens had a strong sense of financial matters. Moreover, Osaka's topography resembles that of Venice. Because of the many canals, people often refer to it as "the city built on water."

In the year following the performance of this adaptation, the Society for Dramatic Improvement was organized. Prominent people who took part in the society included Kenji Yasui, a member

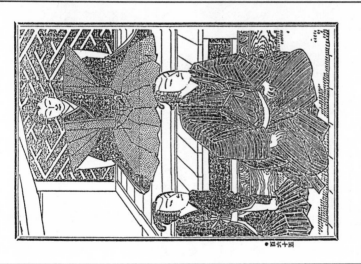

The trial scene of *Sakuradoki Zeni no Yononaka*, a Japanese adaptation of *The Merchant of Venice*, 1885. On the floor Tamaei (Portia) and Kawashima (Judge) sit, while on the ground Aoki (Bassanio) listens to the dialogue between Kinokuniya (Antonio) and Gohei (Shylock). Photo courtesy of the National Diet Library of Japan.

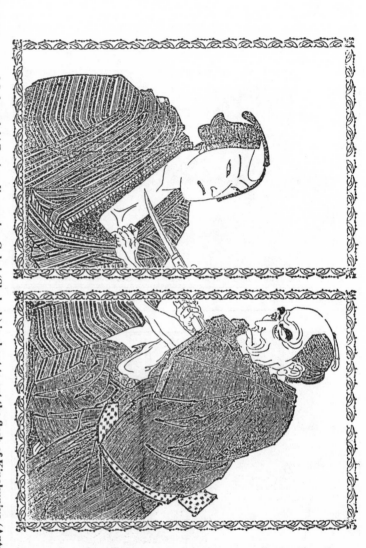

The trial scene of *Sakuradoki Zeni no Yononaka*. Gohei (Shylock) is about to cut the flesh of Kinokuniya (Antonio)'s chest. Photo courtesy of the National Diet Library of Japan.

of the municipal assembly; Bunkai Udagawa, a journalist and writer of this adaptation for the newspaper; Sojuro Nakamura, a Kabuki actor who played the leading role in the stage production of the adaptation; and Genzo Katsu, who adapted the newspaper story for the stage. We do not know whether their efforts to make improvements to Japanese drama by introducing Western elements were completely successful. However, I think it was not entirely accidental that these people, who wanted to improve Japanese drama by introducing the influence of Westernization, chose *The Merchant of Venice* for their first performance in Osaka. Perhaps they thought that it was the easiest to understand of Shakespeare's plays; perhaps they also thought it held the most appeal for audiences in Osaka where the people were deeply interested in earning money and improving Japanese drama.

The third reason this adaptation gained in popularity can be attributed to the women in the play. Portia, a woman of intellect, feelings, and will power, was introduced into Japan as an ideal of European women in the days of Westernization. The differences in the images of Eastern and Western women are significant. I think that to discover in Tamaei the reflection of Portia or to compare Tamaei with Portia is useful for clarifying the status of Japanese women of the Meiji era.

In *The Merchant of Venice,* there are three kinds of social groups: the Jewish community, the Christian male society, and the female group in Belmont. Portia is the queen of Belmont. Anna Brownell Jameson, a pioneer of feminism in the nineteenth century, described the character of Portia as follows:

> She treads as though her footsteps had been among marble palaces, beneath roofs of fretted gold, o'er cedar floors and pavements of jasper and porphyry; amid gardens full of statues, and flowers, and fountains, and haunting music. She is full of penetrative wisdom, and genuine tenderness, and lively wit; but as she has never known want, or grief, or fear, or disappointment, her wisdom is without a touch of the sombre or the sad; her affections are all mixed up with faith, hope, and joy; and her wit has not a particle of malevolence or causticity.[14]

This is a romantic interpretation of Portia; Jameson described Portia as though she were a goddess living in a mythic world. She also stressed Portia's intellect, and mentioned Portia as the first of Shakespeare's intellectual women. She wrote, "The wit of Portia is like attar of roses, rich and concentrated."[15] According to Jameson, "Intellect is of no sex . . . [but] in men, the intellectual faculties exist more self-poised and self-directed . . . than we ever find them in women, with whom talent . . . is in a much greater degree modified by the sympathies and moral qualities."[16] In short, she appraises Portia's intellect and morality as well as her beautiful and graceful figure.

Bassanio says that Portia "is a lady richly left,/ And she is fair, and, fairer than that word,/ Of wondrous virtues" (1.1.161–63). Indeed, Portia is a fair lady such as those painted by Titian and Giorgione of the Venetian School. Her golden hair attracts the suitors' attention just like "a golden fleece," the most valuable and expensive commodity for the Argonauts.

In contrast, Bassanio is a scholar, soldier, and poor gentleman. *Gentleman* is the key term in the stratification of classes. To be a gentleman placed one within the 4 to 5 percent of the population that exercised power in Shakespeare's time. A gentleman did not work with his hands; he could live off his income.[17] However, Bassanio went bankrupt and wanted to borrow money from Antonio, a merchant, in order to marry the fair, rich Portia. In a word, Portia symbolizes wealth. J. R. Brown says, "Shakespeare wrote of love as a kind of wealth in which men and women traffic. Of all the comedies, *The Merchant of Venice* is the most completely informed by Shakespeare's ideal of love's wealth."[18] We find the dynamics of erotic and economic desires at play in this romantic comedy.

Bassanio must choose the casket which contains Portia's portrait, if he is to win her hand in marriage. Portia is a wise woman and an obedient daughter when she says, "I will die as chaste as Diana unless I be obtained by the manner of my father's will" (1.2.103–5). According to Freud, "Caskets are also women, symbols of the essential thing in woman, and therefore of a woman herself, like boxes, large or small, baskets, and so on."[19] If so, in the casket scene, a man selects not only a casket but also a woman. Here a woman is regarded as the object of man's desire, and the casket has a sexual meaning just like Nerrisa's ring.

In the patriarchal society of the English Renaissance, Portia is both an obedient wife and an obedient daughter when she says to Bassanio:

> You see me, Lord Bassanio, where I stand,
> Such as I am. Though for myself alone
> I would not be ambitious in my wish
> To wish myself much better, yet for you
> I would be trebled twenty times myself,
> A thousand times more fair, ten thousand times more rich,

That only to stand high in your account
I might in virtues, beauties, livings, friends,
Exceed account. But the full sum of me
Is sum of something which, to term in gross,
Is an unlessoned girl, unschooled, unpractisèd,

. . . .

This house, these servants, and this same myself
Are yours, my lord's.

(3.2.149–71)

In this speech, where Portia confesses her love through the imagery of wealth, we also see the relationship between marriage and
property. As Lawrence Stone pointed out, one of the objectives of
family planning in pre-Reformation England was the acquisition
through marriage of further property.[20] Moreover, we see that a
woman's body is regarded as a man's possession or a commodity
in this male-dominated society, though Portia herself is an intellectual. I think that one of the themes of this comedy, the exchange
of goods at both the erotic level and the economic level, is illustrated in this passage.

In *Sakuradoki Zeni no Yononaka*, Aoki comments, "Tamaei is
different from ordinary women because she is educated at
home. . . . Although she is not twenty years old yet, she manages
her father's property, uses servants and maids, and leads her life
admirably."[21] Tamaei is as beautiful as Portia, but she seems to be
more independent and more highly educated than Portia. She says
to her first suitor Kawashima, "I do not know who will succeed to
the head position in my family, but I will never rely on my future
husband. I will make my way skillfully in life by means of the
lessons that my father has taught me. I think a wife should have
the spirit of independence."[22]
Kawashima asks, "Why?" and she answers,

"My father always says that men and women are physically different
but that they have the same mind given by the creator, and that the
European people advance the equal rights for men and women. In our
country, however, men regard women as slaves, and women believe
that they should obey their father, husband, and son. In addition,
women are satisfied with learning only the three R's, sewing and danc-
ing. They live meaninglessly, relying on their husbands and sons. This
is not good. I am Dr. Nakagawa's daughter. I am quite different from
the common women. I have studied Japanese, Chinese, and Dutch, and
I will live independently."[23]

From her speech, we discover the progressive thinking of Tamaei's father. As a pioneer of Westernization, he educated his daughter according to equality of the sexes. However, Tamaei is a special woman educated in a family of intellectuals. Her family background and upbringing must have been unfamiliar to audiences living under male hegemony and patriarchal power. In short, she is a model of the "new woman" in the Meiji era. Perhaps the adapter wanted to show what women's education should be in the period of modernization. As a result, Tamaei was described as a fresh but rather radical woman.

Ume, her maid, is a contrast to Tamaei. Representing one type of traditional Japanese woman, Ume reveals how some women living in a feudal society often had to sell themselves for money. When Gohei was going to sell her to the *geisha* house, he regarded her body as a commodity. There were really such women in the Meiji era, so the audiences must have been sympathetic with Ume. In this adaptation, she plays the role of Nerissa, but she is quite different in personality. Nerissa is shrewd enough to test how deeply her husband loves her by using her ring just as Portia does. Ume is also different from Jessica, who is "wise, fair, and true" (2.6.56) and strong enough to deprive her father of his money and jewels and elope with Lorenzo.

The contrasting personalities of Ume and Tamaei show us the two different types of women, old and new. The traditional image of a Japanese woman evolved in response to the influences of Buddhism, Confucianism, and the *samurai* ethic. Ekiken Kaibara (1630–1714), the Neo-Confucian scholar, was the most influential in defining the role of women. He wrote *Onna Daigaku (Great Learning for Women)*, which became the primary text for women because it reinforced the feudal aim of perfecting the family system. In this book published in 1790, he wrote that a woman must look to her husband as her lord and that the great lifelong duty of a woman was obedience.

A woman's legal status during the Tokugawa period was completely dependent first on her father, then on her husband and eventually on her son, as Tamaei points out in the adaptation. If a couple gave birth only to daughters, a son was frequently adopted and married to the oldest daughter. Therefore, Aoki would take the family name of Nakagawa. However, when feudalism finally collapsed in the Meiji era, there were some champions of women's rights. Tsutomu Inoue, the above-mentioned translator of *The Merchant of Venice,* wrote *Joken Shinron (A True View of Women's Rights)* in 1881. While the Confucian concept of the feminine role continued to keep women out of school for a long time, Arinori Mori, the Minister for Education in 1885, supported education for women. Yukichi Fukuzawa, also an educator, championed equality of opportunity for women. He believed that a change of attitude toward women should accompany their education, and he published two critiques of *Onna Daigaku* in 1899. Thus Meiji leaders, realizing that education was essential to modernization, gave it a high priority.

It seems to me that the contrasting images of Ume and Tamaei reflect these confusing social conditions in which people wanted to introduce culture from abroad into Japan without abandoning traditional Japanese culture.

An informative book, *Things Japanese*, written by the Englishman, Basil Hall Chamberlain, introduced Japan to the West. Chamberlain, who arrived in 1873 as a professor of Japanese and philology at Tokyo University, had this to say about the status of Japanese women:

> Japanese women are most womanly,—kind, gentle, faithful, pretty. But the way in which they are treated by the men has hitherto been such as might cause a pang to any generous European heart. No wonder that scme of them are at last endeavouring to emancipate themselves. . . . Two grotesquely different influences are now at work to undermine this state of slavery—one, European theories concerning the relation of the sexes, the other, European clothes! . . . But many resident foreigners—male foreigners, of course—think differently, and the question forms a favourite subject of debate. The only point on which both parties agree is in their praise of Japanese woman. Says one side, "She is so charming that she deserves better treatment,"—to which the other side retorts that it is just because she is "kept in her place" that she is charming. The following quotation is from a letter to the present writer by a well-known author, who, like others, has fallen under the spell. "How sweet," says he, "Japanese woman is! All the possibilities of the race for goodness seem to be concentrated in her. It shakes one's faith in some Occidental doctrines. If this be the result of suppression and oppression, then these are not altogether bad. On the other hand, how diamond-hard the character of the American woman becomes under the idolatry of which she is the object. . . ."[24]

The "well-known author" of the above-mentioned letter is Lafcadio Hearn who came to Japan in 1890 and married a Japanese woman.

When *Sakuradoki Zeni no Yononaka* was performed, the ring episode and Tamaei's disguise were omitted. In the newspaper, the adapter made Tamaei say to Aoki, "I hear there is a custom of exchanging rings for marriage in European countries. You and I

studied Dutch culture, so we had better keep this habit."[25] However, there was no scene where Tamaei gave her ring to Aoki on
the stage. I suspect this omission occurred because the Japanese
of those days were not familiar with this custom, and because
Tamaei did not disguise herself as a lawyer. Consequently, there
was no chance for the ring to be used in a love test.

Next, I wish to consider the omission of the dramatic ploy of
making use of disguises. In *The Merchant of Venice,* Jessica, a
Jewish girl, disguises herself as a boy when she escapes from op-
pressive patriarchy and elopes with Lorenzo, an Italian Christian.
She says, "I am much ashamed of my exchange" (2.6.35), but Lorenzo says, "So are you, sweet,/ Even in the lovely garnish of a
boy" (2.6.44–5). Her festive cross-dressing helps her break down
racial prejudice and cross the boundary between the Jewish community and Christian society.

When Portia and Nerissa go to Venice, they disguise themselves
as a young lawyer and his clerk. Portia says:

> . . . they shall think we are accomplishèd
> With that we lack. I'll hold thee any wager,
> When we are both accountered like young men
> I'll prove the prettier fellow of the two,
> And wear my dagger with the braver grace,
> And speak between the change of man and boy
> With a reed voice, and turn two mincing steps
> Into a manly stride, and speak of frays
> Like a fine bragging youth, . . .
>
> (3.4.61–9)

Belmont is a static space where people are given love and
wealth; Venice is a dynamic world where people must fight for
money and love. Venice is a city full of competition between races,
as well as in economy and religion. Venice is a *topos* of a homosocial bond, "a continuum of male relations which the exchange of
women entails,"[26] while Belmont is a place of marriage. Venice is,
so to speak, a masculine society while Belmont is a feminine
society. Therefore, women, who wish to compete in Venice,
have to wear male clothes. Portia knows well that cross-dressing
potentially involves both inversion and displacement of gender
binaries.[27]

Portia is never ashamed of her transformation, indeed she uses
her exchange effectively. In Belmont she conforms to the Renaissance ideal of womanhood: chaste, obedient, and silent. In the trial
scene, however, Portia as the upright judge is strong, decisive, and

wise. The Portia who speaks about mercy and monarchy in the Venetian court bears some resemblance to Queen Elizabeth who called herself "a prince" in the English Court.[28] In the trial scene, Portia is not only an androgynous justice-figure but also a person of "the supernumerary gender" or "the superior sex."

Portia is also a predecessor of the female pages of Shakespeare's romantic comedies. Rosalind in *As You Like It* wears a skirt for a few minutes. In the Forest of Arden, however, she enjoys the opportunity to play a man. But she has, in truth, no doublet and hose in her disposition. Viola's cross-dressing in *Twelfth Night* makes her feel uncomfortable because she cannot confess her love to Orsino. Portia's disguise, however, is unlike those of Rosalind and Viola. Portia does not choose a disguise for protection. Instead she disguises herself in order to play at being a man. Keith Geary says, "What is most striking about Portia's disguise as Balthazar is the absence of the psychological and sexual ambiguity that informs the disguises of the other heroines."[29] In *The Merchant of Venice,* the complex feelings of female pages are found more clearly in Jessica's speech than in Portia's speech, both of which are quoted above.

The female pages are sometimes discussed from the viewpoint of feminism.[30] Moll Cutpurse, in *The Roaring Girl* by Middleton and Dekker, is a case in point. However, in English Renaissance theaters the female pages were played by boy actors. They were the "little eyases" (*Hamlet,* 2.2.339) who were "not yet old enough for a man, nor young enough for a boy." (*Twelfth Night,* 1.5.151–52). Consequently, the eroticism of the Elizabethan stage was probably different from that of the present-day stage where an actress plays the role of a female page. For example, in Rome, at a performance of Goldoni's *La Locandiera,* Goethe was surprised to see men acting women's parts, and he experienced the unique aesthetic pleasure which Elizabethan playgoers must have felt.[31] Transvestism has such a dramatic effect. In addition, the transvestite stage gives men and women an opportunity to reconsider both the sex-gender system in their society and the ideological meaning of the semiotics of dress.

In Japan, boys played the female roles in the seventeenth century. People called this troupe "Wakashu Kabuki" (Lad Kabuki). They danced, mimicked, and performed a skit or acrobatics. They were effeminate enough to be the partners in homosexual relationships. As a result, the government prohibited their performances in 1652. Now Kabuki actors called *onnagata* play female roles on the stage. The word *onnagata* means "a woman's form" or "the

woman side." An *onnagata* is not a boy but a male actor who plays
the role of a young woman very skillfully and gracefully in a Kabuki play. Even an older actor would play these roles. Japanese
audiences, who are accustomed to this dramatic convention, suspend their belief and forget that the *onnagata* is actually a male
actor.

Of the trial scene where Tamaei disguises herself as a lawyer,
Bunkai Udagawa writes, "Tamaei Nakagawa makes up like a
woman and has her hair dressed like a young man. But nobody
knows whether she is a male or a female."[32] Tamaei herself says,
"I am disguised as a young man, taking the name of Kosaburo
Yoneda. As an official spy, I will go to the court. I encourage
myself in order to imitate a man just like a Kabuki actor imitates
a woman."[33]

It is noteworthy that Tamaei is conscious of the *onnagata* when
she disguises herself as a young lawyer. In the stagescript, however,
there is no cross-dressing. Instead of Tamaei, a young lawyer
named Mizuki appears on the stage. This name reminds Japanese
audiences of a famous *onnagata* named Tatsunosuke Mizuki
(1673–1745). Why did the dramatizer, Genzo Katsu, omit Tamaei's
disguise? I think the main reason was that he thought of the audiences' response: the audiences of those days were more familiar
with a man in woman's disguise than a woman in man's disguise.

Clearly there are many major differences between Shakespeare's
play and the Japanese adaptation. The following are minor differences between them. First, Bassanio borrows money to marry Portia and get her property, while Aoki borrows money not only to
marry Tamaei but also to succeed to the family name and scholarship of Dr. Nakagawa. This change may have occurred because the
adapter was profoundly conscious of Japanese feudalism. Second,
Shylock holds strong principles as a Jew who places more importance on justice than on mercy or on Old Law than New Law,
while Gohei has neither prejudice nor religious theory. Third, while
Gohei is a villain, he does not have the same overwhelming desire
for revenge that Shylock has. Consequently there is little serious
opposition between Kinokuniya and Gohei, while there is much
between Antonio and Shylock. Shakespeare's Antonio says that
Shylock is "a stony adversary, an inhuman wretch/ Uncapable of
pity, void and empty/ From any dram of mercy" (4.1.3–5). But
Heinrich Heine recalls, "A British beauty wept passionately to see
the end of act 4 behind me in the box of Drury Lane."[34] It is
unlikely that anyone wept upon seeing Gohei in the Japanese
theater. This adaptation resembles a morality play in the style

of Kabuki, while Shakespeare's original dramatizes the religious opposition between Judaism and Christianity.

I think these differences between Shakespeare's original play and its adaptation reflect Japan's hasty introduction of European culture during the Meiji era. The Japanese people of those days did not understand Renaissance ideas, English dramaturgy and the Western mode of living as well as Japanese do today. They had no time to value substance above form. They wanted to adapt European culture to the Japanese lifestyle as soon as possible.

We may, therefore, reasonably conclude that *The Merchant of Venice* was introduced into Japan to enlighten the public and improve the standard of culture. In other words, Shakespeare was used as one means of improving Japanese culture. While Udagawa and Katsu did not know European dramaturgy and conventions, they were strongly aware of Kabuki plays when they adapted Shakespeare's comedy to the Japanese stage. Later, Shoyo Tsubouchi, the first translator of Shakespearean works, compared Shakespeare with Monzaemon Chikamatsu, a great Kabuki playwright, and enumerated eighteen similarities between the two great dramatists.[35] Tsubouchi was the first to give serious consideration to what the Japanese people should learn from Shakespeare and how Japanese drama should be improved by a study of Shakespeare's dramaturgy.

A sketch of the stage history of *The Merchant of Venice* in Japan shows a great variety and innovations. *Sakuradoki Zeni no Yononaka* performed by the Kabuki actors acquired great popularity. In this adaptation, Sojuro Nakamura played the part of Kinokuniya, while Jusaburo Bando, an *onnagata,* played the role of Tamaei. Thus the first performance of *The Merchant of Venice* in Japan was an all-male production. However, when Otojiro Kawakami, a star of *shinpa* (New School of Theater), produced the trial scene of this comedy in 1903, Sadayakko, his wife, performed the part of Portia. Kawakami and his wife, who had seen *The Merchant of Venice* in Boston, tried to produce this comedy in the European style for Japanese audiences. Kawakami imitated Henry Irving's Shylock, and Sadayakko copied Ellen Terry's Portia. This production was criticized by Tsubouchi, but it is noteworthy that Kawakami took the lead in staging the translated drama of Shakespeare in Japan for the first time.

The Bungei Kyokai (The Association of Literature and Arts), established by Tsubouchi in 1906, performed only the trial scene at the Kabuki Theater. This was an all-male production, and Shunsho Doi, who had seen Shakespearean plays in America with Ka-wakami, played the role of Portia. His performance was well received. In 1913 Kabuki actors also performed the trial scene. Sadanji Ichikawa played the part of Shylock, and Shocho Ichikawa, an *onnagata,* played the role of Portia. In an essay about this performance, Tsubouchi wrote that Portia disguised as a lawyer was not so manly and that Shylock did not look so cruel.[36]

In 1903, the actress Sadayakko was the first woman to play Portia; in 1915, Ritsuko Mori was the second. In those days actresses were not recognized as professionals by the public. However, Mori was the first student to enter a drama school for women and to become an actress. Since then, the female characters of *The Merchant of Venice* have been acted by women.

In 1926 *The Merchant of Venice* directed by Yoshi Hijikata was performed by the actors and the actresses of the Shingeki (New Drama) troupe. This dramatic group was founded in 1924 and performed mainly modern and realistic dramas such as those by Ibsen, Chekhov, and Gorki at the Tsukiji Small Playhouse in Tokyo.

Modern dramatic interpretations of Shylock have varied between sympathetic portrayals and critical portrayals. In 1968 Keita Asari directed *The Merchant of Venice,* using Tsuneari Fukuda's translation. Osamu Takizawa, a leading actor of the Mingei troupe, played the role of Shylock and expressed his deep sympathy with Shylock. When Asari directed the comedy for the Shiki troupe in 1977, however, Takeshi Kusaka, who played the part of Shylock, was critical of the racial discrimination in the play.

During the 1970's and 1980's, the Shakespeare Theater group displayed considerable activity. They played all of the Shakespearean plays translated by Yushi Odashima at a small underground playhouse called "Jan Jan." Norio Deguchi directed *The Merchant of Venice* in 1976, 1977, and 1978. These performances—given by the players dressed in T-shirts and jeans on a simple stage—were very popular among younger Japanese.

In 1973 Fukuda directed *The Merchant of Venice* for the Keyaki troupe, using his own translation. In 1982 Toshikiyo Masumi directed the same comedy for the Haiyu-za dramatic company, and players in Victorian costumes performed on the modern stage. This performance was moderate; Shylock did not appear at all villainous.

In 1983 the Subaru troupe performed *The Merchant of Venice* directed by Toshifumi Sueki and Asao Koike, who played Shylock. Koike thought that the story of this comedy was the nightmarish experience of Antonio, and he expressed this idea on stage. Five years later, in 1988, the Globe Tokyo, a new arena playhouse, opened. Here Tetsuo Anzai directed the En troupe in *The Merchant of Venice* and *The Jew of Malta* in 1990. He wanted the Japanese audience to compare Shakespeare's Shylock with Marlowe's Barabas.

In 1993 Gerard Murphy, an associate artist of the Royal Shakespeare Company, was invited by the Globe Tokyo to direct a group of Japanese actors in *The Merchant of Venice*. He thought that this comedy had a strong modern aspect because its themes were racial and sexual discrimination and the gap between the rich and the poor. In addition, he was very interested in both the Japanese way of thinking and the Japanese style of acting, and he wished to express both British and Japanese cultures on stage.[37]

Over the years, *The Merchant of Venice* has maintained the attention of Japanese audiences. Since the Meiji era, there have been various productions of this play, and *Sakuradoki Zeni no Yononaka* became a model for adapting Shakespeare's plays to the Japanese stage. In this sense, it is of historical importance. I think that *Sakuradoki Zeni no Yononaka* is the fountainhead of Japanized Shakespeare, such as *Kumonosujo (Throne of Blood)*, *NINAGAWA Macbeth*, and *Ran*. In *Ran*, a film adaptation of *King Lear*, Akira Kurosawa successfully reproduced the atmosphere of feudal society in Japan. He described the life of a feudal *samurai* lord by combining Shakespeare's plot with the style of the Noh play. *NINAGAWA Macbeth*, which received favorable reviews in Edinburgh and Amsterdam in 1985, revealed Yukio Ninagawa's consciousness of the dramatic technique of Kabuki plays. Moreover, his production of *The Tempest*, which also earned high praise in Edinburgh in 1988, represented his boldest experiment in combining Shakespeare's plot with elements of traditional Japanese culture.

Thus the fusion of Shakespeare with Noh or Kabuki plays represents a current trend in today's Japanese Shakespearean theater. I think that adaptation means that many people of different languages and cultures can enjoy the limitless "performability" of Shakespeare's play-texts while searching for their own images of Shakespeare on the stage or in the film. These film or stage adaptations have allowed audiences all over the world to consider a new interpretation of Shakespeare.

While there are obvious gaps in time and space between Renaissance England and modern Japan, Shakespeare is "not of an age, but for all time," as Ben Jonson remarked, and Shakespeare's language is cross-cultural and universal. We should recognize that

Shakespeare is accepted in different cultural and social contexts and that Shakespeare is a criterion by which to determine the cultural standards of the world. From this standpoint, how to produce Shakespeare and what to receive from Shakespeare are important and ongoing problems.

Notes

All quotations from Shakespeare's works are cited from *William Shakespeare: The Complete Works,* eds. Stanley Wells and Gary Taylor (Oxford: Oxford University Press, 1986).

1. Tsutomu Inoue, *Seiyo Chinsetsu Jinniku Shichiire Saiban* (Tokyo: Kinkodo, 1883), 330.

2. Cecil Roth, *The Jews in the Renaissance,* 2nd ed. (New York: Harper & Row, 1965), 49.

3. There is a railway station named "Montebello" near Venice. This is a reversal of "Belmont," which means "a beautiful mountain." As the name suggests, "Montebello" is located in a hilly country.

4. Roth, *Jews in the Renaissance,* 13.

5. Bunkai Udagawa, *Sakuradoki Zeni no Yononaka* (Osaka: Bunpodo, 1886), title page. (Hereafter cited as *Sakuradoki.*)

6. Ibid., 2.

7. Ibid., 3–4.

8. Ibid., 104–5.

9. Joan Ozark Holmer, "Loving Wisely and the Casket Test: Symbolic and Structual Unity in *The Merchant of Venice,*" in *Shakespeare's Christian Dimension: An Anthology of Commentary,* ed. Roy Battenhouse (Bloomington: Indiana University Press, 1994), 85.

10. *Sakuradoki,* 163–66.

11. Monzaemon Chikamatsu, *Shakanyorai Tanjoe,* vol. 4 of *The Complete Works* (Osaka: 1906), 61–63.

12. Joan Ozark Holmer, *"The Merchant of Venice": Choice, Hazard and Consequence* (London: Macmillan, 1995), 33.

13. See Francis Bacon, *The Essayes or Counsels, Civill and Morall,* ed. Michael Kiernan (Oxford: Clarendon Press, 1985), 124–29. Here Bacon wrote that usury was necessary. Furthermore, in England, moneylending became a legitimate commercial activity, and merchants, tradesmen, scriveners, and others involved in trade and business became moneylenders, provided they had the money to lend. Compare E. C. Pettet, "*The Merchant of Venice* and the Problem of Usury," in *Shakespeare: "The Merchant of Venice": A Casebook,* ed. John Wilders, 2nd ed. (London: Macmillan, 1977), 102. (Hereafter cited as *A Casebook.*) Also see Joan Ozark Holmer, "Miles Mosse's *The Arraignment and Conviction of Vsurie* (1595): A New Source for *The Merchant of Venice,*" *Shakespeare Studies,* 21, eds. Leeds Barroll and Barry Gaines (London: Associated University Presses, 1993), 11–54. Holmer regards *The Arraignment and Conviction of Vsurie* (1595) as the most likely source for Shakespeare's decision to stage a debate between Shylock and Antonio in order to present the case for and against usury. A contrasting view may be seen in Ralph Berry, *Shakespeare and Social Class* (Atlantic Highlands: Humanities Press International, 1988), 44. Berry asserts that Antonio and Shy-

lock dramatize the tension between collecting interest and collecting excessive interest.

14. Anna Brownell Jameson, *Shakespeare's Heroines: Characteristics of Women Moral, Poetical, and Historical* (London: G. Bell & Sons, 1916), 35–36.

15. Ibid., 33.

16. Ibid., 31.

17. Berry, *Shakespeare and Social Class,* xii.

18. John Russell Brown, "Love's Wealth and the Judgement of *The Merchant of Venice,*" in *A Casebook,* 163.

19. Sigmund Freud, "The Theme of the Three Caskets," in *A Casebook,* 60.

20. Lawrence Stone, *The Family, Sex and Marriage in England 1500–1800,* 6th ed. (London: Penguin Group, 1988), 37.

21. *Sakuradoki,* 54.

22. Ibid., 61–63.

23. Ibid., 63–64.

24. Basil Hall Chamberlain, *Japanese Things: Being Notes on Various Subjects Connected with Japan* (originally entitled *Things Japanese* and published in 1890), 17th ed. (Tokyo: Charles E. Tuttle, 1987), 500–1.

25. *Sakuradoki,* 113–14.

26. Karen Newman, "Portia's Ring: Unruly Women and Structures of Exchange in *The Merchant of Venice,*" *Shakespeare Quarterly* 38: 1 (Spring 1987): 22.

27. Jonathan Dollimore, *Sexual Dissidence: Augustine to Wilde, Freud to Foucault,* 4th ed. (Oxford: Clarendon Press, 1993), 288.

28. J. E. Neale, *Elizabeth I and Her Parliaments 1559–1581* (1953; reprint, London: Jonathan Cape, 1971), 127, 147–50.

29. Keith Geary, "The Nature of Portia's Victory: Turning to Men in *The Merchant of Venice,*" *Shakespeare Survey* 37 (1984): 55.

30. Juliet Dusinberre, *Shakespeare and the Nature of Women,* 3rd ed. (London: Macmillan, 1985), 231–34.

31. A. M. Nagler, *A Source Book in Theatrical History* (New York: Dover Publications, 1952), 433–35.

32. *Sakuradoki,* 183–86.

33. Ibid., 188.

34. Heinrich Heine, "Shakespeare's Mädchen und Frauen," in *A Casebook,* 29.

35. Shoyo Tsubouchi, "Chikamatsu *vs.* Shakespeare *vs.* Ibsen," vol. 10 of *The Selected Works* (Tokyo: 1977), 769–96.

36. Shoyo Tsubouchi, "Staging Shakespeare's Plays Translated into Japanese," *Sao Fukko (Shakespeare Revival),* 4 (1933; reprint, Tokyo: Meicho Fukyukai, 1990): 4–6.

37. Gerard Murphy, "Gerard Murphy Talks about Himself and His Production," *The Globe 21* (1993): 5.

Money and Sexuality in *Measure for Measure*

YUKARI YOSHIHARA

MEASURE for Measure is much concerned with substitution, exchange and replacement. Angelo is substituted for the Duke as deputy; he proposes that Isabella's maidenhead should be exchanged for Claudio's head or his life; Mariana replaces Isabella in the bed trick; Regozine's head is substituted for Claudio's. In other words, they are exchangeable commodities like money. Furthermore, in the play, sexual reproduction is under surveillance by the state, just as coinage is. Illicit generation is compared to counterfeiting, and the crime of those who get "issues" without the state's sanction is a capital one, just as counterfeiting was a capital crime in Shakespeare's time. The model of monetary exchange informs the characters' bodies and souls. Not only coins, but also the subjects' bodies, their words, even the fluids circulating in their bodies must bear the sovereign's "figure" in order to be legitimately current.

The Duke's "figure" gains omnipotent authority over his subjects' sexual, verbal and mercantile transactions. The Duke assumes that he has absolute authority over metal and mettle; he acts as if his right to "issue" coins in his "figure" automatically authorizes him to regulate the way his subjects use their sexual mettle. I shall argue that his assumption of absolute authority over metal/mettle is quite problematic. I do not believe that the Duke's authority over money authorizes him to monetize his subjects' mettle/metal, to coin, stamp and press it into his "image," to deal with his subjects' sexual reproduction as the mechanical reproduction of his "figure," or to treat his subjects' sexual mettle as if they were ingots of metal.

1

In act 2, scene 4, when asked by Isabella to forgive Claudio's illicit generation, Angelo describes a child conceived in illicit generation as a "false" coin or a counterfeit:

70

> ANGELO   Ha? Fie, these filthy vices! It were as good
>   To pardon him that hath from nature stolen
>   A man already made, as to remit
>   Their saucy sweetness that do coin heaven's image
>   In stamps that are forbid. 'Tis all as easy
>   Falsely to take away a life true made,
>   As to put mettle in restrained means
>   To make a false one.

                                                        (2.4.42–49)[1]

Coinage metaphors are usually employed to account for the physical similarities between a biological father and his child; the father's "image" is said to be "coined" and "stamped" on the child. Yet in the lines above, coinage metaphor is employed to affirm the state's authority over its subjects' sexual reproduction, rather than to describe the physical similarities between Claudio and Juliet's fetus. It should be noted that the fetus Juliet bears is not false or a counterfeit, as far as the physical similarities between Claudio and the fetus are concerned. The fetus would be a sterling coin that bears and coins Claudio's original "image" as far as biological kinship is concerned. In the play, however, the political sovereign appropriates biology as a means to naturalize and legitimatize his political authority over the sexual reproduction of his subjects. According to Angelo's argument, the political sovereign has more claim to authority or authorship of a child than the biological father. In order to be legitimate, a child must bear the sovereign's "image," rather than that of its biological father. In the play, monetary politics assume the state's sexual policy.

Angelo argues that the Duke is authorized to assume the role of a parthenogenetic demi-god who creates everything in his own image, as in the Judeo-Christian myth of the Creation. His subjects must be his copies or clones, monetarily as well as sexually.[2] In this regard, Claudio's crime is the violation of the sovereign's "copyright." Actual sexual reproduction becomes a kind of surrogate reproduction in which the sovereign's image, not the biological father's, is copied and multiplied. In the play, the state, not subject, owns the sexual body. Subjects are standardized, stamped and quantified—in other words, they become the bodies of populating animals which, together with accumulated capital, are used to strengthen the nation's power.[3]

Procreation is imagined as textual inscription by the male member upon the female body, and hence, as male parthonogenesis. Claudio compares Juliet's pregnancy to textual production: "The stealth of our most mutual entertainment/ With character too gross is writ on Juliet" (1.2.143–45). "Character" here means an inscribed, engraved letter, and suggests the biological father's image inscribed on his child; "gross," here, means "large." Claudio is the author, Juliet's body is a blank page on which he inscribes his "character" with large letters; the fetus is a text written by Claudio's male member. Claudio assumes the part of an author who claims an exclusive "copyright" for his child, in the fashion of God in the Creation. Claudio's pen or penis has parthonogenetic power to create art or a biological child out of the "nothing" of the female sexual body.

2

The Duke parthonogenetically re-produces Angelo as his son or a coin that bears his own "figure." Just before appointing Angelo to be his deputy in his absence, the Duke asks Escalus about Angelo: "What figure of us, think you, he will bear?" (1.1.16). "Figure" here suggests both the physical similarities between a father and his child and the sovereign's figure that a sterling coin bears, and hence the amount of the coin: Angelo is to become the Duke's son who bears his "figure" and "image," or a coin, pressed with his "figure," that represents ducal authority in the market. The Duke parthonogenetically "issues" (gives birth to, puts into circulation) Angelo as his own son and a coin of high value. The Duke also assumes the privileged male role of the father or the original "figure" that reproduces itself on the passive and obedient "means" of Angelo's mettle/metal. Will Angelo prove to be the Duke's legitimate son, a sterling coin that reproduces the Duke's "figure" faithfully, or will he be a counterfeit son or coin that distorts the Duke's "figure," misrepresenting and misappropriating his authority?[4]

Angelo follows the Duke's figure of speech, and replies using the metaphor of metallurgy and coinage: "Let there be some more test made of my metal,/ Before so noble and so great a figure/ Be stamp'd upon it" (1.1.48–50).[5] Angelo is an essentialist who believes that the monetary value of a coin ("figure") should correspond to the "essential" value of its ingot. For him, the Duke's "figure" coined on his mettle/metal should be the sign of the Duke's metallurgical estimation of his mettle/metal.

Yet as the Duke soon shows in his conversation with Friar Thomas, he has little faith in the 'essential' value of Angelo's mettle/metal (1.3). Angelo's simple belief that there should be a proper correlation between mettle/metal and the "figure" coined upon it is subverted by the very person whose minted "figure" upon coins is supposed to guarantee the value of coins. Does the issuer of currency who debases the coinage have the authority to punish the two counterfeiters—Claudio, who puts "mettle in restrained moulds," and Angelo who is to be made a counterfeit coin?

The Duke's monetary policy—and hence his sexual policy—resembles a paper money policy in which the substance of the currency has almost no value, and its monetary value is determined solely by the virtue of the figure impressed upon the paper. Even though the metallurgical metaphor is insistently employed to describe the monetary economy of sexuality in the play, the Duke seems to have almost no faith in the genuine metallurgical value of human mettle. Following the model of the Judeo-Christian myth of the Creation, the Duke endeavors to make his "figure" the sole origin of monetary/political authority: his "figure" creates value out of nothing, in his own image.[6]

The Duke's monetary/sexual politics virtually negates "essentialist" ideas about the distinction between the nobleness and the baseness of human mettle. It is not that the essential value of mettle/metal determines the sign that signifies its value, but that the sign actually determines the value of mettle/metal. Angelo's mettle/metal becomes, in effect, a kind of blank paper of *tabula rasa* on which the Duke stamps, inscribes and reproduces his "figure"; it has almost no value in itself; it is a void, a nothing, which can be made to signify whatever the Duke's authorial "figure" forges upon it.

The blankness of Angelo's mettle/metal, however, does not serve to prove its innocence. When Angelo is accused of being a "slip," that is, a counterfeit coin, the question raised is solely about the "corruptible" nature of Angelo's mettle.[7] The fact of the Duke's misappropriating his own authority as an issuer of coins is totally concealed.

> ESCALUS   I am sorry one so learned and so wise
> As you, Lord Angelo, have still appear'd,
> Should slip so grossly, both in the heat of blood
> And lack of temper'd judgement afterward.
>
> (5.1.468–71)

Because of "the heat of blood" and "gross" "intemperate lust" (5.1.98), Angelo's mettle/metal has degenerated into ill-tempered mettle/metal that is only fit for a counterfeit. The Duke, who is said to be "a gentleman of all temperance" (3.2.231), is presented as an all-powerful alchemist who detects the base "temper" of Angelo's mettle/metal.[8] Vaguely occult suggestions of alchemical refinement and degeneration are, I would argue, a cover to mystify the Duke's illegitimate monetary and sexual policy.

At the start of the play, in praising Angelo's "fine" "spirits," the Duke employs alchemical terms. In fact, he assumes the role of an alchemist, a touchstone or a metallurgist, who "assays" and tests Angelo's mettle/metal. Even while he employs the rhetoric of occult alchemy, however, his intention remains capitalistic. The ultimate purpose of his alchemical arts is not to "refine" and "sublime" base mettle/metal, but merely to "multiply" the wealth.[9]

> Spirits are not finely touched
> But to fine issues; nor Nature never lends
> The smallest scruple of her excellence
> But, like a thrifty goddess, she determines
> Herself the glory of a creditor,
> Both thanks and use.
>
> (1.1.35–40)

Angelo's "spirits," being "touched" as by a touchstone, should be used as capital in an economically gainful way, to gain "use" or interest. Similarly, "Nature" is a thrifty usurer who would not neglect "the smallest scruple," or, by extension, the smallest price of gold.

The lines quoted above are clearly suggestive of "spirits" as seminal fluids and of an offspring as interest or "use" begotten through copulation. In the context of usury regulated by the state, these lines imply that even the use of "spirits" must be regulated by the state. Indeed, procreation is imagined as state-regulated usury. Angelo is allowed to have "fine" issues or offspring on the condition that he subjugates himself to the money-issuer's authority.[10] The wasteful "expense of spirit" (*Sonnet* 129:1) is not allowed in *Measure*'s Vienna. Angelo's "fine spirits," the Duke urges, must be used to generate themselves in the form of offspring, closely following the model of capitalist accumulation of wealth and of population.

Through usury and through the subjects' sexual reproduction, the Duke's "figure" multiplies. The Duke implies that it is the sovereign himself with the absolute privilege to "issue" coins and to regulate usury, not Angelo, who has the authority to determine what is proper in using Angelo's seminal fluid. Not only the circulation of coins in the body politic, but also the use of seminal fluid that "issues" from Angelo's body, the Duke implies, must be regulated by the money-issuer. The body politic is eroticized, as the human body is monetized and politicized. Every spirit must be optimized to increase the nation's power, in the form of money and the number of men.[11] The ideology of heterosexuality, under the guise of benevolent recommendation for the proper use of one's body and spirits, coerces the subjects into becoming usurious machines for mass production of the sovereign's "figure."

3

It is ironic that Isabella becomes implicated in money-like exchanges of roles and parts precisely because she refuses the mercenary exchange of her maidenhead with her brother's head. When Angelo proposes that her maidenhead should be used as money to "redeem" and "deliver" her brother from the prison, Isabella firmly resists his mystificating the redemption as an imitation of Christ's redemption, insisting on the mercenary aspects of the exchange between her maidenhead and her brother's head.

> ANGELO   Then must your brother die.
> ISABELLA   And 'twere the cheaper way.
> Better it were a brother died at once,
> Than that a sister, by redeeming him,
> Should die for ever.
>
> (2.4.104–8)

She refuses to be used as a coin to "redeem" her brother's head, and insists on the unique, unexchangeable value of her maidenhead. Yet, when she consents to the disguised Duke's proposal for the bed trick, she becomes implicated in the undifferentiated exchange of her hymen and Mariana's: any maidenhead will do to "deliver" Claudio, just as any coins of the same figure can stand for each other.

As a candidate for a religious sisterhood, Isabella is a kind of "barren metal" that is not current in the market of sexual transactions. Her status exempts her from the market logic of sexual reproduction. However, her view about sexual reproduction in general is not free from the imperative of phallocentrism. She is concomitant with male-centered view about procreation in that she regards women's bodies as mere "means" to reproduce male "forms."

> ANGELO   Nay, women are frail too.
> ISABELLA   Ay, as the glasses where they view themselves,
>   Which are as easy broke as they make forms.
>   Women?—Help, heaven! Men their creation mar
>   In profiting by them. Nay, call us ten times frail;
>   For we are soft as our complexions are,
>   And credulous to false prints.
>
>   (2.4.123–29)

The multiplication of "forms" by a mirror is clearly suggestive of sexual multiplication. Isabella's melancholic tone lamenting women's "frailty," though intended to defend women who are powerless before the assault of phallic aggressiveness, actually degrades women's reproductive capacities. According to Isabella, women's reproductive capacities are merely reflective: just as a mirror cannot produce and create "forms" by itself, so women can only reflect the male "forms" in sexual reproduction; woman has no claim to the authorship of her children; sexual reproduction is capitalistic "profiting." Isabella's phallocentric notions about sexual print pave the way for Angelo's assault.

> ANGELO   Be that you are;
>   That is, a woman. If you be more, you're none.
>   If you be one, as you are well expressed
>   By all external warrants, show it now,
>   By putting on the destined livery. . . .
>   Plainly conceive, I love you.
>
>   (2.4.133–40)

Here Angelo voices biological determinism. He implies that to be a woman is to merely "conceive" a male "figure." Angelo's version of biological determinism allows no rights or possibilities, as far as women are concerned, except for their capacity to "conceive." All women must be silent, obedient passive mettle/metal and bear the male "figure" and "character." Angelo urges women as a group to be reduced to a womb. According to his argument, a woman is not allowed to control her reproductive ability; on the contrary, her womb determines her life. His argument is extreme, yet the ideology of heterosexuality and parthonogenetic ideas about sexual reproduction share Angelo's basic assumptions. The "natural" fact that a woman can conceive a child is appropriated to "naturalize" her passive role in the socio-economic system.

Even the "perverted" desire of Isabella, who says she would prefer "th'impression of keen whips" to Angelo's sexual "impression," might tell us how far she has internalized the phallic mode of sexual imagination. The fantasy image of whipping is clearly eroticized. She talks of whipping as if it were consummation of her erotic desire. Indeed, her fantasy of erotic whipping is disturbingly reminiscent of sexual reproduction imagined as an inscription of the male "figure" upon the blank page of a woman's flesh:

> ISABELLA   [W]ere I under the terms of death,
> Th'impression of keen whips I'd wear as rubies,
> And strip myself to death as to a bed
> That longing have been sick for, ere I'd yield
> My body up to shame.
>
> (2.4.100–4)

It is almost impossible to distinguish "th'impression of keen whips" from the sexual inscription by the male "figure." Whipping in public (a standard punishment for prostitutes) is a sign of the state's overwhelming power to regulate the use of the subjects' sexual bodies and blood. In her fantasy, Isabel's flesh becomes a page on which the political authority impresses and inscribes itself; "keen whips" are pens with which the state presses its "figure" upon its subjects' flesh; the blood Isabella sheds resembles ink on legal papers that legitimatize the state's authority or authorship over its subjects' sexual bodies. For Isabella, all blood—whether shed in cutting off men's heads, breaking hymens, or whipping prostitutes—must be used as ink that testifies the state's authority. Isabella's resistance against unlawful inscription of Angelo's "forms" upon her body does not mean that she is giving a dissident voice to male-centered notions about sexual inscription.

Under the regime of state-regulated birth control, a womb is under the state's surveillance. It becomes analogous to a prison, and to the world imagined as a prison, in the recurrent invocation of ideas about redemption and deliverance. The analogy between a womb and a prison is common; here uniquely both are under surveillance by the state.

Apart from the Christian association, "redemption" and "deliverance/delivery" need socio-political and bio-ideological analysis. As we have seen, Isabella would not allow her redemption of her brother to be mystified as an imitation of Christ's redeeming mankind from original sin.[12] In spite of her resistence, Angelo insistently compares the delivering of her maidenhead to Christ's delivering of humankind from the prison of original sin: "Redeem thy brother,/ By yielding up thy body to my will" (2.4.163–64). He implies the blood Isabel will shed in yielding her virginity must be used to "redeem" her brother from prison, as Christ shed his blood to "redeem" and buy back humankind from the debt of original sin. His argument has the effect of making Isabel's delivering her maidenhead look as if it were her moral and religious obligation.

Isabella's "redemption" or "deliverance/delivery" of her brother from the prison is understood in terms of her biological capacity to "conceive" and "deliver" a child, as well as in terms of religious "deliverance"; she becomes a mother who "delivers" Claudio from the prison cell of her womb. The association of deliverance from prison with deliverance from a womb is most vividly imagined in Isabel's vehement condemnation of Claudio, who asks her to deliver her maidenhead to deliver him from the prison. She condemns Claudio as a "slip" or a counterfeit, and regards such deliverance as incest:

> ISABELLA   Wilt thou be made out of my vice?
>   Is't not a kind of incest, to take life
>   From thine own sister's shame? What should I think?
>   Heaven shield my mother play'd my father fair:
>   For such a warped slip of wilderness
>   Ne'er *issued* from his blood.
>
> (3.1.137–42)

Claudio is a fetus waiting to be 'delivered' from prison. His deliverance is a kind of double incest, for Claudio is either a fetus conceived by incestuous union with his sister, or a fetus conceived by Isabella's incestuous union with their dead father.[13]

Isabella then becomes a demonized mother who refuses either to "conceive" male inscription or, once pregnant, to "deliver" her child from the prison cell of her womb. Pompey's light-hearted comparison between a prison and a bawdy house (4.3.1–20. Cf. 4.2.1–5) and his professional situation—he who once was an executioner of maidenheads becomes an executioner of men's heads—is revealing: as prostitution must be regulated by the state, in a way analogous to the state's policy over usury, so the womb must be under the state's panoptical surveillance, in a way analogous to the state's surveillance over prisons. In the disguised Duke's sermon to Claudio, he describes death as a longed-for deliverance from a world imagined as a prison and a womb. He completely degrades the value of life in the world, yet offers no comfort after the deliverance (3.1.5–41). The world and the womb become claustrophobic prison-like spaces demonized by the dominant ideology. Reproduction-centered bio-ideology degrades the womb as nothing more than a prison for a fetus, while at the same time enforcing sexual reproduction as women's religio-socio-political imperative.

4

At the end of the play, Angelo is condemned as a "slip" or a counterfeit who abuses the Duke's authority. However, there is not much point arguing whether Angelo's mettle/metal is essentially "noble" or "base," in the situation in which the Duke's "figure" reduces his subjects to endlessly exchangeable commodities and in which the "essential" values of mettle/metal do not count for much. In the market where Angelo's authority is current as a coin of high value, there is confusion about the relationship between the monetary value of a coin and the "essential" value of its ingot, between a sign and its meaning. To a large extent "the crisis of representation," in which a sign does not correspond to its supposed meaning, is caused by the Duke's misappropriation of his own authority and of Angelo's mettle/metal when he introduces a gulf between "figure" and the value of mettle/metal, between a sign and its meaning.

The most extreme instance of "the crisis of representation" arrives when Angelo acknowledges his own authority is counterfeit. Urged to tender her maidenhead to redeem Claudio, Isabella threatens to expose Angelo's evil intentions. She condemns Angelo, for his reputation as a virtuous person is false "seeming" (2.4.150). However, she is naive about representational strategies, for she seems to believe that the conflict between "seeming" and 'truth' can be corrected by simply revealing the falsity of "seeming." Angelo is more pragmatic: he knows, in this situation, "truth" is unrepresentable. He retorts:

> ANGELO   Who will believe thee, Isabel?
> My unsoil'd name, th'austereness of my life,
> My vouch against you, and my place i'th'state
> Will so your accusation overweigh,
> That you shall stifle in your own report,
> And smell of calumny. . . .
> Say what you can: my false o'erweighs your true.
>   (2.4.153–58, 169)

Angelo is confident that a false coin will be judged heavier and more substantial than a legitimate coin. As Isabella's testimony against Angelo represents the truth; her words are a metaphorical legal tender, and hence must be heavier than Angelo's words which are a metaphorical counterfeit, made of a "base" or lighter metal/mettle. Angelo acknowledges that his mettle/metal is not equal to his authority, yet he is confident that his authority has currency as a sterling coin, as far as the Duke's "figure" authorizes it. As the title suggests, *Measure for Measure* is full of references to measurement. Even measurement, a seemingly neutral way of just evaluation, does not function properly in this situation.

"The crisis of representation" here paradoxically consolidates the Duke's authority. The disastrous situation in which his "figure" cannot signify what it is supposed to signify, at first might seem to be destructive to his authority over economical and political representation. However, at the very moment the Duke's "figure" is most drastically misappropriated, it becomes omnipotent, for Angelo the "slip" himself acknowledges that the Duke's "figure" can make his mettle/metal become current solely by virtue of its authority, without any reference to the value of his mettle/metal. This is the very situation the Duke has been seeking from the time he issued Angelo as a coin of high value, knowing his mettle/metal was not equal to the "figure" pressed upon it. The Duke's obsessive pursuit of his authority as the author like God in the Creation myth is paradoxically complete at the moment it is thoroughly violated.

5

In the play, "the rebellion of a codpiece" (3.2.110–11) or the rebellion of a sexual member is tantamount to rebellion against the body politic, and hence to legally lead to the execution of the rebellious citizen. Almost endless substitutions of roles in the play imply that not only can any citizen of the community can be substituted for another, but also the bodily part of one person can be replaced with that of another. In *Measure*'s Vienna, the body is a combination of detachable, exchangeable and replaceable bodily parts.

In the bed trick, Mariana replaces Isabella; or, Mariana's private "parts" represent Isabella's. Urging Isabel to join her in pleading for Angelo's life, Mariana says, "sweet Isabel, take my part" (5.1.428). Isabel is asked to take Mariana's "part" or role in public, in exchange for Mariana's having offered her private "parts" in bed. Furthermore, their mutual exchange of "parts" is a representation in a dramatic sense: in the scene where they appear on stage as Angelo's accusers, they are playing parts assigned by the Duke. He is a playwright whose writing member scripts the scenario. When Angelo detects someone behind Mariana and Isabel, he says, "I do perceive/ These poor informal women are no more/ But instruments of some more mightier member/ That sets them on" (5.1.234–37). The Duke is the "more mightier member." His "mightier member" that writes the script of Angelo's accusation scene is tantamount to his male member which reproduces his "character" everywhere, making Mariana and Isabel's "parts" represent his authorial intentions. The women's private "parts," as well as their dramatic and public "parts," is under the direction of the powerful male author's scripting hand.

In the last scene, Claudio appears on the stage as his own son: he is said to be "as like almost to Claudio as himself:" (5.1.487).[14] He is delivered from the prison and a prison cell of the womb, as a son conceived in the sexual intercourse of Angelo and Isabel represented by Mariana. Isabella's horrified fantasy of her brother's incestuous rebirth is finally realized without the sacrifice of her maidenhead. The Duke's surveillance over his subjects' sexual reproduction is disturbingly complete; Isabella is made to "conceive" and "deliver" Claudio, even without her knowledge.

When the Duke proposes marriage to Isabel, the powerful sovereign orders her to become an instrument to reproduce his "figure." After conducting a successful experiment to make every subject a vehicle to reproduce his "figure," the Duke intends to carry out another experiment to see if sexual reproduction of his "figure" through Isabel's body can be as successful as in the cases of other-than-sexual reproductions. Will Isabel accept being made into a sexual mold that reproduces the Duke's sexual "character" by consenting to his marriage proposal?

6

I have tried to delineate the Duke's overwhelming power to multiply his "figure" monetarily and sexually upon his subjects' mettle/metal. In my view, his assumption of authority as the unexchangeable origin of commodity production and procreation is illegitimate. As the exchange value of a coin is partially determined by its content of precious metals, so the Duke's "figure" cannot wholly determine the exchange value of his subjects' mettle/metal. Insofar as the Duke must use his subjects' sexual mettle and molds to multiply his "figure," his authority is radically dependent on and parasitic to his subjects. Therefore, he transgresses his own political authority as an issuer of currency and overseer of his subjects' sexuality when he deals with his subjects' mettle/metal.

Whether the Duke's transgressing his own authority leads to his subjects' resisting is, however, questionable. Many of the characters seem to subjugate themselves to the illusion that the Duke's "figure" is the only reliable source of justice in monetary, sexual and verbal exchanges. In contrast, I would like to invoke the character of Lucio who would not easily, subscribe to the view that various currencies in *Measure*'s Vienna are dependent on the royal countenance for their circulation.

In the last scene, Lucio is punished for his two-fold violation of the sovereign's exclusive authority over sexual and verbal copyright, i.e., for illicit generation and for his slander against the Duke. Earlier Lucio thought if he pursued the economic activity of buying, the only "interest" or "use" would be a bald head or a "French crown" as a result of venereal disease (1.2.46–53. cf. 27–40); but finally, he is forced to take another "interest," i.e. his child. He must marry a prostitute who bore his child. Lucio embodies a model of wasteful "expense of spirits" and the market logic of sexual/verbal/monetary currencies that questions the legitimacy of the notion that all currencies depend solely on the royal countenance for their authenticity. As such, he might be qualified as a subversive critique of the Duke's productivity-centered, authoritarian sexual politics over mettle/metal.

Lucio challenges the authoritarian notion that all verbal and monetary transactions depend on the royal countenance for their authority. In fact he recites an outrageous version of the Duke's life to the disguised Duke himself (3.2.83–183). Perhaps Lucio's estimation and interpretation of the Duke's life is not an honest reading. Nonetheless, the Duke's excessive irritation about Lucio's "gall" is suggestive. He laments, "What king so strong/ Can tie the gall up in the slanderous tongue?" (3.2.181–82). "Gall" suggests slander, black bile, and an ingredient of ink. The Duke is lamenting the inefficacy of his policy over words, bodily fluids and writing. He can successfully regulate neither the circulation of slander in the body politic; nor the circulation of the black bile (which was supposed to beget malcontent and melancholy) inside Lucio's body; nor the circulation of written words or texts. Lucio, a marginal figure, rewrites the texts that tell about the Duke's life, writing his comments in the margin of the text, with ink full of gall. In Lucio, the Duke's attempt to regulate totally the circulation of various currencies faces a serious challenge.

The most farcical moment of the Duke's failure to control sexual/ textual reproduction arrives when he finds he has become a bastardizer of his subjects' fancy and of voluminous piratical texts. His "character," circulating in the body politic, has multiplied itself, in a fashion analogous to sexual reproduction:

> DUKE   O place and greatness! Millions of false eyes
> Are struck upon thee: volumes of report
> Run with these false, and most contrarious quest
> Upon thy doings: thousand escapes of wit
> Make thee the father of their idle dream
> And rack thee in their fancies.
>
> (4.1.60–64)

The phrase, "thousand escapes of wit," conceives (in two senses of the verb) the Duke's "character"; reprinted in the subjects' brain-womb, the Duke's "character" produces "volumes" of its piratical versions. The Duke cannot regulate even the way his own "character" circulates. This is a grievous case for him, for his textual/ sexual/monetary policy requires total surveillance over the production and circulation of "characters." He unwittingly becomes a bastardizer or a counterfeiter of "character," in some ways like Lucio and Claudio.

Lucio shows that the sovereign cannot wholly regulate the way various currencies circulate in the body politic of *Measure*'s Vienna. Even though Lucio is forced to submit himself to the state's regulation of sexual reproduction, even though he must be pressed and inscribed with the figure of the state's authority by whipping (5. 1. 501–21), his subversive power of questioning the legitimacy of the sovereign's authority over sexual/textual/monetary reproduction has not been canceled.

Notes

This paper is based on my presentation of "Metallurgical Metaphors in *Measure for Measure* at the 31st meeting of the Japan Shakespeare Society, October 1992.

1. All citations are from *The Arden Shakespeare: Measure for Measure,* ed. J. W. Lever (London: Methuen, 1965).

2. In his now classic essay on *A Midsummer Night's Dream,* Louis Adrian Montrose remarks about the Aristotelian idea of procreation as male partheno-genesis that: "Shakespeare's embryological notions remain distinctly Aristotelian, distinctly phallocentric: the mother is represented as a vessel, as a container for her son; she is not his *maker*. In contrast the implication of Theseus' description of paternity is that the male is the only begetter. . . . *A Midsummer Night's Dream* dramatizes a set of claims which are repeated throughout Shakespeare's

canon: claims for a spiritual kinship among men that is unmediated by women; for the procreative powers of men; and for the autogeny of men." See "Shaping Fantasies: Figuration of Gender and Power in Elizabethan Culture," in Stephen Greenblatt, ed., *Representing the English Renaissance* (Berkley: University of California Press, 1988), 42. I shall employ Montrose's terms "the autogeny of men" and "male parthenogenesis" to study sexual economy in *Measure for Measure* and apply the term to procreation imagined as coinage.

3. Employing Foucault's concept of modern "bio-power," Richard Wilson remarks that the duke "has grasped the power of the modern state will depend . . . on the optimising of desire for the increase of its population." He also argues that a Shakespearean comedy depicts "the interdependence of economic and political interests in this era when the accumulation of capital and the accumulation of men were geared together. Richard Wilson, "Discipline and Punishment in Shakespearean Comedy," *Will Power: Essays on Shakespearean Authority* (New York: Harvester Wheatsheaf, 1993), 130, 140.

4. The name Angelo suggests angel coins. Although no direct reference to coins appear in the play, Angelo's line, "Let's write good angel the devil's horn" (2.4.16) and the Duke's, "but that frailty hath examples for his falling, should wonder at Angelo" (3.1.185–86) must refer to them. Cf. angel: An old English gold coin (*OED*, n.6).

5. test: to subject gold or silver to a process of separation and refining in a test or cupel; to assay (*OED*, v. 4.1)

6. In terms of monetary policy based on the "essential" value of ingots, the Duke's policy is untenable, for in that policy the royal countenance, expressed by the sovereign's figure impressed upon coins, cannot be the sole basis of the value of the coins. Discussing the Duke's monetary strategy, Paul Yacknin writes: "With regard to the ideology of monetary value in *Measure,* it should be noted that in Tudor England and in Jacobean Ireland the marketplace rather than the royal countenance often served to underwrite the value of the coinage. On several occasions, the government attempted to debase the coinage by reducing or removing its precious metal content; on such occasions, market forces took over and had the effect of forcing the monarch to restore the precious metal content of the coinage. Therefore, *Measure*'s audience would have been aware that the value of coinage did not necessarily depend exclusively on royal authority." See "The Politics of Theatrical Mirth: *A Midsummer Night's Dream, A Mad World, My Masters* and *Measure for Measure,*" *Shakespeare Quarterly* 42 (1992), 42n.

7. slip: a counterfeit coin (*OED*, n.4).

8. temper: to bring steel to a suitable degree of hardness (*OED*, v.14). The official story about Angelo's mettle/metal, scripted by the Duke, is fairly simple. At first Angelo seems to be made of "incorruptible" mettle/metal like gold. This is the primary reason the Duke issues Angelo as a coin of high value. Confronted with Isabella's body, Angelo reveals his "base" mettle/metal and becomes the "corrupt deputy" (2.1.255; cf. corruption: the oxidation or corrosion of metals. (*OED*, sb 1.c). Isabella's attempt to save her brother is fittingly called an "assay" (1.4.76), for it functions as a metallurgical trial of Angelo's metal. Cf. assay: to test the composition of an ore, alloy, or other metallic compound by chemical means, so as to determine the amount of a particular metal contained in it (*OED*, v4.a), and "assay" (3.1.161) and "trial" (3.1.196). In these lines Angelo's temptation to Isabel is compared to a metallurgical experiment on Isabella's metal/ mettle.

9. For the distinctions between common alchemists who pursue only the multiplication of capital and occult alchemists who pursue the refinement and sublimation of base metals, and for alchemical patterns in Renaissance literature, cf. Charles Nicholl, *The Chemical Theater* (London: Routledge and Kegan Paul, 1980). Sometimes the Duke is compared to an alchemist who refines his subjects' "gross" metal/mettle into something like fine incorruptible gold. In my view, his interests lie more in accumulating the "gross" number of his subjects by means of gross sexual reproduction than in refining their metal/mettle.

10. Pompey talks of "two usuries / the merriest was put down, and the worser allowed by/order of law" (3.1.6–8). He pirates the logic of capitalist accumulation, by calling prostitution a means to multiply population. His is critical when both forms of "increase," usury and procreation are held to be legitimate because they are sanctioned by the state, by the Duke's "figure."

11. In *Measure*'s Vienna, overpopulation is also inconvenient for the state. This can be seen in the recurrent references to abortion. For example, "future evils / Either new, or remissness new conceived, / And so in progress to be hatch'd and born, / Are now to have no successive degrees, / But ere they live, to end" (2.2.96–100). "Future evils" are compared to babies who must be aborted.

12. Christ's redemption and deliverance of humanity from original sin was, according to Isabella, an unequal exchange between Christ's blood and human sin; Christ's blood was a kind of currency to redeem and deliver mankind from the prison of sin; Christ did not require that there be the exact equivalent between his blood and human sin (2.2.70–79). She argues that Angelo, as a representative of God on earth, must imitate Christ by not asking the exact payment of Claudio's life for his sin.

13. Isabella remains a faithful daughter of partriarchy when she calls her brother a "slip" or counterfeit. Claudio, a bad "issue" or son, is condemned as a counterfeit-like misrepresentation of their father's "figure." Isabella regards Claudio as a counterfeit "issued" from the contaminated mold of their mother in order to keep their father's "figure" innocent of Claudio's degeneration. As Adelman remarks, Isabella "allies herself with the male voices condemning female contamination" by placing responsibility for Claudio's corruption entirely with her mother." Janet Adelman, *Suffocating Mothers: Fantasies of Maternal Origin in Shakespeare's Plays, Hamlet to The Tempest* (New York: Routledge, 1992), 97.

14. In his inspiring study of various exchanges in *Measure for Measure*, Marc Shell writes, "Claudio is saved . . . in a figurative resurrection through 'a kind of incest' between him and Isabella . . . Claudio is born again . . . as his own new born son." *The End of Kinship: "Measure for Measure," Incest and the Ideal of Universal Siblinghood* (Stanford: Stanford University Press, 1968), 139.

The Stage Tableau and Iconography of *Macbeth*

Soji Iwasaki

I

On the 13th of March 1604, King James I's coronation progress moved through the city of London gloriously adorned with triumphal arches and *tableaux vivants*. For a new sovereign's entry, it was the custom to build arches like castle-gates and set up stages on which to present *tableaux vivants* on themes devised for the celebration. Interlocutors were placed to praise the new sovereign and express the people's wish for peace and justice to come, as had been the case with the royal entrances of Elizabeth and Mary Tudor.[1]

For the royal entrance of James, seven arches were built, the first being erected in Fenchurch Street. Here Tuscane columns supported the five-storied square arch, fifty feet high and fifty feet in the ground line, complete with battlements, turrets and steeples. At the foot of the battlements was inscribed the word "LONDINIUM," and beneath it "CAMERA REGIA." In this arch twelve girls appeared as *tableaux vivants,* the topmost designated as '*Monarchia Britannica.*' She was attended by Divine Wisdom, and by six daughters of *Genius Vrbis:* Veneration, Promptitude and Vigilance on her right, and Gladness, Loving Affection and Unanimity on her left. Below stood the Genius of the City, one of two interlocutors, supported on the right by a person representing Counsel of the City and on the left by a person representing the Warlike Force of the City. Further down, a small room projected in which *Thamesis*, the River, the other interlocutor, was leaning on a gourd, out of which water was running. On the lowest level was a gallery for the musicians.[2]

The third of the seven arches prepared for this occasion was built for Dutch merchants near the Exchange at Cornhill. It had a facade of a mixed style, part castle and part classical edifice. When the new sovereign approached, the musicians, located on the top level, began to play. In the Medieval pictorial and architectural traditions, this type of facade usually had an image of God at its top, but this one presented a picture of King James in his imperial robes, wearing the crown and the sword and holding a scepter. This design probably implied James's idea of the divine right of kings. When the trumpet sounded, the curtain on the middle floor opened to reveal seventeen young ladies representing the seventeen provinces of Belgium. The ladies stood up and expressed homage to the king. Following them a scholar appeared on stage to deliver a Latin welcome address for the king.[3]

Shakespeare's *Macbeth* is closely related to King James I. The first performance of the play most probably occurred at Hampton Court in August 1606, before James and King Christian of Denmark who was visiting the English court.[4] The play is an appraisal of the noble character of Banquo, James's ancestor, and it includes scenes reminiscent of the king's books, *Daemonologie* (1597) and *The Basilicon Doron* (1599). It is likely that Shakespeare, when writing the play, had in mind a castle facade, or more particularly the screen of the great hall of Hampton Court for the background of the action of the play.

George R. Kernodle in his book *From Art to Theatre: Form and Convention in the Renaissance* (1944)[5] argues that many formal conventions of the English Renaissance theater came not from Medieval drama but from the pictorial and sculptural traditions of the Middle Ages. The stage developed in close relation to the castle arches through which the royal processions passed, and the components of the theatre—wing, proscenium arch, inner stage, curtain, side-doors, upper-stage gallery, and canopy—were already familiar in Medieval and early Renaissance pictures, sculptures, stained glass, tapestries, and the staged *tableaux vivants:*

> In England and Flanders, stages grew up which made no such attempt to create illusion as those of Paris and Italy did. In these northern countries the actors were not seen within a picture space surrounded on three sides by the scenery. Instead, they came onto a forestage from doors that never changed, and they acted in front of an architectural facade that had to serve for all kinds of scenes. . . . We have assumed that only by putting elaborate descriptions into the mouths of his characters or by bringing on movable trees, tents, thrones, or other properties could the playwright indicate a particular place. Yet in play after play the facade itself became a visual symbol—it became a castle, a city gate, or a backing for a throne, altar, or tomb. The upper stage and the under side of the penthouse became symbols of the heavens.

Sometimes the facade was, at the same time, a symbol of a castle and a backing for a throne.[6]

What actually happened in the growth of the Renaissance theatre was probably that concurrently with this development from art to theater another tradition was also active, i.e. that ancient philosophical tradition of 'memory theater' which Frances Yates illuminated in her studies in Renaissance neoplatonism.[7] In the following pages, however, the philosophical tradition will be set aside and we shall be more particularly concerned with the stage on which the first performances of *Macbeth* took place—the architectural background, the stage *tableaux*, and the iconography of the play.

2

Throughout the first four scenes of *Macbeth*, two witch-scenes set in bleak country, one in the royal camp, and one in the castle of Forres, the background remains the same architectural facade. In the royal court scenes it serves as a backing for the throne, following the pictorial convention, an example of which is found in an illustration of the tenth or eleventh century manuscript of Prudentius's *Psychomachia*.[8] In the castle of Forres scene, perhaps a tapestry or a curtain is hung on the wall to suggest that the scene is set indoors.[9]

Act I scene 5 is set in Macbeth's castle at Inverness. On the stage, the curtain may have been taken away and a chair put in place. Lady Macbeth enters, reading a letter from her husband informing her of the witches' prophecy. Her invocations to evil "Spirits," "murth'ring ministers" and "thick Night"[10] are literally answered: her body becomes filled with direst cruelty and "with the coming of night her castle is . . . shrouded in just such a blackness as she desires."[11] Macbeth's castle is now a hell castle. The castle facade at the back of the stage assumes an infernal aspect, so it is ironical that on their arrival, King Duncan and his court admire the appearance of the castle, the "heaven's breath" that smells "wooingly," with the peaceful martlet nestling (1.6.3–6).

In the dagger scene, the stage is set indoors. Ironically in the context of Lady Macbeth's wish "That [her] keen knife see not the wound it makes," a vision of a dagger appears to Macbeth on his murderous way to Duncan's room. If, as he says, Macbeth is an emblem of "wither'd Murther," his victim Duncan might be called an emblem of "Sleep" on the same allegorical level, so it is not unexpected that when, absent-mindedly, he comes back with bloody daggers in his hands, he says he heard a voice cry, "'Sleep no more! / Macbeth does murther Sleep'." Because "murther" has killed "Sleep," future sleeplessness is inevitable for the murderer and his wife, their consciences being full of guilt. Once Macbeth's castle has changed into a hell castle, those living there are harassed by continual perturbation and agony.

According to Robert Burton in his *Anatomy of Melancholy,* unrest of mind and insomnia are symptoms of melancholy or its causes. Burton refers to the "thunder and lightning of perturbation," and compares perturbation to "winds upon the sea, some only move as those great gales, but others turbulent quite overturn the ship."[12] The thunder and lightning in the opening witches' scene of *Macbeth* foreshadow Macbeth's perturbation in his wakeful nights. Burton also says that melancholy persons, when imagination rages in them, get "witch-ridden," "walk in the night in their sleep," feel sorrow and fear, and tell, when they come to themselves, "strange things of heaven and hell, what visions they have seen."[13] These symptoms of melancholy are observed in the behavior of the central characters of this play. To contemporaries of Shakespeare, mental perturbations were "hell upon earth,"[14] which is exactly what Macbeth and Lady Macbeth suffer in their haunted hours.

The voice crying, "'Sleep no more! / Macbeth does murther Sleep' . . .," which Macbeth hears in the dagger scene, is in fact imaginary, for the sober Lady Macbeth hears nothing. Macbeth is upset by his own act of bloody sacrilege, and so full of guilt he says, "Look on't again I dare not." Lady Macbeth takes the blood-stained daggers back to Duncan's chamber, and when the knocking on the south door begins, Macbeth's heart beats heavily:

> Whence is that knocking?
> How is't with me, when every noise appals me?
> What hands are here? Ha! they pluck out mine eyes.
>
> (2.2.56–58)

He is so absent-minded that he does not know where the knocking comes from. To him, the sound, like a voice crying, "'Sleep no more! . . .'" (2.2.40) comes from *within,* his consciousness is so utterly absorbed in his inner world. We remember that when Macbeth first thought of murdering Duncan, the horrid image unfixed his hair and made his "seated heart knock at [his] ribs" (1.3.135–

36). The knocking is an "objective correlative" for Macbeth's guilty conscience.

In Shakespeare's time, knocking at one's heart signified God's voice calling at the door of his heart, or Conscience working in his heart. The idea originally came from Revelation 3.20: "Behold, I stand at the door and knock: if any man hear my voice and open the door, I will come in to him, and will sup with him, and he with me." That the idea had long been current we can surmise from such writings as Thomas More's *The Four Last Things* (1552)[15] and King James's *Basilicon Doron* (1603). King James says:

> Conscience . . . is nothing else, but the light of knowledge that God hath planted in man, whiche euer watching over all his actions, as it beareth him a joyfull testimonie when he does right, so choppeth [knocks] it him with a feeling that he has done wrong, when euer he committeth any sinne.[16]

It is because of the divine significance of the knocking that we feel in this sound "a peculiar awfulness and a depth of solemnity" as De Quincey says in his well-known essay.[17] To Shakespeare and his contemporaries "conscience" and "consciousness" were one (as we find in Shakespeare's *Sonnet* 151), and when Macbeth's consciousness begins to work reflectively he acknowledges his inner foulness, which, as it is a spiritual sinfulness deserving eternal damnation, he thinks he cannot wash away even with the waters of "multitudinous seas" (2.2.59).

The facade at the back stage, which assumed an aspect of hell gate when Lady Macbeth invoked evil Spirits, is now changed into a powerful symbol of Conscience, for the knocking comes from within. To Macbeth it is the Inner God knocking at his heart.

3

In the hell-gate scene (act 2, scene 3), the facade represents the south gate of Macbeth's castle viewed from within, which the drunken porter regards as hell-gate. The knocking begun in the preceding scene continues, and the porter half awakened from his drunken sleep plays the hell-gate porter in *The Harrowing of Hell* play in the mystery cycle. The porter is probably recalling the scene of Christ descending to hell, as does the comic Pardoner in John Heywood's *The Four PP.* (1520), who boastingly says that he has been to hell to look after a woman who died without absolution.[18]

The Harrowing of Hell in the York Cycle Plays tells the story of Christ going down to hell on the second day after his crucifixion to release the souls of the patriarchs and prophets. On his arrival at hell-gate, Christ knocks at the door three times but, since the devil-porter will not open the gate, he breaks down the door and, conquering the Devil, delivers the souls who have long been imprisoned there. Many pictures, stained-glass windows and frescoes depict this theme, and among the artists who use it are Fra Angelico, Taddeo Gaddi, Memmi, and Albrecht Dürer.[19]

The Wakefield Cycle (or the Towneley Plays) include the episode of "The Deliverance of Souls," where the devil Rybald answers Christ's knocking:

> . . . What devill is he
> That callys hym kyng ouer vs all?
> hark belzabub, com ne,
> ffor hedusly I hard hym call.[20]

This speech is echoed by the porter in *Macbeth* saying, "Who's there, i'th' name of Belzebub?" (2.3.3–4). More worth our attention are the words, "hedusly I hard hym call," which refer to the fanfare followed by the recitation of Psalm 24: *"Attollite portas, principes, vestras & eleluamini porte eternales, & introibit rex glorie."* ("Lift up your heads, O ye gates; even lift them up, ye everlasting doors; and the King of glory shall come in.")

Later in the same scene, the lines spoken by Lady Macbeth when the bell starts tolling:

> What's the business,
> That such *a hideous trumpet* calls to parley
> The sleepers of the house?
>
> (2.3.81–83; italics added)

suggest her mistakenly identifying the bell with the trumpet of Judgement Day, the latter being implied in Macbeth's speech three lines earlier:

> Up, up, and see
> The great doom's image!—Malcolm! Banquo!
> As from your graves rise up, and walk like sprites,
> To countenance this horror!
>
> (2.3.78–81)

Thus the knocking and the dialog echoing the mystery play, *The Harrowing of Hell,* the clamorous bell, the shrill cries of Lady

Macbeth, together with Lenox's references to the unruly night—
the storm blowing down chimneys, the earth quaking feverishly,
lamenting voices tearing the night air, flaming fire and "strange
screams of death" foretelling destruction, the obscure bird's clamour—and all the other aural images of hell draw the audience
into an infernal ambience.[21]

The three sinners let in by the hell-gate porter in this scene—
the avaricious farmer who hanged himself after his unsuccessful
speculation, the topical Jesuit equivocator, and the English tailor
who stole his customer's cloth—these are prefigurations of the
damnation of the ambitious, equivocating and usurping Macbeth.
At the same time the correspondences between the hell-gate scene
and *The Harrowing of Hell* or *The Deliverance of Souls* play in
the mystery cycles confirm the infernal identity of Macbeth's castle
with hell.

In the banquet scene (act 3, scene 4), the newly-enthroned King
Macbeth invites the lords to dine in the royal palace. They toast
each other's health, and Macbeth says, "Here had we now our
country's honour roof'd / Were the grac'd person of our Banquo
present" (3.4.39–40), when the ghost of Banquo appears as if magically invoked. The ghost sits in the royal seat, invisible to all except
Macbeth, who is upset. Lady Macbeth manages to calm her husband after some effort, but when he again drinks "to th' general
joy o'th' whole table, / and to our dear friend Banquo, whom we
miss" (88–89), the ghost re-enters. Macbeth is again strongly disturbed and the banquet disrupted, so Lady Macbeth hurriedly dismisses the party. The ghost that Macbeth's guilty conscience calls
forth is very like those devils that confront Philologus in Nathaniel
Woodes's moral interlude *The Conflict of Conscience* (c. 1579),
where the protagonist is tempted by Hypocrisy, Tyranny, Avarice,
and Lechery to discard his Protestant faith and, possessed by Terror (also called Confusion), is driven to despair.[22] Thus the play
Macbeth, while it stands in the Catholic tradition of the mystery
plays in the hell-gate scene, is at the same time deeply involved in
the Protestant theology of the Inner God.

In act 3 the scenes are set either in the hall of the castle or some
outdoor place, but the background of the stage remains the same
throughout. The symbolic disruption of the royal banquet and the
resulting dismay of the king and queen occur in front of the architectural facade with the throne center stage, the stage picture being
in accordance with the Medieval pictorial tradition, one instance
observed in Prudentius's *Psychomachia.*

4

In act 4, the cauldron scene is no less emblematic than the hell-gate scene. Here we may properly surmise that the door in the center of the back facade is open, representing hell-mouth with the infernal cauldron inside. In miniatures, frescoes, and Judgement plays in the mystery cycles, hell-mouth is traditionally represented in the shape of a monster opening its jaws, and this and the image of a cauldron both come from the description of Leviathan in Job: "Out of his nostrils goeth smoke, as out of a seething pot or caldron. . . . He maketh the deep to boil like a pot" (41: 20, 31). This passage had so great an influence on the Medieval iconography of hell that, "The thirteenth-century artist put a literal construction on these passages, and carried his scruples so far as to represent a boiling cauldron in the open jaws of the monster."[23] In the Medieval and the Renaissance iconography of hell, the cauldron either constituted a central part of hell, as we see in the copy of the now lost fresco[24] in the Guild Chapel in Stratford-upon-Avon, or it represented hell itself, as is shown in the woodcut illustration of hell in *The Kalender of Shepherdes* (1503).[25] In the English Renaissance theater before *Macbeth,* a cauldron had appeared in Marlowe's *The Jew of Malta* (1589). In the final scene of that play, Barabas the Jew is tricked by Fernez, the governor of Malta; into falling into the cauldron on a fire which he himself had prepared for the Turkish general. From the stage direction "a cauldron discovered"[26] in the 1633 Quarto of *The Jew* and the item "j caudern for the Jewe"[27] among Henslowe's accounts, we can safely affirm that a cauldron was actually on the stage.

In *Macbeth* the cauldron appears as a property of the witches' sabbath. The weird sisters may be those Scottish hags who "are hellish monsters, brewing hell-broth, having cats and toads for familiars, loving midnight, riding on the passing storm, and devising evil against such as offend them [and who] crouch beneath the gibbet of the murderer, meet in gloomy caverns, amid earthquake convulsions, or in thunder, lightning, and rain."[28] Or they may be Shakespeare's inventions concocted from the classical Fates, the Medieval Goddess Fortuna, and the witches of Reformation Europe. Undoubtedly these "secret, black, and midnight hags" (4.1.48) belong to the evil party in the dichotomy of the moral outlook of *Macbeth,* a play much like the Medieval morality in which good and evil are strikingly contrasted. Here, as in Hieronimus Bosch's picture of St. Anthony, the left wing of the triptych

The Retable of the Hermits (c. 1505), the motif of the witches' sabbath is superimposed on the vision of hell. In *Macbeth* the cauldron is placed "at the pit of Acheron" (3.5.15) and such sinister and grotesque ingredients as we find in Bosch's picture are thrown into the broth (4.1.14–31). Thus the boiling cauldron prefigures the hellish downfall of Macbeth who repeatedly sheds blood pursuing his ambition.

Macbeth chooses evil with his "free will," suppresses his conscience to dare murder after murder, and inevitably comes to damnation. What should be noted here is that the hell into which Macbeth falls is not that outer hell which is envisioned in Dante's *Inferno* or in the *"Judgement"* plays in English mystery cycles. The hell in *Macbeth* is the inner hell, the hell "on this shoal of time" (1.7.6), which tortures evil-doers with mental perturbations before their death. Macbeth, with his conscience seared and benumbed, is now in the depth of evil. God's grace has deserted him, and he is deprived of the natural rhythm of life and natural affections. Even the news of his queen's unnatural death stirs no emotion in him: "She should have died hereafter: / There would have been a time for such a word. . ." (5.5.17–18). To Macbeth, a man of vain ambition, life is now an empty "nothing," featureless "To-morrow, and to-morrow, and to-morrow" passing into the dark abyss of shadowy yesterdays.

Here another meaning of the boiling caudron should be noted. In Geffrey Whitney's *A Choice of Emblemes* (1586), the emblem book with which Shakespeare was most probably familiar, the emblem, *"Qui se exaltat, humiliabitur"* ("He who exalts himself is humbled") appears. The caption below the picture of a boiling caldron states:

> The boylinge brothe, aboue the brinke dothe swell,
> And comes to naughte, with falling in the fire:
> So reaching heads that thinke them neuer well,
> Doe headlonge fall, for pride hathe ofte that hire:
>   And where before their frendes they did dispise,
>   Nowe beinge falne, none helpe them for to rise.[29]

The verse provides us with a moral explication of the fall of Macbeth who passionately aspires to rise like a boiling broth, but eventually falls headlong into the fire and comes to "naught," a futility not accompanied by "honour, love, obedience, troops of friends" (5.3.25). This nothingness is the hell on earth Macbeth suffers, and like him Lady Macbeth walks in her own hell on earth saying,

"Hell is murky" (5.1.30). Her spiritual perturbation is beyond the doctor's curative powers (5.1.56).

5

After the sleep-walking scene, the rest of act 5 is made up of successive short scenes running from the second to the ninth, alternately presenting action both inside Dunsinane Castle and out. Scenes 2 and 4 are set in the open air. Malcolm's army marches with drums and colors, and probably several trees are placed at one end of the stage. In scene 6 trees are more than stage properties, for the soldiers are covered with leafy boughs—thus Birnam wood coming to Dunsinane.

Scenes 3 and 5 are set in Dunsinane Castle. There may be a stool or some such piece of furniture on the stage. In scene 5 Macbeth and his soldiers enter with drums and colors. Macbeth says, "Hang out our banners on the outward walls," which probably is, as Kernodle says, "another case where the changing or hanging of symbolic decorations on the facade has been dramatized."[30] Here the facade at the back is just a picturesque background and is not used realistically.

In scene 7, the battle begun in the preceding scene continues. Old Siward, seeing the day will be theirs, leads Malcolm into the castle. In this scene, the facade at the back holds a mimetic reality as the real castle gate of Dunsinane. From an iconographical point of view, however, the facade represents hell-gate, for Malcolm's conquest of Dunsinane is a type of the harrowing of hell, or the fulfilment of the prefiguration of the harrowing in the hell-gate scene, the shrill alarms repeatedly recalling the *Harrowing of Hell* episode in the mystery plays.

The iconographical significance of the gate facade is more clearly revealed in the final scene of the play. It is none other than Macduff who, earlier in the knocking scene, knocked at the infernal gate like Christ in the mystery *Harrowing* and who now, again like Christ the savior-avenger, has harrowed the devilish tyrant's castle.

While the last scene is ritualistic both in its action and the accompanying imagery, the earlier scene of Birnam wood coming to Dunsinane is no less so, for such green branches as are held by the soldiers of Malcolm's army are sometimes used at the consecration of a new church. In Barking, near London, in the *Elevatio* of the monastery, members of the convent are first confined in the church of St Mary Magdalen and then led out, just as the souls are released by Christ in the mystery play *Harrowing of Hell*, and the erstwhile prisoners have palm branches in their hands.[31] The palm tree usually symbolizes triumph and pleasure, and here in the dedication of a new church it symbolizes, as in the procession of Palm Sunday, the triumph of the Church over Satan and Death and the ensuing pleasure. In the First Book of Spenser's *Faerie Queene*, when the Red Cross Knight has liberated Una's kingdom from the vicious dragon, a similar procession is held at the entrance of the castle:

> Forth came that auncient Lord and aged Queene,
> Arayd in antique robes downe to the ground,
> And sad habiliments right well beseene;
> A noble crew about them waited round
> Of sage and sober Peres, all grauely gownd;
> Whom farre before did march a goodly band
> Of tall young men, all hable armes to sownd,
> But now they laurell braunches bore in hand;
> Glad signe of victorie and peace in all their land.
>
> (I.xii.5)

Thus the final and fifth act of *Macbeth*, from the symbolic Birnam wood scene to the ritualistic proclamation of King Malcolm's reign at the very end, seems intended to echo the newly enthroned King James's entrance into London. Or it might better be seen as a dramatic expansion of a *tableau vivant*, possibly of Victory accompanied by Peace, at the coronation procession. A similar form of ritual is still observed at Trinity College, Cambridge, where the newly-elected master knocks at the college gate three times until the door is opened for him.

In *Macbeth*, the architectural facade again and again represents hell-gate like that in the mystery play, *The Harrowing of Hell*, and this, together with the infernal images visual and aural—the cauldron, the witches, trumpets, door knocking, owl's screeching and so on—creates Shakespeare's vision of hell. The stage action of the play is thus involved in the Catholic tradition but, as discussed earlier in reference to God's knocking at man's heart, mentioned in *The Basilicon Doron*, it is also subtly associated with the theology of Conscience of the Reformed Church. The playwright amalgamates these old and new religious viewpoints, taking no certain stance, but the Scottish play is never uncertain in his homage to King James.

Notes

1. As to the processions of Elizabeth and James see John Nichols, *The Progresses and Public Processions of Queen Elizabeth*, new ed., 3 vols. (London,

1823; New York: AMS Pr., n.d.) and the same author's *The Progresses, and Magnificent Festivities of King James the First,* 3 vols. (London, 1828; New York: Burt Franklin, n.d.).

2. Nichols, *Progresses . . . of King James I,* 1: 329–30, 343–44.

3. Ibid., 1. 349–54.

4. See Henry N. Paul, *The Royal Play of Macbeth* (1948; reprint, New York: Octagon Bks., 1971), 317–31. Nicholas Brooke, however, says that Paul has "no evidence whatsoever" for his central thesis and that Shakespeare's "choice of subject has far more to do with public interest, and therefore the public theatre, than with pleasing the king." Brooke's edition of *Macbeth* (The Oxford Shakespeare, 1990), 72–76.

5. George R. Kernodle, *From Art to Theatre: Form and Convention in the Renaissance* (Chicago: University of Chicago Press, 1944).

6. Kernodle, 5.

7. Frances A. Yates, *The Art of Memory* (London: Routledge, 1966; Penguin 1969) and *Theatre of the World* (London: Routledge, 1969).

8. Reproduced in Kernodle, fig. 4.

9. On the pictorial and architectural use of symbolic curtains and tapestries to show that the scene is set indoors, Kernodle has a detailed discussion. See Kernodle, 26–29.

10. Quotations from *Macbeth* are from Kenneth Muir's Arden edition (London: Methuen, 1951, 1961).

11. Walter C. Curry, *Shakespeare's Philosophical Patterns* (Baton Rouge, Louisiana, 1937), 86.

12. Robert Burton, *The Anatomy of Melancholy* [1621] (London: Everyman's Library, 1964), 1: 250–52.

13. Ibid., 1: 253–54.

14. Cf. Joseph Hall, *Heauen vpon Earth, or Of True Peace and Tranquilitie of Minde* [1606], ed. Rudolf Kirk (New Brunswick, N.J., 1948), 85–91.

15. See Thomas More, *The Four Last Things* [1522], ed. D. O'Connor (London, 1935), 39.

16. *The Basilicon Doron of King James VI* (1603), ed. James Craigie (Edinburgh, 1944), 41–43.

17. Thoman De Quincey, "On the Knocking at the Gate in *Macbeth,*" *Shakespeare Criticism 1623–1840,* ed. D. N. Smith (London: Oxford University Press, 1916; 1964), 331.

18. John Heywood, *The Play Called The Four PP.* (1520); J. Q. Adams, ed., *Chief Pre-Shakespearean Dramas* (Cambridge, Mass.: Riverside Press, 1924, 1952), 367–84. Cf. Glynne Wickham, "Hell-Castle and its Door-Keeper," *Shakespeare Survey* 19 (1966), 74, n. 1. For my iconographical reading of the hell-gate scene here, I am indebted to Wickham's brief but illuminating explication.

19. See Willi Kurth, ed., *The Complete Woodcuts of Albrecht Dürer* (New York: Dover Publications, 1963), plates 217, 247.

20. *The Towneley Plays,* ed. George England (EETS, 1952), 297; *The Wakefield Mystery Plays,* ed. Martial Rose (1961; New York, 1969), 449.

21. Cf. Wickham, 73.

22. Nathaniel Woodes, *The Conflict of Conscience* (printed 1581 by Richard Bradock), eds. Herbert Davis and F. P. Wilson (Malone Society Reprints, 1952).

23. Emile Male, *The Gothic Image: Religious Art in France of the Thirteenth Century,* trans. Dora Nussey (New York: Harper, 1958), 380.

24. Reproduced by Wickham in *Shakespeare Survey* 19 (1966), plate II (facing 65), and in S. Schoenbaum, *Shakespeare: The Globe and the World* (New York: Oxford University Press, 1979), 41.

25. Reproduced in G. K. Hunter, "The Theology of Marlowe's *The Jew of Malta*," *Journal of the Warburg and Courtauld Institutes*, xxvii (1964), fig. b (facing 234).

26. Christopher Marlowe, *The Jew of Malta*, ed. N. W. Bawcutt (Manchester University Press, 1978), 5.5.62.s.d.

27. *Henslowe Papers*, 118; cited in Hunter, 234, n.

28. Gunnyon, *Illustrations of Scottish History, Life, and Superstition* (1879), 322; cited T. F. Thiselton Dyer, *Folk-Lore of Shakespeare* (c. 1883; New York, 1966), 26.

29. Geoffrey Whitney, *A Choice of Emblemes* (Leyden: C. Plantyn, 1586), 216.

30. Kernodle, 138.

31. Wickham, 69–70.

"And Left Them More Rich for What They Yielded": Representation of Woman's Body and the Heterogeneous Economies in *The Winter's Tale*

MIKI SUEHIRO

1

RECENTLY several critics have pointed out the significance of economic terms repeated in *The Winter's Tale*. Stanley Cavell, for example, notes his own impression that the text is "engulfed by economic terms," enumerating them in detail:

> In *The Winter's Tale*—beyond the terms [*sic*] tell and count themselves, and loss and lost and gain and pay and owe and debt and repay— we have money, coin, treasure, purchase, cheat, custom, commodity, exchange, dole, wages, recompense, labor, affairs, traffic, tradesman, borrow, save, credit, redeem, and—perhaps the most frequently repeated economic term in the play—business.[1]

As the repetition of these economic terms suggests, almost all the characters in the play, from Leontes and Polixenes, and the courtiers in Sicilia to Autolycus, preoccupy themselves in economic principles. In examining the discursive practices of the play, however, we can detect a change of economic principles from the first part to the latter part of the play. In the critical history of the play, its two-part structure has often been problematized; some critics have discussed how the generic differences between the first part and the second part of the play function; others have found fault with the wide gap of time between them. Examining the shift of economic principles, however, registers an ideological discontinuity in the play which could illuminate a discussion of the play's two-part structure.

With the advent of the trend of body criticism, several critics have noted a change in the significance of the female body in

99

Shakespeare's romances. For example, Richard Wilson, critically reflecting on the tendency of liberal criticism which "has long identified an accommodation with motherhood in the romances," points out that "the romance, by disclaiming actuality, recounts what the history obscures: patriarchy's inability to impose mastery on the female body."[2] Those critics whose views are similar to Wilson's, however, tend to overstate the function of patriarchal licensing of the maternal body. In *The Winter's Tale,* the shift of the economic principles, to a large extent, affects the representational mode of women's body. Therefore, we should also examine the ideological shift of representation of the female body in the play. In order to reexamine the structural differences, it is necessary to focus on the relationship between the representational modes of women's body and the economic principles.

The opening scenes of *The Winter's Tale* provide no detailed clues to Leontes' fantasies of sexual betrayal. The exchange between Archidamaus and Camillo, however, suggests a certain kind of anxiety latent in the court of Sicilia which would lead to the abrupt outbreak of Leontes's jealousy:

> *Arch.* . . . you shall see, as I have said, great difference betwixt our Bohemia and your Sicilia.
> *Cam.* I think this coming summer, the King of Sicilia means to pay Bohemia the visitation which he justly owes him.
> *Arch.* Wherein our entertainment shall shame us: we will be justified in our loves: for indeed—
> *Cam.* Beseech you—
>
> (1.1.3–10)[3]

Here the courtiers' comparison of Sicilia and Bohemia should be understood as something much more than a mere exchange of courtesies. As Michael D. Bristol notes,[4] gift-giving, hospitality and expenditure are the dominant economic preoccupation of the first part of the play. Leontes and Polixenes "were twinn'd lambs that did frisk i' th'sun,/ And bleat the one at th' other" (1.2.66–68) during their childhoods. Even after they are separated, they keep a close friendship through "interchanges of gifts, letters, loving embassies" (1.1.28). These gifts and letters function as their proxy, as if they were *present* by means of these representatives where they are actually absent. Despite their protestations of love and friendship and despite their nostalgia for the prelapsarian nature of mankind, Leontes and Polixenes are in a potentially deadly *rivalry* for honor and prestige.

When Hermione urges Polixenes to postpone his departure, both of them apparently speak of the nature of love and friendship. They, however, often employ economic imagery, as if they were engaged in a commercial transaction:

> *Her.*   Verily,
> You shall not go; a lady's Verily's
> As potent as a lord's. Will you go yet?
> Force me to keep you as a prisoner
> Not like a guest: so you shall pay your fees
> When you depart, and save your thanks! How say you?
> My prisoner? or my guest?
>
> (1.2.49–55)

Hermione's argument here obviously proves to be decisively impelling to Polixenes; Polixenes chooses to be a guest rather than a prisoner, and agrees to extend his stay for another week. Although Hermione and Polixenes use commercial terms when they negotiate with each other about his departure, neither wants to engage in a commercial transaction. As Bristol points out, "To submit to the position of prisoner, to pay fees and settle accounts, would profoundly dishonor Polixenes, since it would transform the relationship into an impersonal exchange of equivalents or commodity transaction."[5]

Leontes does not want Polixenes to go home because he wishes to exceed his friend in honor and prestige. Polixenes wants to leave Sicilia without too much debt so that he can compensate Leontes for his hospitality when he visits Bohemia. This economic principle of gift-giving is dominant in the first part of the play, although the struggle for honor and prestige is always the source of male anxiety. This relationship of gift-giving is the cause of an inequality between men; at the same time, gift-giving helps to strengthen the male homosocial bond between Leontes and Polixenes. Paradoxically, Hermione's body is represented as at once establishing and disrupting this male homosocial bond. As Eve Kosofsky Sedgwick explains, the theory of a male homosocial bond is derived from René Girard's discussion of the erotic triangle in which two males are rivals for a female: in this erotic triangle, the bond between male rivals is "stronger, more heavily determinant of actions and choices, than anything in the bond between either of the lovers and the beloved." Furthermore, Sedgwick, borrowing Gayle Rubin's influential anthropological discussion, points out that "patriarchal heterosexuality can best be discussed in terms of one or another form of the traffic in women: it is the use of women as exchangeable, perhaps symbolic, property for the primary purpose of cementing the bonds of men with men."[6] In the play Hermione structurally, if not emotionally or subjectively, positions herself within the erotic triangle in which both Leontes and Polixenes take the positions of a desiring male subject. Within the male bonding between Leontes and Polixenes, however, Hermione is hardly represented as "exchangeable property." If Hermione were to become a commodity circulating between Leontes and Polixenes, she might give rise to an unbridgeable gap between them which no symbolic exchange could recompense. In fact, Polixenes refers to a kind of devilry in women which would split a close relationship between Leontes and Polixenes:

> *Pol.*   O my most sacred lady,
> Temptations have since then been born to's: for
> In those unfledg'd days was my wife a girl;
> Your precious self had then not cross'd the eyes
> Of my young play-fellow.
> *Her.*   Grace to boot!
> Of this make no conclusion, lest you say
> Your queen and I are devils!
>
> (1.2.76–82)

In the idyllic picture of boyhood, women are accused of being devils, seductive and corrupting to men's pre-sexual innocence.

Women not only disrupt male bonding but also transgress the threshold of private territories, that is, of the household. The jealous Leontes represents women's bodies as breaking the boundaries of a community and freely communicating with the outside:

> There have been,
> (Or I am much deceiv'd) cuckolds ere now,
> And many a man there is (even at this present,
> Now, while I speak this) holds his wife by th'arm,
> That little thinks she has been *sluic'd* in's absence
> And his pond fish'd by his next neighbour, by
> Sir Smile, his neighbour: nay, there's comfort in't,
> Whiles other men have *gates*, and those *gates open'd*,
> As mine, against their will. Should all despair
> That have revolted wives, the tenth of mankind
> Would hang themselves. Physic for't there's none;
> It's a bawdy planet, that will strike
> Where 'tis predominant; and 'tis powerful, think it,

> From east, west, north, and south; be it concluded,
> *No barricado for a belly.*
> (1.2.190–204. Italics mine.)

"Sluic'd", "gates opened," a "barricado": these images Leontes uses to represent women's bodies are derived from the assumption that women's bodies are naturally grotesque. As Mikhail Bakhtin says, woman's body is "unfinished, outgrows itself, transgresses its own limits. The stress is laid on those parts of the body that are open to the outside world, that is, the parts through which the world enters the body or emerges from it, or through which the body itself goes out to meet the world."[7]

Woman's grotesque body should be subject to constant surveillance because it transgresses not only the limits of private territories but also the body politic. In fact, the image of the opened gate is reiterated in the play: when Polixenes escapes from the Sicilian court through a back gate by Camillo's "great authority," Leontes's authority is symbolically usurped by Camillo.

In the first part of the play there are two modes of representing women's body. First, Hermione's body is represented as disrupting male bonding in that her body becomes the object of male desire. Secondly, Leontes characterizes women's body as if it were Bakhtin's "grotesque body," the image of the impure corporeal bulk opened to traffic through orifices. Leontes is so obsessed with sexual jealousy that he tries to contain the grotesque of Hermione's body. To borrow Peter Stallybrass's phrase, in the action of the first part of the play Leontes, representing woman's body as naturally grotesque, tries to "enclose" it. Leontes's jealousy is admittedly groundless, therefore completely unjustified. However, if we pay attention to the relationship between the economic principle and representation of women's body, motivation for his extreme jealousy would reside in an anxiety of the self-closed male bonding.

In his extreme sexual jealousy Leontes attempts to contain Hermione's grotesque body; consequently, he has to sever his close connections with Polixenes, and exclude Hermione from his own world, as if he could remove impurities from the world. Significantly, Leontes separates Hermione from his close relationship with Mamillius. As Carol Thomas Neely notes, Leontes, rejecting the need for the male to share the creative process with the female, seems to be wishing that Mamillius had been created by some variety of "male parthenogenesis."[8] As a matter of fact, Leontes supposes Mamillius has been already contaminated by Hermione's blood:

> *Leon.*   I am glad you did not nurse him:
> Though he does bear some signs of me, yet you
> Have too much blood in him.
>
> (2.1.56–58)

The tragic action of the first part of the play consists in the death of Mamillius. The death of Mamillius has a decisive effect on the discursive practices throughout the play. He by no means plays such symbolic roles as "innocence slain by evil" or "frustrated youth and growth,"[9] in the play. As Leonard Tennenhouse puts it, "[a]t stake in Mamillius's death is not inversion of a family relationship but the disruption of political order—the survival of the state itself."[10] The opening scene of the play calls our attention to the role of Mamillius in the thematic structure of the play. As, according to the law of primogeniture, he is the only son and legitimate heir to Leontes, he is "a gentleman of/the greatest promise" (1.1.35–36). Camillo and Archidamus emphasize Mamillius's promising future, which ironically suggests the seriousness of the political crisis caused by his death. The exchange between them also predicts the action of the second half of the play which inevitably follows his death, Leontes's waiting for his heir:

> *Cam.*   . . . they went on crutches ere he was born
> desire yet thir life to see him a man.
> *Arch.*   Would they else be content to die?
> *Cam.*   Yes; if there were no other excuse why they should desire
> to live.
> *Arch.*   If the king had no son, they would desire to live on crutches
> till he had one.
>
> (1.1.39–45)

In his attempt to enclose Hermione's grotesque body, Leontes expels her from his own world in order to maintain a male homosocial alliance with Polixenes and a close relationship with Mamillius. The result is, ironically, that Polixenes's Bohemia severs diplomatic relations with Leontes's Sicilia, and that Mamillius dies "with mere conceit and fear of / the queen's speed" (3.2.144–45). Sicilia has become a temporally and spatially self-closed space.

2

It should be noted that the location of the second part of the play, a rural area of Bohemia, is not a purely traditional pastoral space. As the Clown, Perdita's brother, goes toward a market place, calculating the cash income from wool, this seemingly idyllic space has been already permeated by a market economy. In the first part of the play, Polixenes tries to maintain a boundary between a gift economy such as hospitality, and a market economy such as commodity exchange. In the second part of the play, the sheepshearing is a popular culture festival contaminated by a market economy; it is an opportunity for lavish expenditure in which Perdita offers the guests luxurious commodities bought in the market place. The figure of Autolycus symbolizes both the infiltration of a market economy in the country and the predominance of the commodity form. According to Robert Weimann, Autolycus's speech, "My traffic is sheets" suggests the complexity of his social identity."[11] J. H. P. Pafford interprets this speech as "My merchandize is stolen sheets" and concludes that he is "the traditional tinker and petty thief."[12] Weimann, however, points out that, during the seventeenth century, the word "sheet" already had the meaning of "an oblong or square piece of paper or parchment, *esp.* for writing or printing" or a "broadsheet,"[13]; he concludes that Autolycus here uses a pun to announce that he deals with ballad-broadsides. As a matter of fact, Autolycus is represented as a ballad-monger as well as a petty thief. These social identities seem quite different, but, in fact, they overlap:

> . . . they throng
> who should buy first, as if my trinkets had been hallowed and brought
> a benediction to the buyer: by which means I saw whose purse was
> best in picture; and what I saw, to my good use I remembered.
>
> (4.4.601–5)

Here Autolycus sells trifles, as if they were "hallowed," and at the same time looks for gulls. As Bristol notes, he is "a versatile economic opportunist who preys upon the typical consumer psychology of wealthy *arrivistes*."[14]

These fraudulent transactions are not limited to vagabonds, but are characteristic of merchants in Shakespeare's England. Autolycus himself recognizes this when he says, "Let me have no / lying: it becomes none but tradesmen, and they / often give us soldiers the lie" (4.4.722–26).

Autolycus seems to have versatile social identities: a ballad-monger and entertainer, and petty thief. In fact, Autolycus embodies "the placeless market" in Jean-Christophe Agnew's term. Ag-

new observes how the meanings of "market" had multiplied and
grown more abstract in the development of a market economy:

> Market now referred to the acts of both buying and selling, regardless
> of locale, and to the price or exchange value of goods or servicers. A
> culturally confined site was no longer the precondition of a market so-
> called. Rather, the topography of exchange had been made to depend
> on a market now understood to be the mere presence of marketable
> items or disposable items.[15]

The figure of Autolycus is closely associated with the function of
the market no longer confined to a particular place in seventeenth
century England.

Autolycus puts on several disguises and freely transforms his
own social identity; at the same time, he is a kind of trickster who
makes "liquid" stable social relations. In other words, Autolycus
represents theatricality of the market economy. As Agnew notes,
in Shakespeare's England, "theatricality itself had begun to acquire
renewed connotations of invisibility, concealment, and misrepresentation, connotations that were at once intriguing and incrimi-
nating."[16] The market had become opaque and invisible, and begun
to make opaque its participants' identities; the market had begun
to misrepresent itself and to bring about a social mobility. The
power of a market economy and theatricality Autolycus symbolizes contribute to restore the relationship between Bohemia and
Sicilia severed in the first part.

The power of a market economy and theatricality are, however,
not always encouraged in the second part of the play. We must note
that Perdita and Florizel often attempt to restrain these impulses.
Perdita who plays the role of a "mistress of the feast" is reluctant
to misrepresent her own identity and is suspicious of the sheepshearing festival itself:

> *Per.*   Your high self,
> The gracious mark o' th' land, you have obscur'd
> With a swain's wearing, and me, poor lowly maid,
> Most goddess-like prank'd up: but that our feasts
> In every mess have folly, and the feeders
> Digest it with a custom. I should bluish
> To see you so attir'd; swoon, I think,
> To show myself a glass.
>
> (4.4.7–14)

Although Perdita, who asks the Clown to buy luxurious commodities at a market, indirectly participates in a market economy, she

does not consent to the symbolic functions of the market, that is, commodification and misrepresentation of identities. When she has to disguise herself in order to escape to Sicilia, she says with resignation that, "I see the play lies / That I must bear a part" (4.4.655–56) which Pafford interprets in the following way: "I see that we're all play–acting (dressing up) and that I have to take a part." Perdita never commits herself to the theatricality Autolycus embodies.

Unlike the other participants in the sheepshearing, Florizel does not buy Autolycus's commodities to attract his lover. Florizel is reluctant to take part in the network of exchanges in a market economy. When he gives up the status of a prince and agrees to exchange clothes with Autolycus he, for the first time, participates in the network of a market economy. As a matter of fact, in the second part of the play, the impulse of a market economy is at once enhanced and restrained.

After all, the relationship between Sicilia and Bohemia is restored, but their political, economic and representational systems do not substantially change. In the opening scenes, similarities between Sicilia and Bohemia are noted but, at the same time, differences between them are equally emphasized. Throughout the play, however, differences between Sicilia and Bohemia have gradually been repressed. Leontes commands Antigonus to cast his newly-born baby to a strange country, not to Bohemia:

> As by strange fortune
> It came to us, I do in justice charge thee.
> On thy soul's peril and thy body's torture,
> That thou commend it strangely to some place
> Where chance may nurse or end it.
>
> (2.3.178–82)

However, Bohemia, where Antigonus has cast Perdita, is, not a strange country. Furthermore, from an economic point of view, Sicilia and Bohemia are by no means different countries. In fact, in a strict sense, there is no commodity exchange between them. Those things and people which move from Sicilia to Bohemia return to Sicilia in the end: Perdita. Camillo and the basket which contained a baby and a quantity of gold. The only exception is Antigonus who is eaten by a bear. The fact of his loss, however, is ideologically forgotten and concealed when Camillo, as if he played the part of Antigonus' substitute, gets married to Paulina.[17] In the narrative, the income and outgo in Sicilia and Bohemia are misrepresented as balanced. Perdita is called a "changeling"

(3.3.117) by the old shepherd. A changeling is supposed to be a kind of commodity to be exchanged with the other like fairies. However Perdita, who is reluctant to participate in any network of a market economy, circulates in the closed relationship between Sicilia and Bohemia. When social mobility is accomplished in the end, it does not lead to any danger of social instability. The old shepherd and the Clown who have already become rich by means of a quantity of gold "beyond the imagination" of their neighbours are promoted to gentlemen. However, they are only contained within the closed aristocratic system of the Sicilian court. Autolycus as a trickster indeed helps Perdita and Florizel, the old shepherd and the Clown to move to Sicilia. However, the power of the placeless market and theatricality Autolycus symbolizes are repressed and concealed when the action draws to a close.

3

In the denouement the statue of Hermione is the focus. According to Peter Stallybrass and Allon White who formulate Bakhtin's paradigm of the body, the grotesque is contrasted with the classical in early modern somatic concepts. Stallybrass and White explain Bakhtin's vocabulary of the classical body this way:

> Taking formal values from a purified mythologized canon of Ancient Greek and Roman canon . . . the classical body was far more than an aesthetic standard or model. It structured, from the inside as it were, the characteristically 'high' discourses of philosophy, statecraft, theology and law, as well as literature, as they emerged from the Renaissance. In the classical body were encoded those regulated systems which were closed, homogeneous, monumental, centered and symmetrical.[18]

Bourgeois individualist ideology finds its image and legitimation in the classical body which stands in opposition to the grotesque body. Then, is the statue of Hermione represented as such a classical body? Is Hermione reduced to the symbol of harmony and order in the patriarchal family with the success of Leontes's strategy of enclosing the grotesque body? Before discussing these questions, I want to consider the process of representation of Hermione's body.

When Leontes represents Hermione as a grotesque body, he enumerates her improper behavior in detail, observing how Hermione entertains Polixenes:

> This entertainment
> May a free face put on, derive a liberty
> From heartiness, from bounty, fertile bosom,
> And well become the agent: 't may, I grant:
> But to be paddling palms, and pinching fingers,
> As now they are, and making practis'd smiles
> As in a looking-glass; and then to sigh, as 'awere
> The mort o' th' deer—O, that is entertainment
> My bosom likes not, nor my brows.
>
> (1.2.111–19)

Here it doesn't matter whether she should actually make such gestures on stage. Significantly, Leontes tries to represent Hermione as the object of male gaze. Through this strategy of visualization, Leontes reduces Hermione to a kind of spectacle. In the trial scene of act 3, scene 2, Hermione is exposed to public view. She attempts to resist Leontes by appealing to the visually unrepresentable:

> You, my lord, best know
> (Who least will seem to do so) my past life
> Hath been as continent, as chaste, as true,
> As I am now unhappy; which is more
> Than history can pattern, though devised
> And play'd to take spectators.
>
> (3.2.32–37)

Here Hermione speaks of antitheatricalism. She gives priority to the theatrically unrepresentable over the spectacle of her own body which is inscribed with any meaning by men. In the language of Hermione the idea of "honor" is set against that of "life": "for honor/'Tis a derivative from me to mine/And only that I stand for" (3.2.43–45). The significance of succession from Hermione to her children precedes the worth of her own body; in contrast, Leontes recognizes the newly-born child only as evidence of her adultery. Rather than the rigor of the Sicilian law, Hermione invokes "powers divine" revealed as the Delphic Oracle, that is, the theatrical representation of the law of genealogy. In the discursive practices of the second half of the play, the law of genealogy is closely connected with the representation of Hermione. As the Oracle predicts, the consequence of Leontes's tyranny is not his personal ruin, but the political crisis caused by the death of his only legitimate heir: "and the king shall/live without an heir, if that which is lost be not/found" (3.2.134–36). In the narrative, however, it is ambiguous who is "that which is lost." Perdita is of course etymologically "that

which is lost." But Shakespeare much more dramatically represents another recovery of "that which is lost," that is, that of Hermione. When the statue of Hermione begins to move, in addition
to mutually exclusive categories of the grotesque body and the
classical body, the third iconography of the representation of the
body is introduced: the reproductive body.

Paulina reminds Leontes of the Oracle's prophecy when the
courtiers propose the idea of Leontes's re-marriage in order to
overcome the political crisis of an heirless state:

> There is none worthy
> Respecting her that's gone. Besides, the gods
> Will have fulfill'd their secret purposes;
> For has not the divine Apollo said,
> That King Leontes shall not have an heir,
> Till his lost child be found?
>
> (5.1.34–40)

Surprisingly, Paulina gives precedence to the Oracle's prophecy
rather than the actual measures against the crisis of the state. Here
Paulina interprets "that which is lost" as Perdita. At the same
time, however, she persuades Leontes to give up the idea of his
re-marriage, reminding him of the distinguished quality of Hermione as queen:

> *Leon.*   Good Paulina,
> Who hast the memory of Hermione,
> I know, in honour,—O, that ever I
> Had squar'd me to thy counsel! Then, even now,
> I might have look'd upon my queen's full eyes,
> Have taken treasure from her lips,—
> *Paul.*   And left them
> More rich for what they yielded.
>
> (5.1.49–55)

Both Leontes and Paulina speak of the miraculous economy of
Hermione's lips. As *The Oxford English Dictionary* notes, however, the word "yield" has also means "to produce, bear, generate
(fruit, seed, vegetation, minerals, etc.); to bring forth, to give birth
to, bear (offspring)." Therefore, we could read the image of a reproductive body in Paulina's representation of Hermione's body. As
Paulina declares to Leontes that the date of his re-marriage "shall
be when your first queen's again in breath" (5.1.83), Paulina awak-
ens Leontes into realizing the significance of the restoration of

harmony in the patriarchal family through the recovery of a reproductive body.

Mentioned above, the statue of Hermione is something more
than a classical body. To be sure, it may be represented as a classical body when its coldness and painting are referred to. However,
when the statue begins to move by means of Paulina's white magic,
it is no longer a classical body.[19] Unlike the spectacle seen by men,
Hermione is now a seeing and speaking subject as well as an object
seen by Leontes, Perdita and Florizel. Beyond the framework of
patriarchal visual economy, Hermione has acquired a discursive
and visual reciprocity. She ascertains family ties with Perdita in
the following brief passage:

> . . . for thou shalt hear that I,
> Knowing by Paulina that the Oracle
> Gave hope thou was in being, have preserv'd
> Myself to see the issue.
>
> (5.3.125–28)

Because of multiple meanings of the word "issue," Hermione's
speech here could be interpreted in several ways. Significantly,
although the word "issue," repeated fourteen times in the play, is
one of the key words in the play, Hermione speaks this word only
here. The word used here by Hermione could be interpreted in
several ways. First, the issue means the result of the Delphic Oracle's prediction. Second, as Hermione here speaks to Perdita, the
issue could be Hermione's daughter and Leontes's only legitimate
heir. Third, as Sandra K. Fischer notes, in Shakespeare's plays the
word often means "a certain mint of coins, with a pun on progeny,
as the coins of copulation, and concerns, as issues."[20] Therefore
the word here could mean money with a pun on the line of descent
for an inheritance. The dynamic power of a market economy which
has been repressed and concealed toward the end of the play un-
cannily surfaces here.

In the critical history of the play, even feminist critics like Valerie Traub cannot find any site of women's resistance in the statue
scene. As a matter of fact, Traub concludes that, "To the extent that
a statue's function is commemorative, Hermione-as-statue safely
remembers, but does not embody, the threat of female erotic
power"[21]: in the end Hermione's female erotic power is contained
within the patriarchal frame work. My point, however, is that the
statue scene does not lead to the self-closed patriarchal relationship of a gift economy. With Hermione's transformation from a

classical body to a reproductive body, she is linked with the dynamic power of a market economy which helps to produce children and economic surplus. Both Hermione and Autolycus, although quite different in class, have a particular consciousness of time in common. In fact, they live in expectation of the transformative and reproductive power of time. Although it seems that the dynamic power of a market economy is repressed in the end, the radically transformative power of time, "To o'erthrow law, and in one self-born hour/To plant and o'erwhelm custom" (4.1.8–9) lies latent.

Notes

1. Stanley Cavell, "Recounting Gains, Showing Losses: Reading *The Winter's Tale*," in *Disowning Knowledge: In Six Plays of Shakespeare* (Cambridge: Cambridge University Press, 1987), 200.

2. Richard Wilson, "Observations on English Bodies: Licensing Maternity in Shakespeare's Late Plays," in *Will Power: Essays on Shakespearean Authority* (Hemel Hempstead: Harvester Wheatsheaf, 1993), 158–83; 170–71. For other readings of the romances sceptical about liberal criticism, see Peter Erickson, "Patriarchal Structures in *The Winter's Tale*," *PMLA* 97 (1982), 819–29, and Janet Adelman, "Masculine Authority and the Maternal Body: The Return to Origins in the Romances," in *Suffocating Mothers: Fantasies of Maternal origin in Shakespeare's Plays, Hamlet to The Tempest* (London: Routledge, 1992), 193–238.

3. All citations are from the Arden edition of *The Winter's Tale*, ed. J. H. P. Pafford (London: Methuen, 1963).

4. Michael D. Bristol, "In Search of the Bear: Spatiotemporal Form and the Heterogeneity of Economies in *The Winter's Tale*," *Shakespeare Quarterly* 42 (1991), 154. With regard to the discussion of the economic principles in the play I am very much indebted to Bristol's argument, but he does not deal with the question of the representation of the female body.

5. Ibid., 156.

6. For the definition and discussion of the term "a male homosocial bond," see Eve Kosofsky Sedgwick, *Between Men: English Literature and Male Homosocial Desire* (New York: Columbia University Press, 1985), especially chapter 1, "Gender Asymmetry and Erotic Triangles," 21–27.

7. Mikhail Bakhtin, *Rablais and His World,* trans. Hélène Iswolsky (Cambridge, Mass: MIT Press, 1968), 26. For a particularly illuminating discussion of the "natural grotesqueness" of woman's body, see Peter Stallybrass, "Patriarchal Territories: The Body Enclosed," in *Rewriting the Renaissance: The Discourses of Sexual Difference in Early Modern Europe,* eds. Margaret W. Ferguson, Maureen Quilligan, and Nancy J. Vickers (Chicago: The University Chicago Press, 1986), 123–42.

8. Carol Thomas Neely, "Women and Issue in *The Winter's Tale*," in *William Shakespeare's The Winter's Tale: Modern Critical Interpretations,* ed. Harold Bloom (New York: Chelsea House, 1987), 78.

9. J. H. P. Pafford's introduction to the Arden edition of the play, xxi.

10. Leonard Tennenhouse, *Power on Display: The Politics of Shakespeare's Genres* (London: Methuen, 1986), 175.

11. Robert Weimann, "Shakespeare and the Broadside: Traditions of Elizabethan Culture Revisited" (paper given at the 5th World Congress of Shakespeare held in Tokyo, 1991).

12. Pafford's commentary, 81.

13. See the entry of the word "sheet" *sb.* 5. in *The Oxford English Dictionary,* Second Edition.

14. Bristol, 163.

15. Jean-Christophe Agnew, *Worlds Apart: The Market and the Theater in Anglo-American Thought, 1550–1750* (Cambridge: Cambridge University Press, 1986), 41.

16. Ibid., 40.

17. Presentation of the self-closed relationship between Sicilia and Bohemia may have something to do with the politics of insularity. Discussing colonialism in *The Tempest,* Jeffrey Knapp points out the significance of homebodiedness to Shakespeare: "Shakespeare, it seems, wants to recommend American colonies as essential to England's well-being, and essential because of the dangerous treasure those colonies may secure, but he must "remove" such motives and even America itself from direct consideration in order to promote the temperate homebodiedness without which, he believes, a colony cannot last." (235) In *The Winter's Tale* Shakespeare, dealing with the negotiation between Sicilia and Bohemia, hardly dramatizes an expansionist movement. See Jeffrey Knapp, *An Empire Nowhere: England, America, and Literature from Utopia to The Tempest* (Berkeley: The University of California Press, 1992), especially 220–42.

18. Peter Stallybrass and Allon White, *The Politics and Poetics of Transgression* (London: Methuen, 1986), 22.

19. In her discussion of early modern patriarchy's suspicion about pregnancy, birth, maternal surrogacy and nurture, Gail Kern Paster asserts Hermione in the statue scene as a reproductive mother no longer subject to "the shame and the juridicial disciplines that attended motherhood in the tragic action." See her *The Body Embarrassed: Drama and the Disciplines of Shame in Early Modern England* (Ithaca: Cornell University Press, 1993), 260–80.

20. Sandra K. Fischer, *Econolingua: A Glossary of Coins and Economic Language in Renaissance Drama* (Newark: University of Delaware Press, 1985), 88.

21. Valerie Traub, *Desire and Anxiety: Circulations of Sexuality in Shakespearean Drama* (London: Routledge, 1992), 45–46.

Canibal and Caliban: *The Tempest* and the Discourse of Cannibalism

TED MOTOHASHI

1

NAMING is a contentious issue in *The Tempest*. According to Caliban, whose account of the first days of Prospero's arrival on the island is not refuted by the latter's alternative explanation, the two started their mutually accountable relationship amicably:

> When thou cams't first,
> Thou strok'st me and made much of me, wouldst give me
> Water with berries in't, and teach me how
> To name the bigger light and how the less,
> That burn by day and night; and then I lov'd thee,
> And show'd thee all the qualities o' th'isle,
> The fresh springs, brine-pits, barren place and fertile.
> (1.2.331–37)[1]

This seeminglly mutually beneficial relationship between the precursor and the newcomer is based on the exchange of knowledge—on the one hand, naming of the planets, acknowledged within an European discourse and legibly represented by signs such as "sun" and "moon"—and on the other, revelation of the island's topographical information, only locally accountable as substantial "facts" and unrepresented as a sign yet easily translatable into vital knowledge for a would-be colonizer. This representational gap between the two discourses lies at the heart of the play's representation of the struggle between the dominant and the subordinate. Prospero is endowed by the play with a power to name, transfiguring the natural heterogeneity of the island into a hierarchical order, whereas Caliban is allowed an ability to question and undermine that naming process by revealing the subaltern hybridity as discursively unrepresentable.[2]

Among the character's names in the play, one stands out—"Caliban." One could even argue that "Caliban" is a sign—with other names such as "water," "berries," "sun," and "moon"—created by Prospero to mark the "qualities" of this aboriginal boy.[3] We may never know for certain whether Shakespeare intended "Caliban" as an anagram of "Canibal," but the uncertainty does not lessen the name's significance. It is a generic term for the man-eater introduced into European languages for the first time by Christopher Columbus in *The Journal* of his first voyage. On the 23rd of November, 1492, Columbus wrote:

> and beyond this cape there stretched out another land or cape, which also trended to the east, which those Indians whom he had with him called "Bohio." They said that this land was very extensive and that in it were people who had one eye in the forehead, and others whom they called "Canibals." Of these last, they showed great fear, and when they saw that this course was being taken, they were speechless, he says, because these people ate them and because they are very warlike. The admiral says that he well believes that there is something in this, but that since they were well armed, they must be an intelligent people, and he believed that they may have captured some men and that, because they did not return to their own land, they would say that they were eaten. They believed the same of the Christians and of the admiral, when some first saw them.[4]

This entry is worth quoting in length not only because it provides the first appearance of the word "Canibals" but because we here glimpse, along with Columbus's doubt about the Indians' claim about the man-eaters, a kind of dialogical reciprocity in the discourse of cannibalism: the first encounter with an alien race, European or Amerindian, produces fear and suspicion that the strange visitor might eat man's flesh. The encounter between different cultures hinges on the reciprocal (though not symmetrical) nature of cannibalistic discourse. "Canibals" colonized the European imagination as they were being colonized.[5]

The present paper attempts to analyse, through an examination of statements by Columbus about man-eaters and of *The Tempest*, a play constructed around the displaced center of the (non-)cannibalistic figure of Caliban, the process in which a mutual accountability is replaced by a monologic and Eurocentric representation of the native people as "Other." In this analysis, *The Tempest* will emerge as an instance of dialogic negotiation between an historicizing attempt by the European master to legitimize conquest and an endeavour of rehistoricizing, dehistoricizing, and so

decolonizing by the indigenous slave in order to question this legiti-
mizing process. While it is true that this kind of analysis, to put
the play into a colonial context, is itself as historicizing an attempt
as Prospero's directorial staging of the island's history for a redemption of lost harmony and sovereignty, my reading, is justified
by subsequent history of colonial expansion, which has been
underlined by the discourse of cannibalism.

In *The Tempest,* Prospero calls an indigenous boy "Caliban,"
while he leaves the island nameless. In Columbus's *Journal,* by
contrast, the native name of the island "Bohio" is replaced by
another signifier "Canibals" which may or may not have meant
man-eaters. In *The Tempest,* "Caliban" is an ambiguous name that
not only indicates the slave's subjection to the white master but
also evokes a topos of resistance against him; in the *Journal,* a
native name is translated by the recorder into another term signi-
fying the savageness and inferiority of the indigenous population
(there was of course a counter-tradition via Montaigne and Jean
de Léry which would stress their comparative innocence). If "Caliban" involves both displacement and retention of the subversive
power of the man-eaters, "Canibal," as subsequent history of colonization manifests, merely marks a site of deceptive reciprocity, of
translation and uprooting.

The dialogism detected in Columbus's *Journal* is reiterated in
Sebastian Munster's account of Columbus's voyage included in
Cosmographie, which was translated into English by Richard Eden
in 1553. This provides one of the first English references to the
"canibals" in America (the first *OED* entry), which was rapidly
displacing the Greek term "anthropophagi." Here, the reason for
the natives' fear of Europeans is said to be "that they suspected
them [the Europeans] to haue been *Canibals,* that cruel and fearse
people which eate mans fleshe."[6] However, this sense of reciprocity
was suppressed as the term "Canibals" gained popularity. For instance, Peter Martyr's "Preface" to his "Decades" translated also
by Eden in 1555, rationalizes the bondage of the native people, as
"theyr former libertie . . . was to the cruell Canibales" and "they
were euer in daunger to be a prey to those manhuntynge woolues."[7]
According to this logic based upon the binary distinction between
the "gentle Arawaks" and "cruell Canibales," the European conquest was mutually beneficial, even more so to the natives who
were given a true "libertie" free from "cruell" and "licencious
Canibales."

When Columbus thought he heard that word for the first time
on 23 November 1492 and acquired a surprising amount of informa-

tion for a man who had been in this region for less than six weeks
without any previous knowledge of its languages and customs, he
had some doubt about the authenticity of the information. But after
three months' experience in the region, Columbus came to claim
that he was able to "identify" the man-eating "Caribes," whom he
claimed he *met* on the northern coast of Hispaniola, because they
looked so different from—"uglier" than—the others. In his *Journal*, Columbus described how he encountered one of the "Caribs"
for the first time on 13 January 1493:

> they found some men with bows and and arrows, . . . and asked one
> of them to go to speak with the admiral in the caravel, and he came.
> The admiral says that he was more ugly in appearance than any whom
> he had seen. He had his face all stained with charcoal, although in all
> other parts they are accustomed to paint themselves with various col-
> ours; he wore all his hair very long and drawn back and tied behind,
> and then gathered in meshes of parrots' feathers, and he was as naked
> as the others. The admiral judged that he must be one of the Caribs
> who eat men and that the gulf, which he had seen yesterday, divided
> the land and that it must be an island by itself.[8]

In a way, this entry is more remarkable than the previous one,
for this is the day when the hitherto mythical "Canibales" were
personified into the "Caribes,"[9] hence establishing not only the
mythical tale of the "island of Canibales" which fascinated so many
voyagers/writers after Columbus, but also the Carib/Arawak binarism, each term of which was separated by the "gulf" dividing the
two regions inhabited by them. Apart from Columbus's observation that the man had "many arrows"—the feature that might
match one of the characterics of the "Canibals" reported by the
natives on 23 November—, his judgement depended solely on the
man's external appearances such as dressing habits and facial
decorations. What is more disturbingly predictable is that, as Columbus himself admitted ("he was as naked as the others"), there
was no way of telling *ipso facto* the difference between the "gentle
Arawak" and the "cruel Carib." The only way to distinguish between the two was their *intrinsic* characteristics: the one was *by
nature* gentle and servile, hence cooperative with the Spanish, attentive to Christian dogmas and fearful of and victim to the "Canibales"; the other was definitely its opposite—most likely because
they possessed and were ready to use their "weapons." Columbus
confidently stated on the same day, when he learned that the "Caribs" had unsuccessfully assaulted the Spanish: "they would be
afraid of the Christians, *for without doubt,* he says, the people

there are, as he says, evil-doers, and he believed that they were those from Carib and that they eat men. . . ."[10] Christianity, as it frequently did during the course of his voyage, came to provide a rational explanation for the internal nature of the "Carib."

Furthermore, the *actual* identity of the fierce tribe did not matter here: it was sufficient to know that they were fearless and consequently likely to pose an obstacle to the European desire for God, Gold and Groom, as the diary continued: "and he says that if they were not Caribs, at least they must be *neighbours of them and have the same customs,* and they are a fearless people, not like the others of the other islands, who are cowardly beyond reason and without weapons."[11] In fact, this category of "neighbours" could limitlessly expand as the Europeans set new boundaries between the "fearless" and the "cowardly". The "customs" were "discovered" wherever they were "a daring people" with weapons in their hand.[12] After all, what was "discovered" by Columbus was, rather than the Indians or America, in fact a sign of "Canibales" which had not and needed not a body.

2

If "Canibal" is a sign that elliptically contains a void within itself, how was it appropriated by English writers of the age and transformed into the 1611 text by Shakespeare? Out of Shakespeare's five uses of "Cannibal" and its derivatives in his works, one of the most interesting examples is found in *The Third Part of Henry VI,* when York accuses Margaret of disdaining his son Rutland's death:

> That face of his the hungry cannibal
> Would not have touch'd, would not have stain'd with blood;
> But you are more inhuman, more inexorable—
> O, ten times more—than tigers of Hyrcania.

$$(1.4.152)^{13}$$

Here the main function of the sign "cannibal" is that of *differentiation:* York, by comparing Margaret's cruelty with that of the "hungry cannibal" (which is at once marginalized and animalized into "tigers" living beyond human habitation), emphasizes the degree of the atrocities she committed.[14] "Cannibal" in this context no longer disguises itself to inscribe ideological messages through an invention of intrinsic features: it plainly represents unmatchable bloodthirstiness, for the real target of this discourse is not an entity to which this sign is applicable, but a woman present at the scene, whose demeanour, as a queen and a warrior heroine, exhibits what is totally alien even to "cannibals." The speech's point lies in differentiation between those who appear to hold the same rank as the speaker, rather than in marginalization of those who are manifestly inferior to the producer of the discourse.

Similar examples can be found in accounts of English expeditions in the New World. Latecomers by some 100 years to the region, early English businessmen in America were more piratical than commercial, justifying their pillage of Spanish gold by emphasizing *natural* differences between the Spanish "conquistadors" and the English "liberators." They invented the myth of the Motherly love of Queen Elizabeth who, as they claimed, contrary to the evil Catholic King Philip II, truly cared for the well-being of the native population.

According to Richard Hakluyt the elder (of Middle Temple), one of the foremost colonial ideologues, in order to attain the three ends of the Virginia enterprise—"to plant Christian religion," "To trafficke," and "To conquer"[15]—, the English had to take "a gentle course," which should distinguish them from the precursor Spaniard. In order to draw the native population "into love with our nation," Hakluyt writes, "we become not hatefull unto them, as the Spaniard is in Italie and in the West Indies, and elsewhere, by their maner of usage."[16] The most important aspect of the English colonial enterprise was to expel the native people from their lands with minimum force, preferably without recourse to violence. According to these pragmatic considerations, indulging in a philosophical argument about the Indians' humanity would have been seen as a waste of time, as in the argument between Bartolomé de Las Casas and J. G. de Sepúlveda from 1550 to 1551 in Valladolid. For the English, the "cannibal" was useful so long as it served to differentiate between the rival colonists, as the following passage from Walter Ralegh's *The Discovery of Large, Rich and Beautiful Empire of Guiana* typifies. According to Ralegh, the Spaniards:

> buie women and children from the *Canibals,* which are of that barbarous nature, as they will for 3 or 4 hatchets sell the sonnes and daughters of their owne brethren and sisters, and for somewhat more euen their own daughters: heerof the Spaniards make great profit for buying a maid of 12 or 13 yeeres for three or fower hatchets, they sell them againe at *Marguerita* in the west Indies for 50 and 100 pesoes, which is so many crownes.[17]

Here the "Canibals" are naturalized as "barbarous," but their barbarity is interpreted as crude commercial greed influenced by the Spanish, rather than as natural bloodthirstiness. The "Canibals" are to blame because they forsake their family ties at the expense of material profit gained from their commerce with the Spaniard. The barbarity of the "Canibals" comes not only from their intrinsic features but from the influence of the intruding European economy. The binary opposition is squarely set between the bad Spanish and the good English (who would never encourage the "Canibals" into this kind of inhuman barter, but conduct honest business with the "good Arawaks"), with the exclusion of the culturally alien "Canibals" who are both inhumanly callous and economically instrumentalized.[18] For Ralegh, these "Canibals" need not be a representation of man-eaters at all: he just has to insist that they are inhuman and evil enough to be associated with the Spaniards.

When this rhetorical strategy was employed to degrade England's most immediate foe in the sixteenth century (and its first "successful" colony), Ireland, the term's symbolic power declared itself. Sir John Davies, the Attorney General of Ireland, wrote in 1612 of the Irish customs which he considered vile:

> As for oppression, extortion, and other trespasses, the weaker had never any remedy against the stronger: whereby it came to pass that no man could enjoy his life his wife, his lands or goods in safety, if a mightier man than himself had an appetite to take the same from him. Wherein they were little better than cannibals, who do hunt one another; and he that hath most strength and swiftness, doth eat and devour all his fellows.[19]

According to Davies, the most culpable are "the stronger" soldiers of Ireland, who consume the husbandry of "the weaker" ordinary people of the land, but his comprehensive indictment of the *whole* Irish people as a "barbarous" nation is empowered by the indiscriminate use of the "cannibal" sign.[20] This observation leads Davies to the conclusion that "the mere Irish were not only accounted aliens, but enemies; and altogether out of the protection of the law," and that their land was made "waste" and "the people idle."[21]

These English appropriations of the "cannibal" sign undermine the possible reciprocity—first detected in Columbus's account—in the discourse of cannibalism. The intrinsic feature of man-eating is conspicuously absent in the English usage of the term in the sixteenth century. From the English viewpoint, the "cannibals" did not necessarily *have to* eat human flesh: they were just barbarous, corrupt and evil, being a crucial part of the Spanish colonial design. In these English discourses, the "cannibals" were represented as docile and servile creatures, deprived of their internal and sub-versive characteristics—the power to eat enemies and strike back on their own terms.

This process of repressing reciprocity in the discourse of canni-balism can be more clearly illustrated by another example from Ralegh, when he attempts to establish a clear moral distinction between "us"—the English—and "them"—the Spanish. Here the same rhetorical strategy is employed with more complexity in which the distinction is underlined in economic and sexual terms. The imaginary tour-de-force of this passage deserves a lengthy quotation:

> This *Arawacan* Pilot with the rest, feared that we would haue eaten them, or otherwise haue put them to some cruell death, for the Span-iards to the end that none of the people in the passage towards *Guiana* or in *Guiana* it selfe might come to speech and vs, perswaded all the nations, that we were men eaters, and *Canibals:* but the poore men and women had seen vs, and that we gaue them meate, and to euerie one some thing or other, which was rare and strange to them, they began to conceiue the deceit and purpose of the *Spaniards,* who indeed (as they confessed) tooke from them both their wiues, and daughters daily, and vsed them for the satisfying of their owne lusts, especially such as they tooke in this maner by strength. But I protest before the maiestie of the liuing God, that I neither know nor beleeue, that any of our companie one or other, by violence or otherwise, euer knew any of their women, and yet we saw many hundreds, and had many in our power, and of those very yoong, and excellently fauored which came among vs without deceit, starke naked.
>
> Nothing got vs more loue among them then this vsage, for I suffred not anie man to take from anie of the nations so much as a *Pina,* or a *Potato* roote, without giuing them contentment, nor any man so much as to offer to touch any of their wiues or daughters: which course, so contrarie to the Spaniards (who tyrannize ouer them in all things) drew them to admire hir Maiestie, whose commandment I told them it was, and also woonderfully to honour our nation.[22]

The "Canibals" sign is here said to be designated by the Spanish towards the English in a plot to prevent the natives from trading with the newcomers. The reciprocity seems to be recovered—but only just. In this case, because the referent of the sign is the Eng-lish, the dialogism, a possible mutual accountability between the dominant Europeans and the subordinate Indians totally collapses. In this tit-for-tat linguistic game within the European rival factions to gain the natives' approval and to justify their colonial activities

on the grounds that their purpose was to save them from the evil-
doers, it is the "Canibals" themselves who are wholly marginalized
and depersonalized. If any reciprocity exists in Ralegh's imaginary
"Large, Rich and Beautiful *Republic* of Guiana" (a glittering commonwealth not unlike the fool's gold his men were reported to
have brought back from the region), it is between the "poor men
and women" and the subjects of "her Majesty." In this nation there
is simply no place for the "Canibals," who are now not only displaced but also discursively nullified. When the term "Canibals"
is applied to one European *by* another European national, the sign
functions as an ordinary derogative which has no intrinsic sense
of agency as a man-eater. It is reported that first the Spaniard
employed the "Canibals" sign as a common denominator of cruelty;
then the English more subtly manipulated the term as a symbol of
evil by at once distancing themselves from the "Canibals" and
from the Spanish. Instead of recognizing the potentially subversive
ability to devour human flesh and resist colonization, Ralegh here
creates the notion of the "Other" (now inclusive of the "Canibals"
and the "Arawacan" alike) as an innocent subordinate devoid of
cultural specificities outside of an assigned role as a boundary
marker fabricated by the dominant culture. In this process, the
term "Canibals" becomes a mere sign of the "Other's Other," while
another candidate for the "Other's Other"—the native woman—
is foregrounded in Ralegh's verification of the English generosity
towards them. Giving the people paltry gifts is, according to Ralegh, is a sign of English respect for the female sex, and the sexual
language forcefully and uneasily takes over the discourse of cannibalism only to be finally replaced by a de-sexualized rhetoric sanc-
tifying "her Majesty."[23]

For Ralegh, then, the Canibals" serve two distinctively ideological purposes. One is to confirm the absolute and essential difference between the English and the Spaniard. The other is to create
an illusion of congruence between the natives and the English,
both of whom revere and idealize the chaste, daughterly and the
motherly. He even valorizes the unlikely pair of wives of the native
men and Queen Elizabeth who now stands in God's place. Here it
is implicitly assumed that the Arawacan women "belong" to their
men (as the Other's Other), waiting and willing to be conquered in
their sexual nakedness by the English, just as the English company
of gentlemen are subject to their captain Ralegh and ultimately to
the Queen. (From Ralegh's point of view, then, the English soldiers
are at once a composite part of his "self" and "others" whose
sexual and monetary desire are felt to be hard to cope with.) At

the crossroads of racial, gender, class and religious difference, one difference—between the English and the Spanish—is formalized, while the other differences—between the Arawak and the English, between the soldiers and the captain—are suppressed. As a result, the original binarism by Columbus between the "good Arawak" and the "bad Carib" (who is here so marginalized that it is almost impossible to find a trace) is reinforced in Ralegh's rhetorical strategy. If any notion of reciprocity exists in Ralegh's account, it is profoundly deceptive, because the native population is deprived both of a voice expressing suspicion that it is not the natives but the conquering Europeans who are cannibalistically manipulative, and of the threatening power of man-eating in their resistance to colonization. In the quintessential figure of the sexually desired and desiring women, the natives are there to be seen, not to act. In this neatly divided scheme of differentiation, it is the "Canibals" who are discursively expelled, leaving no trace of dialogical relationship between the eater and the eaten.

It can be generally observed in English texts about colonization that, while they evoke an illusory reciprocity, the "Canibal" sign is dissociated from their (imaginary) intrinsic feature, man-eating. Through this rhetorical strategy, the original equation, the "Canibal/Carib" = man-eater = the native of the Antilles, is dismantled. This results, on the one hand, in strengthening the Arawak/Carib binarism; on the other hand, as the "Canibal" sign is deprived of its original referent, the text becomes suffused with the complacent members of the illusory Republic—the "large" and bountiful Queen, the "rich" and gentle Englishmen, the "beautiful" and innocent maids of Guiana. Where would be a place for "Canibals" in this con/text? This question leads us to a text which allows us to read it as a colonialist text containing the rhetorical strategy of suppressing the "Canibals" while in many ways resisting that reading—*The Tempest*.

3

Why is Caliban devoid of any substantial traits of "Canibals," so commonly employed in the early literature about the New World? Despite constant attempts by virtually every other character in the play to animalize and demonize him, Caliban is in fact stressed by the play as a human being in many respects—sometimes in a contradictory fashion. The first reference in the play to Caliban—

by Prospero—is one of such impressive occasion as to present a peculiarly *humanized* image:

> Then was this island—
> Save for the son that she did litter here,
> A freckl'd whelp, hag-born—not honour'd with
> A human shape.
>
> (1.2.281–84)

If we have a preconception about Caliban's character as "non-human," the last few phrases (which might reflect the speaker's unconscious wish to deny Caliban's humanity) may misguide us to a false conclusion. Taken altogether, this statement is a clear, if ambivalent, admission that Caliban was the only human being preceding Prospero's residence on the island. This recognition understandably irritates Prospero, as he responds to Ariel's calling of the creature's name:

> *Ari.*   Yes, Caliban her son.
> *Pro.*   Dull thing, I say so; he, that Caliban
>   Whom now I keep in service.
>
> (1.2.285–56)

As his name is repeated, two of Caliban's vital qualifications—Sycorax's son and Prospero's servant—are revealed. Before they see Caliban in person, the audiences are given three basic pieces of information about him. First, Caliban is an ugly boy (in Prospero's eyes). Second, he is the son of an Algerian witch (as Prospero judges her).[24] Third, he is Prospero's servant (as Prospero forces him to be). If we allow ourselves to acquire further information about Caliban's character from the list of *Dramatis Personae* first attached to the First Folio of 1623, there we find Caliban is described as "a salvage and deformed slave"—a tag indicating an "uncivilized" bondman with an extraordinary appearance, information which makes an interesting contrast to Prospero's emphasis on "service." This information, augmented by a wide range of appellations thrown at him by other characters, allows us to see Caliban in an enormously wide range of roles from a noble savage, a revolutionary mutineer, and a dull-witted fool, to an uncanny monster. Solely on the basis of the play's own evidence, however, one thing seems to be incontestable—that Caliban is the former occupant of the island, but now unwilling subject of the newcomer Prospero.

Miranda also, however unwittingly, acknowledges Caliban's humanity. When she sees Ferdinand for the first time, she confesses: "This / Is the third man that e'er I saw" (1.2.445–46). Because her only memory of other human beings before she arrived at the island is that of four or five tending women (1.2.47), two men she has seen must be her father and Caliban.[25] Yet the strongest proof of Caliban's humanity—and at the same time the gravest cause of his suffering—is his education by Prospero and Miranda, and consequently his servitude to them.

Why does Prospero need Caliban as a servant? The magician whose "Art," according to his own words, can cause tempests, shake the earth, uproot trees and even wake the dead from their graves (5.1.41–50), cannot (or will not) do the simplest task like catching fish, collecting wood, preparing food and tidying up, jobs for which he totally relies on Caliban. At least one point is certain: that these menial tasks Caliban carries out for Prospero will teach both the master and the servant the *absolute* difference between them. A conversation between Miranda and Prospero reveals more reasons for his keeping Caliban:

> *Mir.*   'Tis a villain, sir,
> I do not love to look on.
> *Pro.*   But as 'tis,
> We cannot miss him: he does make our fire,
> Fetch in our wood, and serves in offices
> That profit us.
>
>   (1.2.311–13)

Here and elsewhere, Prospero's repeated use of "we/our/us," betrays his possessiveness.[26] Caliban whose "offices" profit "us" cannot but be "he" or the "Other" in an unsymmetrical binary opposition. Within this definite "we/they" relationship, the "slave" marker—like the "Canibal" sign—contains the other two labels for Caliban—"salvage = uncivilized yet human," and "deformed = monstrous." To represent the subjugated as a "human beast" justifies slave labour, and slavery refigures a human being as a "real" monster.[27]

Slavery normalizes the distinction between the "civilized" and the "monstrous," serving an educational function by teaching the master and the slave their respective positions, to the point that the slave becomes him/herself aware of his/her own monstrosity. The aim of Caliban's education is to construct his subjectivity in a deceptive form of reciprocity.

Language teaching is at the heart of any education. In this case
Caliban was taught an European language, and on the basis of the
play's evidence, he mastered it superbly. According to Miranda,
Caliban had no language before he was taught her native tongue:

> I pitied thee,
> Took pains to make thee speak, taught thee each hour
> One thing or other. When thou didst not, savage,
> Know thine own meaning, but wouldst gabble like
> A thing most brutish, I endow'd thy purposes
> With words that made them known.
>
> (1.2.355–60)

There is a body of European literature which attests that "primitive" languages sounded like a "brutish gabble" to European ears.[28]
Moreover, Miranda's confident statement serves to suppress the
fundamental reciprocity in language teaching/learning. History
shows that white masters were also influenced by the tongues of
both indigenous and imported slave-labourers. Colonizer's children, like Miranda, who were allowed to mix with the slaves, were
most susceptible to this influence, and they soon began to speak
the slaves' appropriated languages—Pidgin and Creole—themselves; the first tongue the children heard would be one of these
languages as child care and wet-nursing were the work of slaves.

Since Antonio de Nebrija, presenting his *Gramática* to Queen
Isabella of Castile in 1492, made clear that "language is the instrument of empire," language has been the primary site of contention.
For example, the colonizer's fear of the hybridization of languages,
of adulteration of "pure" English names and customs motivated
John Davies's condemnation of the English colonizers who adopted
the Irish customs, and "not only forgot the English language, and
scorned the use thereof, but grew ashamed of their very English
names, though they were noble, and of great antiquity."[29] Similarly,
the "meaning" and "purposes," which Miranda tries to guard,
through her seemingly impartial and compassionate act of "teaching," against infiltration by the alien culture, are in fact produced
by an unsymmetrical socio-linguistic relationship, however "civil
and honourable" they seem to the eyes of the educator.

From the instructor's point of view, it would be useless to teach
a language to a tortoise or fish: the target of education must be
those who understand the instructor's will and enable human communication. In return for passing on the capacity to articulate,
Prospero acquired from the aboriginal Caliban geographical information—vital to any colonizer—about the island. This seeming

reciprocity—whether based on a happy misunderstanding or on a sinister deception—was bound to collapse, as Caliban became aware of his servile and oppressed status as a consequence of education. Caliban's first words replying to Prospero's command—"speak"—are: "There's wood enough within" (1.2.316). For Caliban, to speak this taught language is to carry out a menial task—to accept his slavery. The paradox is that language both enslaves Caliban and makes him aware of his slavery. This awareness of the distinction between the governing and the governed is now so intrinsic a part of Caliban that he simply sees a new master in Stephano, who is, as Caliban hopes, more conducive to his wish.[30]

Caliban's learned language is both a binding shackle and an instrument of resistance. Caliban who may now have forgotten his native language has recourse to his master's tongue as the only available discursive rebellion which rejects Prospero's version of the island's genesis—a myth of uncontestable origin underlined by the act of naming; as he says, "You taught me language, and my profit on't / Is, I know how to curse" (1.2.365–66). The taught language gives him power to retort, abuse, parody (note his use of "profit" which echoes Prospero's own at 1.313), refigure the political issue in its most fundamental aspect ("I must eat my dinner" [1.2.332]), and above all to present an alternative history to Prospero's (1.2.333–44). This aboriginal version of the sovereignty of the island, though compelling and retaining a certain transgressive potential, is used by Prospero as this discourse itself indicates the devilishness and inferiority of Caliban's contestory claim;[31] for it states that Sycorax's power derives from her witchcraft and that his lack of fellow subordinates undermine any prospect of nationalistic revolution (though the lack of large-scale labour force may be a reason for Prospero's ultimate abandonment of the island). Caliban's insistence on his own rights inherited from Sycorax's prior residence is reversed into the superiority of Prospero's claim on the basis of his moral authority and socio-familial connections secured through Miranda.

The inadequacy of Caliban's claim (although in fact his claim of blood inheritance is valid in common law) is further "proved" by his moral ineptitude as manifested in his alleged assault on Miranda's virginity.[32] Prospero's plan to marry his daughter to Ferdinand in order to secure his rights to the Milanese dukedom, which is politically parallel to Caliban's attempt to recover the island through his possession of Miranda's body, is an example of what Stephen Orgel calls "imperial rapes," which "once they get into history, are a source not of shame but of national pride."[33] As

Caliban's answer to Prospero's accusation ("I had people else / This isle with Calibans" [1.2.352–53]) suggests, it is hard to distinguish Caliban's sexual desire from his political vengeance, as the issue of procreation is so crucial to dynastic and nationalistic claims.[34] As far as Prospero is concerned, however, the most important "fact" is that everyone concerned admits that Caliban's attempted rape failed, for this instantly achieves at least three closely related objectives: demonization of Caliban, prevention of an usurpation by Caliban who is without any offspring to whom he might bequeath his kingdom, and confirmation of Miranda's virginity which will guarantee her position as an heir to his dukedom. As Ralegh's attempt to distinguish the honourable English from the lustful Spaniards demonstrates, an accusation of rape justifies the accuser's moral authority over the others—both the accused and the potential victim. If we are allowed here to juxtapose *The Tempest* with *The Discovery of Guiana,* we might glimpse a first hint of Caliban's refiguration from "Canibal": Prospero's policy that valorizes Miranda's honor and demonizes Caliban's desire is on the same plane as Ralegh's linguistic maneuver to idealize the Arawakan women while demonizing the Spanish. Miranda becomes the symbol both of native innocence and European civility—at once the Maid and the Queen—while Caliban is transfigured into a deceitful yet powerless Spaniard from a subversive man-eater who can retaliate.

The displacement of Caliban's "cannibalistic" ability can be illustrated through the way technology is represented in the play. We tend to presuppose European superiority in technological advancements as a crucial element in European conquest of the native population. However, it is a fallacy to magnify the power of European firearms above native skill in collecting food, cultivating land and forecasting weather. What cannot be denied is the "discursive" power of firearms whose sound and fury kept the native population in awe.

In order to survive in an alien climate, the early English colonizers were almost totally dependent on native food provision.[35] This is emphatically the case in the relationship between Prospero and Caliban, too: for anything to do with survival in the potentially hostile environment of the island, the master and his family have to depend totally on the slave. If so, the only way—and the surest one too—for Prospero to assure his overall superiority in technological competence is his linguistic magic—"Art" which solely relies on the power of his words.[36] Prospero's magic is of a profoundly rhetorical nature: it verbally insists on the supremacy of his own technology—hypnotism, illusionism and scare tactics—over the others. Because of this overtly discursive quality of his "Art," he has to impress the audience on and off stage not only with its effect but with its cause—his "so potent Art":

> I have bedimm'd
> The noontide sun, call'd forth the mutinous winds,
> And 'twixt the green sea and the azur'd vault
> Set roaring war: to the dread rattling thunder
> Have I given fire, and rifted Jove's stout oak
> With his own bolt; the strong-bas'd promontory
> Have I made shake, and by the spurs pluck'd up
> The pine and ceder: graves at my command
> Have wak'd their sleepers, op'd, and let 'em forth
> By my so potent Art.
>
> (5.1.41–50)

In the context of European encounters with the alien aspects of the New World, this celebrated speech reveals Prospero's linguistic dependence on native terms: apart from the last claims which show an obvious Christian—and somewhat Devilish—reflection, Prospero's language here echoes descriptions by early European recorders of one the most striking and novel natural phenomena—the hurricane. As Peter Hulme convincingly argues, this new phenomenon—along with "cannibals"--was interpreted and linguistically appropriated by Europeans in "that general process whereby the discursive and the economic mirrored one another in the establishment of a central civility . . . surrounded by a variety of savage phenomena whose individual characteristics were less important than their definition as 'other' than the central civility."[37] We find figures of speech similar to those of Prospero in Peter Martyr's *The First Decade* translated by Eden in 1555, describing the horror of *"Furacanes"*: it "plucked vppe greate trees by the rootes" and "where so euer the sea bankes are nere to any plaine there are in maner euery where, florishing medowes reaching euer vnto the shore."[38] While the European writers gradually translated "Furacanes" into "hurricane," thus discursively appropriating the hostile natural phenomenan, Prospero's rhetorical power suppresses a naming that connotes the unbridled power of a native phenomenon. The paradox is that his "Art" derives from a discourse that inevitably involves refiguration which undermines his claim of all-in-all self-sufficiency.

Prospero's magic ultimately depends on the art of persuasion. Magic can only function within a language system that admits magic: a miraculous event is always prone to being dismissed as a mere coincidence. Therefore Prospero has to take special care in concealing the magical source of his technological competence in his own logical linguistic codes. It is his "Book" that embodies this strategy. Words which are potentially mutually accountable are transformed into ciphers by the "Book" which turns reciprocity essential to any human communication into an unequal relationship of domination and subjection. Through this socio-linguistic transformation, Caliban's inherently superior technology for survival is appropriated into the invader's geographical information, and a person who has been able to subsist on his own is transfigured into a slave who cannot even eat what he himself produces.

Caliban does not and will not manipulate this kind of verbal magic as an instrument of subjection. Terence Hawkes has noted in Caliban the "absence of reciprocity, of the ability to venture beyond himself" on both levels of "intercourse"—language and sex.[39] We may go further by saying that Caliban reveals and rejects the unsymmetrical "reciprocity" involved in Prospero's discursive construction of others' and his own subjectivity. Instead, using the taught language, whose main profit he says is cursing, he can evince a rare poetical moment, totally unknown to his educators who are too bound to the idea of property to hear his private voice. His celebrated speech (3.2.133–41) transmutes the oppressor's magical language into some murky "noises" free of possessiveness. He appropriates the long European tradition of *locus amoenus* and dream vision into an untranslatable language of the island's woods and brooks that no proper noun can denote. These "voices" reverberate over the island like a universal language which defies a standard—canonical and ideological—language produced by the state education system. The "sounds and sweet airs" Caliban delights in echoe the Mother tongue—at once singularly united and plurally diversified—which denies the nationalistic rhetoric of a mother tongue. Caliban's dream is not a longing for a lost myth of European genesis. Though his lyricism depends on the conqueror's language which determines his ultimate exclusion from that which he conjures, Caliban's "dream" proposes an alternative to Prospero's "Art" of governing others that constantly tries to set cultures in a competitive context of possession and domination. Here out of the language he is forced to use for survival, Caliban excavates rhythm and pleasure that are yet to become information and technology which, under the guise of mutuality, profit one and subjugate the other.

We may further argue that, in a previous scene, Caliban's reemployment of his own name—"'Ban, 'Ban, Cacaliban" (2.2.184)—attempts to wash away from the "riches" the deceptive glitter of gold and silver—to regain the opaque glow of raw ores still hidden under the earth's surface. Deconstructing the name given by the others, Caliban recreates himself as an adaptable agent who belongs to aural/oral and libidinal/laughing culture. "Caliban" and "Canibal" are involved with transgression of the boundary between the eating and the eaten, between the seeing and the seen, between the representing and the represented.[40] At some precious moments in the play, through physical, rather than linguistic intercourse, the "Caliban/Canibal" ceases to be a demonized sign attached from one culture to another, and becomes a metaphor of the ongoing process of hybridization and transformation.[41] Caliban takes all the abuses thrown at him—"earth," "beast," "demi-devil"— and turns them back against his accusers. We can heartily laugh at him and *with* him: our relationship with Caliban, for a moment at least, can be truly reciprocal.

Columbus interprets phenomena before him in the binary sign system between the good Arawak and the bad Carib; Ralegh appropriates this binary framework into an English representation of the harmony between the colonizer and the colonized. Caliban recovers the man-eater from the demonized state to make it an agent of cultural hybridization. At this point, however rare it may be, the island is free of self-enclosed possessiveness, and turned into a popular theatre where diverse voices can cross. This theatrical space even enables us to question Columbus's strategy of marginalizing the "Carib" which identifies the "Carib" with "Canibal"; for Caliban has revealed himself to be a potential "man-eater" who resists a sign system which aims to translate his "noises" into magical ciphers fixing him in an ideological scheme of binary representation. Despite his appalling and prolonged sufferings, he ventures to devour the sign and fight back.

4

All this still does not answer the original question: why did Shakespeare name a native Caliban, an anagram of "Canibal," while broadly refusing to characterize him as a man-eater? In other words, why is the carnivalesque moment in *The Tempest* so momentary? A simple answer seems to be: because Caliban's emancipatory movement is, at every level, doomed to failure.

The ending of the play tells us all. One might argue that even from Prospero's point of view all is not quite what he has wished it to be: Antonio seems unresponsive to his call for repentance and reconciliation, and Prospero has paid a price in order to attain his heart's desires—re-establishing himself in Milan during his lifetime and marrying off Miranda properly and prosperously. At the end, having forsaken his tripartite technology for representing others—"mantle," "staff", and "book"—, his presence on the bare stage is particularly vulnerable, and one senses that his departure for Milan is a voyage not only for his personal freedom but for death. The price for regaining dukedom is abjuration of his linguistic domination of others.

Yet these are no comfort to Caliban. Admittedly, another rare moment of relativization comes just before the debacle of the conspiracy, when Caliban dismisses the courtly attire as "but trash" (5.1.224). His instinctive discrimination, however, totally dissipates at the sight of "real" courtiers ("O Setebos, these be brave spirits indeed! / How fine my master is!" [5.1.261–62]), and he sounds resigned to being at the mercy of Prospero's final judgement. Not unlike the Arawacan "poor men and women" described by Ralegh, Caliban is now devoid of his cannibalistic/carnivalesque voice. His final words are those of a repentant Christian who realizes the difference between the true god and a heathen one:

> . . . I'll be wise hereafter,
> And seek for grace. What a thrice-double ass
> Was I, to take this drunkard for a god,
> And worship this dull fool!
>
> (5.1.294–97)

Indicating his bitterness about betrayal, the lines comply with Prospero's religion as they forestall punishment and suggest recrimination against Stephano and Trinculo.

The play as a whole, then, hardly enhances the cannibalistic vision created momentarily by Caliban. We could even argue that on the background of the English colonizing enterprise which was far behind Spanish counterpart, The Tempest employs an anagrammatic strategy in refiguring the "Canibal = man-eater" as "Caliban = colonial slave." If Ralegh marginalized the "Canibals" as nonentities while foregrounding the innocent and docile women of the Arawaks, the text of The Tempest investigates (and partly undermines) this strategy in which the chiastic relationship is simplified into the binary scheme that creates an "absolute" difference between good and bad, between new and old.

To examine further this text's "anagrammatization"—a tactic to name but, at the same time, obfuscate subversiveness implied by that naming—we need to uncover the absent entities concealed by the text: in other words, we have to ask, "where are the 'real' man-eaters, if any, in the play?" This question leads us to our final quest in the play's problematics of naming—an attempt to discover "real" agency concealed under the surface of its text, which presents itself as a site of contention between male versions of *his*-story. In seeking an alternative both to Prospero's and Caliban's claims, we are led to another, largely undramatized, site of struggle between the three under-represented women—Claribel, Sycorax, and the nameless wife of Prospero.

Stephano's "scurvy tune" which is little noted by critics[42] suggests a misogynistic undercurrent in the play:

> The master, the swabber, the boatswain, and I,
> The gunner, and his mate,
> Lov'd Mall, Meg, and Marian, and Margery,
> But none of us car'd for Kate:
> For she had a tongue with a tang,
> Would cry to a sailor, Go hang!
> She lov'd not the savour of tar nor of pitch;
> Yet a tailor might scratch her where'er she did itch.
> Then to sea, boys, and let her go hang!
>
> (2.2.49–55)

In terms of naming, the song's message is revealing: "those girls whose names start with 'M' are fine," because they all suggest the Maternal, loving and comforting. On the other hand, "those women whose name start with a 'K' sound are shrewish," probably due to an association of the letter K with an unusually subversive force in the English language, for instance in words like "cruel" or "cantankerous." Miranda is an ideal woman for men because she has grown up seeing her own image and listening to her father's language, as she confesses, perhaps to further allure Ferdinand:

> I do not know
> One of my sex; no woman's face remember,
> Save, from my glass, mine own; nor have I seen
> More that I may call men than you, good friend,
> And my dear father.
>
> (3.1.48–52)

For men, Miranda is a safe investment as her "tautological" up-bringing—like a marginalized "Carib"—is very unlikely to subvert male dominance. On the contrary, we may be right to suppose that Claribel was forced to marry Tunis despite her 'loathness' (1.1.126) to the marriage because she was a shrew and considered a good match for a barbarous African, possibly for the political gain of Naples. Her uncle Sebastian, far from sympathetic to her plight, represents the racist and anti-feminist view (2.1.119–23). Thus the text elliptically marks and conceals a distinction between the two women possessed and used by their fathers—*M*iranda of *M*ilan and *C*laribel of *C*arthage. The text's anagrammatic tactics that turn a substance into a cipher even play with history and classical literature: Tunis *is* Carthage; chaste Dido of Petrarch *is* lustful Dido of Virgil.[43] On the one hand, absolute differences are established between the chaste and the shrewish, between the civi-lized and the barbarous; on the other, the real agent of barbarity—whether the King of Tunis or the cultural man-eater Caliban—is marginalized and displaced as the third term in this neatly binary scheme.

Other English texts about a daughter of another king shed light on the dimension of sexual difference in the play. According to a myth created by Captain John Smith, Pocahontas was the ultimate saver of his life, a kind of mother who bore him again in the New World. Smith remembered the dramatic moment of his last-minute escape from execution, "when no intreaty could prevaile," Poca-hontas "got his head in her arms, and laid her owne vpon his to saue him from death."[44] At the expense of Powhatan and his Algonquians, Pocahontas—like the Arawak women in Ralegh's ac-count—is raised above the rest, for she "not only for feature, contenance, and proportion, much exceedeth any of the rest of his people: but for wit and spirit, [is] the only *Nonpareil* of his Coun-try."[45] Later Smith, in a letter to Queen Anne explaining the inci-dent, added that the natives who were affected by the grace of Pocahontas saved the English from starvation: "such was the weaknesse of this poore commonwealth [of Virginia], as had the Saluages not fed vs, we directly had starued. And this reliefe, most gracious Queene, was commonly brought vs by this Lady *Pocahon-tas*."[46] The Indian princess is given the status of "Ladyship" within the English courtly hierarchy presided over by the "gracious Queene." Thanks to Pocahontas's "Christian" virtue, the Algon-quian "Saluage Courtiers" were also raised to a "civilized" status to merit Smith's recognition of debt.

The myth of Pocahontas is a story of a woman who was ennobled and glorified as a princess crossing the boundary of two different cultures, yet inevitably displaced when she came to England to become an English citizen. As a princess, she was first introduced to the enthusiastic English court but—unlike Claribel who marries an African king—she had been married to a commoner John Rolfe, another colonist and an avid protestant. Moreover, she was re-named "Rebecca"—a name whose sound is anagrammatically simi-lar to that of "Carib." Having married her, Rolfe's love of her was torn between godly devotion and carnal desire, as she remained a stranger beyond his understanding sexually as well as religiously. As Rolfe confessed, "marrienge of straunge wyves" like "Pohahun-tas" made him wonder what "shoulde provoke [him] to be in love with one, whose education hath byn rude, her manners barbarous, her generacion Cursed, and soe discrepant in all nutriture from [him] selfe." He suspects that "theise are wicked instigations hatched by him whoe seeketh and delighteth in mans distruc-tion"—"diabolicall assaultes" in other words.[47] As Rolfe's moral confusion indicates, Pocahontas was at once a chaste wife to the Virginia colonist and an enchantress who had bewitched the Eng-lish protestant. Because of this ambiguous representation cast upon her by the colonizer, she was to become neither an Indian Queen nor an English Mother; unlike Ralegh's Queen Elizabeth, Pocahontas could never fulfill the role of the fertile Virgin Mother of the Virginia colony.

One does not have to seek far to find a woman who can perfectly fit this role—the nameless wife of Prospero, the second unrepre-sented woman in *The Tempest,* whom Miranda knows only through her father's account of her. At the same time, however, it is only through *her words* that Prospero "knows" that Miranda is his "non-pareil" (3.2.98) daughter:

Mir.   Sir, are not you my father?
Pros.   Thy mother was a piece of virtue, and
           She said thou wast my daughter; and thy father
           Was Duke of Milan; and his only heir
           And princess, no worse issued.

(1.2.55)

This is a moment where we can detect a crack in the seemingly tautologically self-referential structure of Prospero's family: it is solely his wife's testimony that maintains his claim to sovereignty through Miranda's filial authenticity. His emphatic confirmation of his wife's chastity underlines that patriarchal anxiety. Arguably, her namelessness is a cause and an effect of his repressing that anxiety; but taking the play's English colonial context into account, her name cannot be but "Virginia," the Virgin Mother of the Old and New World (if one wants a full name, it may be something like "Virginia Elizabeth Grace of Milan"). Her "grace" obviously extends not only over Caliban's but over all the marginalized "Canibals" in the realm.

At the end of *The Tempest*, Caliban himself seeks for that Mother "Grace": yet unlike her daughter Miranda, he will never be able to recognize Virginia's colour on his own skin. What he should truly seek for is not "grace" but Sycorax, his *own* and *only* mother—the third hidden woman—and the most displaced one—in *The Tempest*. Possibly associated with a "cannibal" race, Scythian (Sythian),[48] a "damn'd witch" (1.2.263) from "Argier," "left by th' sailors" (1.2.270) on the island possibly after her servile role as a prostitute, the devil's bedfellow—the representations of Sycorax are of the most degraded kind in every human category that constitutes the play's political horizon, ethnicity, class, nationality, religion, age, gender and sexuality.

Acknowledging Sycorax as a cannibalistic mother of the colonized involves questioning the anagrammatical process that names "Canibal" "Caliban." Let us return to the point where we started, 23 November 1492, and detect there the deceptive reciprocity in Columbus's paradigm shift from "anthropophagi" to "cannibal". From the viewpoint of the named, it is, after all, the same substance represented by these signs: as the black state "servant" Othello aptly indicates (*Othello*, 1.3.143–44), the "Cannibals" *are* the "Anthropophagi"—there is no distinction between the two in their agency as man-eaters. That distinction and further distinctions, however elaborate, are but linguistic differences—products of magical representations through the strategy of anagram.

Notes

I wish to thank Stephen Clark, Shoichiro Kawai, Paul Harvey, Peter Hulme, Tsuneo Masaki and Manabu Noda, who were all generous enough to comment on an earlier version of this essay.

1. All quotations refer to *The Arden Shakespeare: The Tempest*, ed. Frank Kermode (London: Methuen, 1958).

2. In Western discourse, there has been, and still is, a strong tendency to conflate its colonial counterparts into a homogeneous sociopolitical entity, e.g., "African negroes," "American Indians," "Orientals," denying the whole range of their social, cultural, religious, economic and linguistic diversity. If I have to use,

in what follows, terms such as "natives," "aboriginal," "West Indians," because I have no other way than employing these signs to refer to the vast range of people, I deliberately use, at the same time, collective terms such as "Europeans," "Spaniards," and "English" in order to create a sense of reciprocal discomfort arising from being discursively reduced to a cultural homogeneity from the "Other" point of view.

3. It was a common practice in the American colonies—and indeed the first step in disciplinary measures—for white masters to re-name their slaves in an attempt to transform their identities rooted in their native lands. New names were not only convenient for white owners but indelible signs confirming their superior power to regulate the lives of the subordinate.

4. *The Journal of Christopher Columbus*, trans. Cecil Jane, rev. L. A. Vigneras (London: Anthony Blond, 1968), 68–69.

5. For the dialogical nature of cannibalistic discourse, two articles stand out: one is Gananath Obeyesekere, "'British Cannibals': Contemplation of an Event in the Death and Resurrection of James Cook, Explorer," *Critical Inquiry* 18 (Summer 1992), 630–54, where he argues for "the possibility that where there is fantasy there could be slippage into reality and from there into human institutions" (630); the other is Kaoru Yamazaki, "Cannibalism and the Problem of Other," *Shisou (Thought)*, 70 (May 1983), 17–35, which examines the European cannibal discourse within its inversionary rhetorical strategy.

6. "The Second English book on America. A treatyse of the newe India, with other new founde landes and Ilandes, . . . after the descripcion of Sebastian Munster in his boke of vniversall Cosmographie: . . . Translated out of Latin into Englishe. By Rycharde Eden. [London, 1553]" in Edward Arber, ed., *The First Three English Books on America*. [?*1511*]–*1555* A.D. (Birmingham, 1885), 29.

7. "The Decades of the newe worlde or west India, conteynyng the nauigations and conquests of the Spanyardes, . . . Wrytten in the Latine tounge by Peter Martyr of Angleria, and translated into Englysshe by Rycharde Eden (1555)" in Edward Arber, ed., *The First Three English Books*, 50.

8. *Journal*, 146–47.

9. A linguistic history of these "modern" terms referring to man-eating can be summarized as follows: first "Canibales" which Columbus heard on 23rd November, 1492 was introduced into Spanish and the other European languages, referring to a group of existing "tribes" called the Caribs as Columbus later heard from those who feared them. The implication of man-eating was the lynchpin of the two identical words. Gradually a distinction between "cannibal" (man-eater) and "Carib" (native of the Antilles) came into being. Much later, "Cannibalism," the general term referring to the custom, was introduced (*OED*'s first entry is dated 1796), completing the distinction between the bahavior and the people.

10. *Journal*, 148 (emphasis mine).

11. *Journal*, 148–49 (emphasis mine).

12. After several years of Spanish settlement in the islands, it was no longer possible to know what that fatal word "Canibales" really *meant* in the native language, because the "Caribs" were annihilated either by direct conflict against the Spanish, by disease, or by slave labour. Nevertheless, as the *OED* exemplifies, the tautological dilemma that has caught the Carib/cannibal since Columbus identified the two became synonymous with those who were against European invasions. The main *OED* entry for "Carib" reads: "One of the native race which occupied the southern islands of the West Indies at their discovery: in earlier times often used with the connotation of *cannibal*." On the other hand, "Cannibal"

is defined as: "In 16th c. pl. *Canibales,* originally one of the forms of the ethnic name *Carib* or *Caribes,* a fierce nation of the West Indies, who are recorded to have been *anthropophagi,* and from whom the name was subsequently extended as a descriptive term. . . . A man (*esp.* a savage) that eats human flesh; a man-eater, an anthropophagite. Originally proper name of the man-eating Caribs of the Antilles." *OED* defines "Carib" as "cannibal," and "cannibal" as "Carib," without mentioning their complex historical circumstances. Here under the name of scholastic impartiality—manifested in the phrase "who are recorded to have been"—the "historical principle" of the dictionary concocts a truth discourse about the origin of words which accidentally "originated" from Columbus's misunderstanding—or wilfull misinterpretation—of a native word possibly referring to anything from the name of a tribe to an ingenious gadget. (One can even argue that this historical principle does not take the words' "origin" seriously enough, because Columbus's *Journal* specifically claims that they are of native origin, not Greek origin.) As the historical origin is invented, so the very identity of the "recorder," as well as his motive for the act of recording, is withheld.

13. *The Third Part of Henry VI,* ed. Andrew S. Cairncross, *The Arden Shakespeare* (London: Methuen, 1964).

14. Later in the play, the same tag—"bloody cannibals" (5.5.59)—is employed, this time, by Margaret towards Edward, York's son, who has killed her son, Prince Edward. The parallelism indicates the already established trope of cruel butchery associated with the term "cannibal."

15. Richard Hakluyt of Middle Temple (the elder), "Inducements to the Liking of the Voyage intended towards Virginia in 40 and 42 degrees of latitude, written 1585. by M. Richard Hakluyt the elder, sometime student of the Middle Temple" in *The Original Writings & Correspondence of the Two Richard Hakluyts,* Hakluyt Society, second series, no. LXXVII, 2 vols. (London: Cambridge University Press, 1935), 2: 332.

16. Ibid., 334.

17. *The Discoverie of the Large, Rich and Bewtifvl Empyre of Gviana, With a relation of the great and Golden Citie of Manoa (which the Spanyards call El Dorado) And of the Prouinces of Emeria, Arromaia, Amapaia, and Other Countries, with their riuers, adioyning. Performed in the yeare of 1595. by Sir W. Ralegh Knight, Captaine of her Maiesties Guard, Lo. Warden of the Stanneries, and her Highnesse Lieutenant generall of the Countie of Cornewall.* (London: Robert Robinson, 1596), sig. Fr–Fv.

18. Logically, there are four terms mapped onto each other: good/bad European; good/bad native. The good European subsumes and overrides the good native, which becomes a kind of blank space required by the conceptual logic of colonialism. Edward Said in his *Culture and Imperialism* regards this logic as the doctrine of retrospective consent, where conquered nations come to realize that they needed to be subjugated: *Culture and Imperialism* (London: Chatto & Windus, 1993), 196–204.

19. "A Discovery of the True Causes why Ireland was never brought under Obedience of the Crown of England, until the Beginning of his Majesty's happy Reign" (1612) in *Historical Tracts: By Sir John Davies,* ed. George Chalmers (London: John Stockdale, 1786), 135.

20. Davies here follows the tradition of conceding the cannibals' "virtuous" qualities such as "strength and swiftness." For example, Peter Martyr wrote, "Tenne of the *Canibals* are able to ouercome a hundreth of them [the adjoining

tribesmen] if they encountre with them." (*The First Three English Books on America*, 67.)

21. "A Discovery of the True Causes" in *Historical Tracts*, 83; 141.

22. *The Discoverie of the Large, Rich, and Bewtifvl Empyre of Gviana*, sig. H2r–H2v.

23. Louis Montrose, discussing the "self-laudification" of the Englishman in this passage, detects the convergence of "misogynistic sentiments" and "anti-Spanish ones, in a project aimed at mastering native Americans" ("The Work of Gender in the Discourse of Discovery," *Representations* 33 [Winter 1991], 21).

24. Later he further alleges that Caliban was born as a result of an intercourse between the witch and the devil, but this might be another of his disparaging allegations, for Prospero, who has never seen Sycorax in person (and whose knowledge of her is acquired solely from Ariel, hardly an impartial witness on this matter), is in no position to know for certain the circumstances of Caliban's birth, let alone his conception.

25. At 3.1.50–2, Miranda calls only Ferdinand and her father "men." Addressing Ferdinand here, she seems to imply that Caliban is not human.

26. Prospero's extraordinary possessiveness has been noted by critics, one of whom is Peter Hulme who neatly summarizes a few political and psychoanalytical explanations of it in his *Colonial Encounters: Europe and the Native Caribbean, 1492–1797* (London and New York: Routledge, 1986), 126.

27. Recall Las Casas's harrowing description of the Indian slaves who "seeme to bee a kinde of monsters in the shape of men, or els some other kinde of men." (*The Spanish Colonie, or Briefe Chronicle of the Acts and gestes of the Spaniardes on the West Indies, called the newe World, for the space of rl. yeeres*, trans. by M. M. S. [London: for William Brome, 1583], sig. J1r.)

28. Pedro de Quiroga in his *Dialogues of Truth* calls the Amerindian language "the most outrageous gibberish." (Quoted in Anthony Pagden, *European Encounters with the New World: From Renaissance to Romanticism* [New Haven & London: Yale University Press, 1993], p. 120.) For an excellent study of the "linguistic colonialism," see Stephen J. Greenblatt, "Learning to Curse: Aspects of Linguistic Colonialism in the Sixteenth Century" in Fred Chiapelli, ed. *First Images of America: The Impact of the New World on the Old*, 2 vols. (University of California Press, 1976), 2: 561–80.

29. "A Discovery of the True Causes" in *Historical Tracts*, p. 147.

30. Caliban's awareness of the class distinction also makes him subtly exploitative, through his sycophancy, of Stephano's class antagonism to Prospero: Caliban is not just after a new master; he intends to set one master in conflict with another.

31. Cf. Peter Hulme's contention that Caliban's claim is *never* adequately challenged by Prospero who tries to obfuscate the issue by simply saying, "Thou most lying slave" (1.2.346): *Colonial Encounters*, 124.

32. Some critics have cast doubt on Prospero's allegation, suggesting that this might simply be a result of his rejection of an alien code of ethics or of his wilful interpretation of Caliban's normal forms of courtship acceptable to the Europeans and the aborigines alike: see Sister Corona Sharp, "Caliban: The Primitive Man's Evolution," *Shakespeare Studies*, XIV (1981), 276; Mark Taylor, *Shakespeare's Darker Purpose: A Question of Incest* (New York: AMS Press, 1982), 143.

33. Stephen Orgel, "Shakespeare and the Cannibals" in Marjorie Garber, ed., *Cannibals, Witches, and Divorce: Estranging the Renaissance* (Baltimore and London: Johns Hopkins University Press, 1987), 55.

34. Cf. Laura E. Donaldson on Caliban's sexism against Miranda, which "reinforces, rather than weakens, the chains of their mutual enslavement" (*Decolonizing Feminisms: Race, Gender, & Empire-Building* [London: Routledge, 1993], 17).

35. One of the best arguments of the "topos of food" is Hulme, *Colonial Encounters,* 128–31.

36. As Terence Hawkes notes (*Shakespeare's Talking Animals: Language and Drama in Society* [London: Edward Arnold, 1973], 202), Prospero constantly urges others to *listen:* his linguistic spell depends on the presence of attentive listeners.

37. *Colonial Encounters,* 100.

38. "The Decades of the newe worlde or west India" in *The First Three English Books on America,* 81.

39. *Shakespeare's Talking Animals,* 205–7.

40. For the kinship between "cannibals" and "carnivals," see Robert Stam, "Of Cannibals and Carnivals" in *Subversive Pleasures: Bakhtin, Cultural Criticism, and Film* (Baltimore: Johns Hopkins University Press, 1989), 122–56.

41. For the concept of hybridization, which deconstructs the Bakhtinian binarism, see Peter Stallybrass and Allon White, *The Politics and Poetics of Transgression* (London: Methuen, 1986), 43–4, 56–8.

42. My attention was first drawn to this song by Shuntaro Ono, to whose unpublished paper on the dimension of post-colonial feminism in the play I owe a great deal for what follows.

43. For a lucid account of these conumdrums, see Stephen Orgel, "Shakespeare and the Cannibals," 58–64.

44. John Smith, *The Generall Historie of Virginia, New = England, and the Summer Isles: with the names of the Adventurers, Planters, and Governours from their first beginning An: 1584 to this present 1624* (1624) in Captain John Smith, *Works. 1608–1631,* ed. Edward Arber, *The English Scholar's Library, no. 16* (Birmingham: 1884), 400. The incident was likely to have been a well-rehearsed ritual of mock-execution.

45. John Smith, *A Trve Relation of such occurrences and accidents of noate as hath hapned in Virginia since the first planting of that collony* (1608) in Smith, *Works 1608–1631,* 38.

46. *The Generall Historie of Virginia,* in *Works,* 531.

47. John Rolfe, "Copy of John Wolfe's Letter to Sir Thomas Dale Regarding His Marriage to Pocahontas" (1614) in Philip L. Barbour, *Pocahontas and her World: A Chronicle of America" First Settlement in Which Is Related the Story of the Indians and the Englishmen—Particularly Captain John Smith, Captain Samuel Argall and Master John Rolfe,* Appendix 3 (London: Robert Hale & Company, 1971), 249.

48. See Stephen Orgel's "Introduction" to his Oxford edition of *The Tempest* (Oxford: Clarendon Press, 1987), 19, note 1.

Representations of Female Subjectivity in Elizabeth Cary's *The Tragedy of Mariam* and Mary Wroth's *Love's Victory*

AKIKO KUSUNOKI

1

REPRESENTATIONS of women's sense of self in the plays of women writers in early seventeenth-century England provide interesting new perspectives on the construction of female subjectivity in the early modern period. In recent years much important work has been done on women writers in the English Renaissance. Some of their works are now available in modern editions, while the strategies and negotiations these women writers employed to cope with the dominant and residual ideologies of their time have been studied from theoretical, historical and cultural points of view.[1] However, many critics, apart from a few such as Barbara Kiefer Lewalski and Elaine V. Beilin, tend to find that their works largely conform to the dominant ideological system of the society in which they lived.[2] Some critics like Gary Waller find their writings rather unilluminating unless we make "the silences" of their texts speak by means of post-structuralist theories of the late twentieth century.[3]

Nonetheless, when we examine representations of female subjectivity in plays by women writers in light of dramatic representations of women's self-consciousness by their male contemporaries, the significance of women's dramatic creations becomes clear in both historical and literary terms. Investigations of how female and male playwrites treat the same issues are particularly useful in this respect. In view of the exceedingly patriarchal society in which these women writers lived, and of the fact that they did not have the advantage of the cultural or psychoanalytical theories of our post-modern age to resort to, their courage in struggling against dominant ideologies and their resilience in attempting to

rewrite the position of women in their plays are not only remarkable but also very important in historical terms. They were in
many ways "governed" by dominant and residual ideologies, to
use Althusser's term, but they made a breakthrough by entering
the male arena of writing and publishing their works, and they
were forerunners in the emergence of female discourse which has
developed subsequently in various cultural contexts.

This essay examines the construction of female subjectivity in
early modern England, focusing on two plays written by women,
Lady Elizabeth Cary's *The Tragedy of Mariam* (c. 1603) and Lady
Mary Wroth's *Love's Victory* (c. 1621). Both plays are landmarks
in the history of women's writing in England: Cary's play is the
first extant original tragedy written by an English woman, while
Wroth's work is the first pastoral play by a woman writer.[4] The
discussion of these plays in this essay includes comparisons with
works by contemporary male writers which deal with the same
issues. *The Tragedy of Mariam* is examined with reference to
Philip Massinger's *The Duke of Milan* (1621/2), as well as Thomas
Lodge's translation of Josephus's *The Antiquities of the Jews*
(1602), which both Cary and Massinger used as the major source of
their plays. *Love's Victory* is contrasted mainly with Shakespeare's
plays, in particular, *A Midsummer Night's Dream*. Finally, in order
to highlight the characteristics of women's writing in the English
Renaissance, the essay glances at representations of woman's
sense of self in the works of women writers in tenth- and the
eleventh-century Japan, a period in the long history of Japanese
literature in which women's writings particularly flourished.

2

Elizabeth Cary's *The Tragedie of Mariam, the Faire Queene of
Iewry* was published in 1613, but had been written much earlier,
around 1603. In the previous year Elizabeth married Sir Henry
Cary, later Viscount Falkland, at the age of seventeen. After their
marriage Sir Henry went to fight in Holland in 1603. While her
husband was away, Elizabeth lived first at home with her authoritarian parents, and then with her mother-in-law, Lady Katherine
Cary, with whom she soon found she was incompatible.[5] She probably started writing *Mariam* either while she was still living with
her parents or when she was already with her exceedingly domi-
neering mother-in-law. The play consists of a clash between
Mariam's strong, though often contradictory, sense of self

and the dominant ideologies which correspond to those in early seventeenth-century England. Lewalski and many others have pointed out the parallel with Cary's personal life.[6] As shown in the biography probably written by her surviving eldest daughter,[7] Cary's whole life was marked by a constant struggle against domestic and social pressures which acted to keep her within the confines of contemporary female ideals of wife and mother; her struggle eventually led to her conversion to Catholicism in 1626, which resulted in domestic, social and even political turmoil.

Her father, Sir Lawrence Tanfield, was a successful lawyer who, after 1607, became Chief Baron of the Exchequer. Her mother was Elizabeth Symondes, descended from country gentry. Elizabeth was their only child and grew up in Burford, Oxfordshire. She was a precocious child who loved learning and voraciously read books from her father's library; she mastered five foreign languages on her own when very young. Her attraction to learning was not necessarily approved of by her parents, especially by her mother, so she had to bribe her servants to bring her candles so that she could read at night. When she was twelve, her father gave her Calvin's *Institutes* to read, to which she made many objections, pointing out various contradictions in Calvin's argument. Sir Lawrence is said to have been bemused by his daughter's aversion to Calvinism.[8] During the time that Sir Henry was away in Holland, Elizabeth's mother, apparently considering her daughter incapable of composing a properly wifely letter to her husband, hired someone to ghostwrite letters to Sir Henry for her.[9] We do not know how Elizabeth reacted to this humiliating arrangement by her own mother which denied her authorship of her personal letters to her husband, but Sir Henry seems to have been quite impressed by the letters she herself wrote to him later on.[10]

As she had been a person of such intellectual independence since childhood, her new status as wife, and the new circumstances of her life with Sir Henry, who is said to have been "absolute,"[11] and with her autocratic mother-in-law, must have caused her to question contemporary ideas of wifely submission. Yet, ironically, even such repressive patriarchal situations sometimes bore unexpected fruit. We are told that because her mother-in-law opposed Elizabeth's fondness for learning and took all her books away from her chamber, she started writing verses.[12] As its author was "governed" by social values in many ways, *The Tragedy of Mariam* is replete with gender anxieties and statements of stereotypical ideas of womanhood. Furthermore, Mariam's emerging sense of self is presented as contradictory in many respects. These aspects of the play have led some critics to see the play as chiefly endorsing the dominant ideological system.[13] Catherine Belsey takes a more positive attitude, but interprets Mariam's vacillating attitudes as evidence that she has not yet quite established her subjectivity.[14] On the other hand, critics such as Lewalski and Beilin stress the significance of the subversive elements in Mariam's rebellion against her husband's authority. And yet these critics see Mariam's resistance mainly in relation to the intellectual or religious milieu of the time. Lewalski recognizes the play's subversive elements by noting its parallel with contemporary French Senecan dramas and with histories in the Tacitean mode, which allow for the conflict of ideological positions and for sympathetic attitudes to resistance.[15] Beilin sees Mariam's resistance and her execution by Herod as a Christian allegory, the martyrdom of Christ.[16] These studies are of tremendous importance in opening new perspectives on a play which has been so long neglected in the traditional history of English literature. Yet, at the same time, more attention should be paid to the significance of the play's structure, which points to the emergence of a new discourse on womanhood.

The play is structured in such a way that each scene presents itself as a site of the clash between woman's sense of self and various dominant ideologies. When the play opens, the Jewish people are faced with the possibility of a great change, due to the news of the death of their tyrannical king, Herod. People react differently to this new situation, but the most complicated reaction comes from Mariam, Herod's beloved and beautiful wife. The play begins with Mariam's soliloquy, in which she eloquently articulates her own baffling psychological state. The play shows her constantly trying to analyze her inner state by means of the dominant ideologies of her society. First of all, she has come to consider it wrong to condemn the changeability of the human mind, although she herself supported this common attitude before, for her feeling for Herod has suddenly changed at the news of his death. She hated Herod, who, despite his infatuation with her, had murdered her brother, Aristobolus, and plotted against her grandfather, Hircanus, in order to ensure his own political power. Furthermore, when, on a previous occasion, he was called to Rome by Antony, he left secret orders with Josephus, the former husband of his sister, Salome, to kill Mariam if he failed to return, so that no one else could possess her. Josephus, however, revealed this secret to her. On Herod's return, Mariam protested against this command, but, at the suggestion of Salome, Herod executed Josephus immediately on the false charge of his having had a liaison with Mariam. When

Herod was again called to Rome, this time by Caesar, who had recently triumphed over Antony, he not only left the same orders with his servant Sohemus, but imprisoned Mariam in a room with Sohemus as her guardian. Out of pity for the great queen, Sohemus also revealed Herod's secret order about her. Indeed Mariam had good reasons to hate her husband:

> When *Herod* liu'd, that now is done to death,
> Oft haue I wisht that I from him were free:
> Oft haue I wisht that he might lose his breath,
> Oft haue I wisht his Carkas dead to see.
>
> (1.1.17–20)[17]

However, for all her hatred of Herod, to her embarrassment she suddenly feels love for him, remembering the ardent passion he bestowed upon her while he was alive. Now she cannot stop her tears, and realizes that, contrary to the general assumption about human nature, the mind can feel "both griefe and ioy" (1.1.12) for the same person.

Seen from the perspective of the post-modern theories of Lacan and Foucault,[18] the complex feelings Mariam suddenly finds in herself for the supposedly dead Herod is obviously the unstable drive of desire, which springs from her lack of fulfillment at his death. Yet, having no access to such theories, Mariam, or rather the author, has no discourse to elucidate this complicated drive Mariam suddenly recognizes in herself. Instead, Mariam tries to explain her contradictory state of mind by drawing on the dominant ideologies of womanhood in the society she lives in. First, she tries to rely on the stereotypical idea of irrational female passion, blaming herself for having neglected Herod's love because of her rage against his having murdered her brother and grandfather. Then she brings in the dominant ideology of wifely submission, which leads her to regard her hatred for him as a failing in her wifely duty: "Hate . . . kept my heart from paying him his debt." (1.1.23–24) She also tries to excuse herself for this failure through another stereotypical idea, that of women's intellectual weakness:

> My Sexe pleads pardon, pardon then afford,
> Mistaking is with vs, but too too common.
>
> (1.1.9–10)

However, Mariam is not entirely convinced by her own explanations. She still feels love for Herod and, at the same time, extreme rage against his possessiveness which she thinks denies her personal independence:

> And blame me not, for *Herods* Iealousie
> Had power euen constancie it selfe to change:
> For hee by barring me from libertie,
> To shunne my ranging, taught me first to range.
>
> (1.1.25–28)

Mariam considers Herod's command to kill her in the event of his own death so exorbitant that not only her hatred for him but even her adultery with another man could be justified, though, bound up by the contemporary concept of woman's chastity, she does not dare to resort to such a deviant retaliation:

> But yet too chast a Scholler was my hart,
> To learne to loue another then my Lord:
>
> (1.1.29–30)

Thus Cary talks about dominant ideologies of womanhood not to endorse them, but to demonstrate whether or not they can explain Mariam's confused state of mind. The result is, as has been shown, that the dominant ideological system can explicate neither her love for Herod nor her strong resistance to him. Without the help of post-modern psychoanalytical theories or feminist thinking, Elizabeth Cary could provide no discourse to systematize Mariam's complicated feelings. And yet, this absence of systematizing discourse denotes a failure in the power of the dominant ideological system, and thus points to the emergence of subversive forces in Mariam's self-consciousness which cannot be contained by the system, and which, in a post-modern cultural context, could have led to an alternative view of womanhood.

Like Elizabeth Cary herself, Mariam is "governed" by dominant ideologies. This is most clearly shown in those scenes which focus on her, her mother, and Salome. At the close of her soliloquy in the first scene, Mariam temporarily comes to terms with her divided self, deciding to dismiss her hatred for Herod on the grounds of the norm of wifely submission:

> And more I owe him for his loue to me,
> The deepest loue that euer yet was seene:
>
> (1.1.57–58)

However, right after this her mother, Alexandra, enters and starts to impose both residual and dominant ideologies upon Mariam, trying to make her look at her problems from different points of view. She insists on the inappropriateness of Mariam's lament for Herod's death for three reasons: first, their familial obligations to Aristobolus and Hircanus, whom he murdered, and the consequent necessity of revenge against him; second, Herod's racial inferiority to them; third, the unreliability of men's affection, which might cause Herod to go back to his former wife, Doris, whom he divorced in order to marry Mariam. Moreover, resorting to the common idea that women can obtain power only through their relationships with powerful men, Alexandra regrets that she did not send Mariam's portrait to Antony when he was in power; if she had done, Alexandra thinks, Antony would have forsaken Cleopatra, thus avoiding his tragic defeat by Caesar, and in the celebration of Antony's triumph over Caesar, Mariam might have been set in the place of honor instead of Cleopatra.

Mariam can respond to most of these conventional arguments only in conservative ways. She does not have an available language which would allow her to retort to her mother in a more radical way. Yet her flat denial of the possibility of her becoming Antony's mistress underlines her strong sense of self:

> Not to be Emprise of aspiring *Rome*,
> Would *Mariam* like to *Cleopatra* liue:
> With purest body will I presse my Toome,
> And wish no fauours *Anthony* could giue.

> (1.2.204–7)

Here again Mariam's sense of personal integrity is based on the dominant ideology of woman's chastity, but unlike the chaste wives depicted by male Renaissance playwrights, she insists on maintaining the purity of her body not for the sake of her husband's honor, but for her own sense of integrity. Here we can observe the emergence of woman's sense of self, independent of her husband; this concept of female subjectivity contains the potential to challenge the husband's authority.

At the same time, not only Alexandra but also Mariam is presented as preoccupied with notions of race and class. Alexandra's racial prejudice against Herod and his ancestors has already been mentioned. Mariam's strong sense of superiority in race and class is stressed in act 1, scene 3, where Mariam and Alexandra on one side, and Salome on the other, start bickering. Mariam's response to Salome's slander against her is strongly charged with dominant

ideologies of class and race in Elizabethan and Jacobean England,
though they are transported to the Palestinian context of the play:

> Though I thy brothers face had neuer seene,
> My birth, thy baser birth so farre exceld,
> I had to both of you the Princesse bene.
> Thou party Iew, and party Edomite,
> Thou Mongrell: issu'd from reiected race,
> Thy Ancestors against the Heauens did fight,
> And thou like them wilt heauenly birth disgrace.
>
> (1.3.240–6)

Salome refutes Mariam's insult with an emerging egalitarian idea:

> Still twit you me with nothing but my birth,
> What ods betwixt your ancestors and mine?
> Both borne of *Adam,* both were made of Earth,
> And both did come from holy *Abrahams* line.
>
> (1.3.247–50)

Again, faced this time with an emerging view, Mariam has no language to argue back with. She therefore shifts the point, and blames
Salome for having made the false allegation of a love affair between
her and Josephus, Salome's former husband. Alexandra is worse.
She even refuses to continue her conversation with Salome on the
grounds of her inferiority in race and class: "let vs goe: it is no
boote/ To let the head contend against the foote." (1.3.267–68)
    However, despite the difference in race and class, Salome makes
an interesting parallel with Mariam. It is true that the author, in
this case drawing on the Biblical description of Salome[19] rather
than on Josephus's account, makes her a foil to Mariam, portraying
her as an utterly wicked woman, whose sexual indulgence destroys
not only her husbands, but many others around her. Elizabeth Cary
makes the contrast between them clear through the conventional
use of the difference in their complexions. As Dympna Callaghan
has pointed out, whether the real color of the historical Mariam,
who was a Jew, was white is uncertain, but Cary portrays her
throughout the play as a traditional female beauty, symbolized by
her white complexion with "rosy" cheeks.[20] Salome's black complexion, on the other hand, is stressed throughout the play. Salome,
moreover, is described as constantly driven by desire. Once her
sexual urge, whether for Josephus or Constabarus, was fulfilled
through marriage, she was driven by desire for another man; she
is now plotting to get rid of Constabarus in order to marry Silleus.

Nevertheless, Salome's constant sexual drive is basically the same as the love which Mariam suddenly feels for her supposedly dead husband; both arise from the unpredictability of desire. Moreover, the way in which Salome defies social pressures recalls Mariam's refusal to submit herself to wifely obedience. Furthermore, both women are blamed by others for being too outspoken. Salome's outspokenness is harshly criticized by her present husband, Constabarus (1.6.), whereas Sohemus is afraid that "Vnbridled speech is *Mariams* worst disgrace." (3.3.1186) Thus the contemporary notion of race and class presented by Cary is in fact deconstructed in the text through the similarities between Mariam and Salome.

What makes a great difference between Mariam and Salome is that since the latter is characterized as a wicked woman, the author gives her a language in which to expound her desire and justify her breach of the moral code. Having killed her first husband by manipulating Herod, Salome finds no meaning whatsoever in the dominant value system; she no longer feels that a sense of shame or honor is important to her. She even challenges the unfair society in which women cannot initiate divorce:

> Why should such priuiledge to man be giuen?
> Or giuen to them, why bard from women then?
> Are men then we in greater grace with Heauen?
> Or cannot women hate as well as men?
>
> (1.4.315–18)

Under Jewish law at that time, women were strictly forbidden to initiate a divorce.[21] Yet Salome's challenge has a wider implication here, since it has relevance to marital conditions in early seventeenth-century England; a man could divorce his wife on the grounds of her adultery, while a woman could not divorce her husband unless he was proved to be sexually impotent.[22] That not all English women in this period were satisfied with this unfair legal system can be illustrated by a few actual historical cases in which women obtained divorce on the evidence, though dubious, of their husbands' physical impotence; the most notorious case was Lady Frances Howard's divorce from the third Earl of Essex in 1613.[23]

It is also interesting to note that Salome's challenge to the authority of the husband invites an accusation of her masculinity, which recalls typical Jacobean reactions against female self-assertion, such as those observed in King James's order against women wearing mannish clothes in 1620, or in contemporary

pamphlets against female masculinity such as *Hic Mulier.*[24] Constabarus, Salome's second husband, criticizes Salome's assertion of
autonomy in similar terms:

> Are Hebrew women now trãsform'd to men?
> Why do you not as well our battels fight,
> And weare our armour? Suffer this, and then
> Let all the world be topsie turued quite.
>
> (1.6.435–38)

Thus, while Salome, since she is a wicked character, is given a
language which can accommodate women's emerging sense of self,
Mariam's self-awareness is presented through the discrepancy between what dominant ideologies define as femininity and what Mariam actually feels.

This is also the case in act 3, scene 3, in which the Chorus
delivers its criticism of Mariam's decision not to submit to Herod
any longer, when she hears the news of his safe return. The un-
steady drive of desire in Mariam immediately disappears at this
unexpected news. She decides never to subject herself to his authority, even forswearing his bed. She knows that she can captivate
Herod with her charming smiles and gentle words; she also knows
that if she does not accept the role of wifely submission, Salome
and her mother, taking advantage of the discord between Mariam
and Herod, will plot against her. Neither of these thoughts, however, make Mariam conform to the dominant ideologies of wifehood. Placed in parallel with Salome's similar decision, Mariam's
bold decision points to her emerging sense of self which, like Salome's actions, challenges the dominant ideologies of womanhood
and the husband's authority. But here again, as is not the case in
the portrayal of Salome, Elizabeth Cary can furnish Mariam with
no alternative discourse to articulate her state of mind. Instead,
she makes Mariam prove her personal integrity by depending upon
her confidence in her "innocence," a vital element in the contemporary notion of goodness in women:

> Oh what a shelter is mine innocence,
> To shield me from the pangs of inward griefe:
> Gainst all mishaps it is my faire defence,
> And to my sorrowes yeelds a large reliefe.
> . . . .
> Let my distressed state vnpittied bee,
> Mine innocence is hope enough for mee.
>
> (3.3.1174–83)

"Innocence" is, however, not an appropriate term for describing Mariam's feelings here. It can be interpreted as her innocence of the false charge of her liaison with Sohemus. It can also be seen, as by Belsey and Fischer,[25] to imply her innocence of the hypocrisy derived from the divergence of her true feelings from her duty of wifely submission. Yet, in either interpretation, the term "innocence" is not quite adequate to explain the situation. Here what makes Mariam decide to defy Herod's authority is her belief that in doing so, she does nothing wrong in the situation she is in; she is "innocent," she insists, in challenging the dominant ideology of wifehood, because she finds it invalid in her circumstances. This clearly indicates the most subversive attitude possible for a woman in Cary's historical context, especially when we think that wifely obedience constituted the cornerstone of the whole patriarchal system at the time, by virtue of the analogy between kingly and divine authority and that of the husband.[26] Although Elizabeth Cary has no language—except for the conventional word "innocence,"—to explain this exceedingly subversive concept emerging in Mariam, she imposes the dominant concepts of wifehood upon Mariam through the Chorus, thereby showing that Mariam's sense of self cannot be contained by these views.

The Chorus at the end of act 3, scene 3 first advocates an Elizabethan and Jacobean commonplace that a woman must keep herself spotless, and that it is equally important for her to keep herself free from suspicion. She, therefore, should not disclose her private feelings to a man other than her husband, as Mariam did to her custodian, Sohemus. Then the Chorus asserts one of the most important ideologies of the time; that, once married, a woman should entirely submit herself to her husband's authority and that, to possess her own sense of self constitutes a usurpation of his right:

> When to their Husbands they themselues doe bind,
> Doe they not wholy giue themselues away?
> Or giue they but their body not their mind,
> Reseruing that though best, for others pray?
>> No sure, their thoughts no more can be their owne,
>> And therefore should to none but one be knowne.
>
> (3.3.1237–42)

Some critics take these views expressed by the Chorus as the author's endorsement of contemporary ideologies.[27] However, as has been shown, when we put the Chorus's speeches into the whole dramatic context, a subversive meaning emerges.

In the next scene, when Herod comes back, ardently wishing to see his beautiful Mariam, she appears in a somber dress and demonstrates her resistance to his authority. He gets extremely upset, but tries to appease her in various silly ways; he promises her titles, land, or wealth, without even trying to understand her feelings. Cary presents this point clearly by making Mariam blame him for not caring for her as a person, but simply treating her as a beautiful object:

> No, had you wisht the wretched *Mariam* glad,
> Or had your loue to her bene truly tide:
> Nay, had you not desir'd to make her sad,
> My brother nor my Grandsyre had not dide.
>
> (4.3.1376–79)

In plays written by male playwrights during the English Renaissance, we often hear men claiming their wives as "my goods, my chattels,"[28] but rarely have a chance to know women's reactions to this treatment. By juxtaposing the ideologies of wifehood articulated by the Chorus and embodied in Herod's attitudes to Mariam on the one hand, and Mariam's reaction to them on the other, Elizabeth Cary shows that these ideologies are not relevant to her sense of personal integrity.

At this point it is useful to compare Cary's representation of Mariam's sense of self with those portrayed by male contemporary writers. Thomas Lodge, in his translation of Josephus's *The Antiquities of the Jews,* on which Cary drew heavily for her play, depicts Mariam's assertion of self simply as a fault:

> she was both chast and faithfull vnto him; yet had she a certaine womanly imperfection and naturall frowardnesse, which was the cause that shee presumed too much vpon the intire affection wherewith her husband was intangled; so that without regard to his person, who had power and authoritie ouer others, she entertained him oftentimes very outragiously: All which he endured patiently, without any shew of discontent. But *Mariamme* vpbraided and publikely reproched both the Kings mother and sister, telling them that they were but abiectly and basely borne.[29]

Philip Massinger also used Thomas Lodge's translation of Josephus's *The Antiquities of the Jews* for one of the sources for *The Duke of Milan,* although he transported the whole scene into Renaissance Italy. Centering his play on the infatuation of Lodovico Sforza, the Duke of Milan, for his beautiful wife, Marcelia, Massin-

ger presents the tragic turning point in the play as the moment
when Marcelia hears from Sforza's right-hand man, Francisco, that
her husband commanded him to kill her at the news of his own
death, so that no one else could possess her affection. As Philip
Edwards has pointed out, Sforza seems to believe that even in
heaven he can enjoy his wife sexually.[30] Marcelia is shocked to
discover the possessive nature of her husband's passion, which
does not acknowledge her as a person, but only as a beautiful
sexual object:

> that my Lord, my *Sforza* should esteeme
> My life fit only as a page, to waite on
> The various course of his vncertaine fortunes,
> Or cherish in himselfe that sensuall hope
> In death to know me as a wife, afflicts me. . .
>
> (3.3.58–62)[31]

Like Mariam, Marcelia protests against her husband's demand for
her self-effacement through both her words and actions, which
results in her death. However, unlike Elizabeth Cary, Massinger
does not specifically present this as a clash of the heroine's sense
of self with the dominant ideologies of wifehood, but simply treats
the issue as a problem of possessive male love.

Even though Elizabeth Cary did not have a language in which
to put forward a new concept of womanhood, probably only someone like her, who had constantly struggled against domestic and
social pressures, could present woman's sense of self in such an
unique way, a way in which the heroine tests her feelings and
thoughts against the dominant ideologies and then realizes that
these ideologies do not accommodate her sense of self.

In the face of her execution, Mariam realizes that her sense of
integrity, which is derived from her confidence in her own beauty
and chastity, and which has taken no account of the importance of
the humility society requires of women, cannot override the dominant ideologies: it has not been able to make her live "wisely":

> Had I but with humilitie bene grac'te,
> As well as faire I might haue prou'd me wise:
> But I did thinke because I knew me chaste,
> One vertue for a woman, might suffice.
> That mind for glory for our sexe might stand,
> Wherein humilitie and chastitie

> Doth march with equall paces hand in hand,
> But one if single seene, who setteth by?

(4.8.1833–40)

These lines illustrate another example of the contradiction in Mariam's sense of self. Although the speech expresses regret, and appears to be an endorsement of the importance of the humility required of women by the dominant ideologies, this is not Mariam's final word: she immediately makes clear her sense of integrity independent of the dominant values in society:

> . . . tis my ioy,
> That I was euer innocent, though sower:
> And therefore can they but my life destroy,
> My Soule is free from aduersaries power.

(4.8.1841–44)

Then, according to the messenger, she dies nobly. Herod regrets that he executed Mariam and laments her death in almost the entire final scene of the play. Cary's way of presenting female integrity through Mariam's constancy in the face of her death to what she has perceived right, and her acknowledgement of the "reality" of the ideological requirement for humility in women, is similar to the way in which Mary Sidney, the Countess of Pembroke, portrays Cleopatra's integrity in her translation of Robert Garnier's *Antonie, Antonius* (1592)/ *The Tragedie of Antonie* (1595). In this respect, in her description of Mariam, Cary seems to have been influenced by Mary Sidney.[32]

3

In her way of dramatizing women's emerging sense of self, Lady Mary Wroth is quite different from Elizabeth Cary. In *Love's Victory,* as in her romance, *The Countess of Montgomery's Urania,* and her sonnet sequence, *Pamphilia to Amphilanthus,* all of which make use of the pastoral mode, Wroth tries to present a discourse on desire distinct from the pastoral conventions established by male writers, in particular, by her uncle, Sir Philip Sidney. To use Gary Waller's phrase about Petrarchan love poetry in general, *Love's Victory* is "a theatre of desire."[33] In its theme and settings Wroth's play often recalls plays written by her male contemporaries, especially Shakespeare. As in *A Midsummer Night's*

Dream, the characters are completely under the control of super-human figures of desire, in this case Venus and Cupid, who, like Oberon and Puck, provide the framework of the whole work by entering at the beginning of the play and at the end of each act. All the characters, except for the aged mother of Musella, are driven by sexual desire, which, again as in *A Midsummer Night's Dream,* is presented as a constant state of inadequacy due to not being fulfilled.

Philisses and Musella are in love with each other, but Philisses is in deep despair, thinking that she loves his best friend, Lissius, while Philisses himself is loved and pursued by several other women. Musella is also desired by many other men; toward the end of the play she is almost married off to a stupid but rich shepherd, Rustick. Silvesta, who used to pursue Philisses, finding it impossible for her desire ever to be fulfilled, has sworn eternal chastity, and yet she is passionately desired by Forester. Lissius, who has disdained such irrational erotic desire in human beings, is punished by Venus for his defiance of her authority, and is suddenly awakened to passion for Simeana, Philisses' sister. She, on the other hand, at first accepts Lissius's love, but soon comes to be possessed by strong jealousy as a result of the intrigue of a villain, Arcas, who, like Iago, feels threatened by assertive women and also hates to see other people's happiness. Thus, the pastoral world in the play, which is called "Arcadia,"[34] is in a state of confusion caused by the unstable and destabilizing drive of desire which emanates from Venus and her son, Cupid. Like the lovers in *A Midsummer Night's Dream,* the lovers in *Love's Victory* have to undergo trials and difficulties before their libidinous energy finally finds its right object.

A major difference between Lady Wroth's play and the pastoral plays written by her male contemporaries is, as Ann Rosalind Jones has argued with respect to *Urania,* the absence of court life or even courtiers.[35] Drawing on Louis Adrian Montrose's discussion of the pastoral in the English Renaissance, Jones thinks that in England the pastoral was seen "as a potentially critical and satirical genre,"[36] which offered discontented courtiers a chance to express their criticism of the current state of the Court. This certainly was the case with many writers of pastoral romance and poetry, such as Philip Sidney and Edmund Spenser. In these writings women are usually represented in Petrarchan terms, either as a symbol of perfect beauty which enhances male virtues or as a cruel mistress who denies the fulfillment of male desire, and love often functions as a means by which men articulate their unfulfilled

ambition for political power. Similarly, in the case of Sidney's sonnet sequence *Astrophel and Stella,* we hear, as has often been
pointed out, a great deal about Astrophel's frustrations with political affairs at the Court through his portrayals of Stella, while we
hardly ever know what she really feels or thinks.[37]

By contrast, in *Love's Victory,* Wroth eliminates all elements of
court life, presenting a pastoral world which centers on desire. The
framework of the play created by the goddess of desire and her
son makes this point clear. The characters cannot escape into a
life where love is only a peripheral concern, as is the case in pastoral writings by men. Some male characters, such as Philisses and
Lissius, still retain Petrarchan concepts of love. The female characters, on the other hand, are free from these courtly values and
candid in admitting their own desire. They are also more seriously
committed to their passion than the male characters, although they
are not always accepted by the men they love; and their situation
is made more difficult by the dominant ideology of womanhood in
early seventeenth-century England which defined women's sexual
approaches to men as deviant.

Many female characters created by male playwrights, such as
Shakespeare's Cressida in *Troilus and Cressida* or Helena in *All's
Well That Ends Well,* find their situations extremely frustrating, a
frustration caused by the requirement that women should not take
the initiative in their relationships with the men they love. Although
Wroth's female characters live in a pastoral world, they are also
quite conscious of this code of female propriety. For instance, Musella feels sorry for Philisses, who is suffering from the delusion
that she loves Lissius, and wants to confess her love to him, but
thinks it improper for a woman to do so:

> Somtimes I faine would speak, then strait forbear
> Knowing itt most unfitt; thus woe I beare.

> (3.77–78)

Silvestra agrees with Musella: "Indeed a woman to make love is
ill" (3.79). Yet, they are resourceful enough to devise a situation in
which Musella can reveal her love to Philisses without breaching
the code of female propriety. Although outspoken in admitting their
love, the female characters in the play continue to share friendship
and mutually support each other despite their rivalry in love; Silvesta is still the best friend of Musella in spite of her unrequited
love for Philisses, and guides them to marriage by helping them to
resolve their problems. Furthermore, the female characters in

Love's Victory do not play tricks upon men to titillate their desire by frustrating their passion, something which female characters often do in plays or love lyrics written by male writers. Dalina, who is called "a fickle lady" in the cast list of the play, mentions this strategy to keep men's love (3.268–70), but even she is portrayed as simply frank in admitting the imperative of her desire (3.134–49: 153–61), not as a destructively promiscuous woman, such as the Countess in Marston's *The Insatiate Countess* or Middleton's Beatrice-Joanna.

It is also important to note that in *Love's Victory*, as in *Urania* and the sonnet sequence, Wroth presents women as sexually autonomous. In *Urania*, some women, like Limena, are driven into forced marriages which cause them great misery, but at the same time they are always capable of loving someone they themselves choose. Moreover, they often articulate their sexual attraction to male beauty, and thus men are sometimes made objects of their gaze. For instance, the opening scene of *Urania* presents an interesting contrast to *Arcadia*. In the latter the shepherds, Strephon and Claius, lament the disappearance of a beautiful shepherdess, Urania, uttering their admiration for her in Petrarchan terms, whereas Urania at the beginning of Wroth's pastoral is presented as a woman searching for her self-identity, and a little later as admiring in elegantly simple language the male beauty and sexual attraction of the young prince, Perissus, whom she has just found in a cave.[38] This is by no means the only example of male beauty being subjected to the female gaze in *Urania*.[39]

These presentations of women's sexual autonomy in Wroth's works can be seen as an intentional defiance of the dominant ideology of womanhood, which defined obedience, chastity and silence as the prime female virtues. Mary Wroth's own life story illustrates her defiant attitudes to these norms. Not only did she breach the code of woman's silence by publishing *Urania*, which caused a great scandal at the Court, but she also bore two illegitimate children to her first cousin, William Herbert, the third Earl of Pembroke.[40]

In *Love's Victory*, men like Philisses and Lissius still talk of their love in the Petrarchan terms established by male tradition. However, the author underlines the ridiculous aspects of their attitudes to love. For instance, Philisses' love for Musella is like Orsino's passion for Olivia in *Twelfth Night;* he is in love with the concept of being in love. Right after his first entrance on the stage, Philisses laments his unrequited love for Musella. Yet, soon afterwards Philisses learns from Lissius, whom he has regarded as his rival in love for Musella, that Lissius does not love her, but does love his sister, Simeana. And yet Philisses continues to moan for love. Even after having conformed with Musella that she loves him, he is still sunk in melancholy. Moreover, in his song in act 2, he divides love from reason in Petrarchan terms, insisting that reason should control human passion (2.213–24). And yet, it is Philisses himself whose passion overrules his reason, and who is at the mercy of the illusion that Musella and Lissius are in love with each other.

The women in the play, in contrast, do not create a dichotomy between love and reason. They accept desire as integral to the human condition. Thus Wroth, influenced perhaps by Montaigne's views on sexuality,[41] launches an alternative discourse to the dominant description of humanity, which divided the human constitution into body and soul. She makes it clear in her play that women are subjects of desire, not objects, and thus tries to present the possibility of female integrity through honesty to their own desire. This concept of desire is explored in more depth and greater detail in *Urania*.

What differentiates Lady Wroth's play from Shakespeare's is the fact that she assigns female characters roles as agents and initiators of action. As is also the case in *Urania* and the sonnet sequence,[42] male characters in *Love's Victory* who function as agents of change are notable by their absence. It is the goddess, Venus, rather than the King of the Fairies, Oberon, who manipulates the characters' amorous situations. Musella, Silvesta and Simeana, not the central male characters, Philisses or Lissius, are resourceful and resolve their amatory entanglements. It is especially interesting to see how Wroth often reverses Shakespeare's allocation of male and female roles by assigning to the women in her play the roles usually given to men in the works of her male predecessor. In act 4, thanks to Silvesta's stratagem, Musella, like Romeo in the balcony scene, has a chance to overhear Philisses confessing his love for her. In the forest scene, Silvesta ponders the nature of love, as Orlando does in *As You Like It*. The final scene presents the faked death of Philisses and Musella, which is designed to avoid the latter's forced marriage to Rustick. This situation obviously recalls a similar scene in *Romeo and Juliet*, but it is Silvesta, not the Priest of the Temple, who reminds us of Friar Laurence by furnishing the lovers with the potion that causes their mock death.

Moreover, although patriarchal power is still, even in this pastoral world, accepted as absolute, it is Musella's mother, not her father (who is absent throughout the play), who directly represents that power by trying to force Musella into a mercenary marriage with Rustick. However, Wroth displaces the responsibility for Musella's mother's actions on her absent husband. Thus, Musella tells Silvesta that her mother is forcing her into marriage because of her father's will (5.11–14), while in the final resolution scene her mother apologizes to her by saying: "Pardon my fault, injoye, and blessed bee,/ And children, and theyr children's children see" (5.501–2). The blame is also displaced on the male villain, Arcas, who told Musella's mother that, "Musella wantonly/ Did seeke Philisses' love" (5. 391–92).

Thus, in *Love's Victory,* the women are always practical and initiate actions, while the men are incapable of resolving problems or of bringing about happiness; Philisses and Lissius limit themselves to deploring their predicaments through the medium of Petrarchan poetry, and Arcas plots to destroy others' happiness, while the insensitive Rustick shows no interest in anything other than country affairs.

Unlike Lady Elizabeth Cary, who could not provide a language to articulate female sexuality in *The Tragedy of Mariam,* Lady Mary Wroth, who wrote her play nearly twenty years afterwards, succeeded in presenting a discourse on desire in *Love's Victory* by making use of the popular literary pastoral mode. Even though still influenced by the social values of the early seventeenth-century England, Wroth challenges general assumptions about womanhood and rewrites women's position as agents of love through this discourse. The genre of the play, tragicomedy, allows it to have a happy ending.[43] This is different from the ending of the published part of *Urania.* This part, generally called *Urania* Part I, after describing the endless complications of Pamphilia's love for the inconstant Amphilanthus, whose name signifies "the louer of two" (*Urania,* 250), finishes with their temporary happiness in each other's love. However, the romance suddenly ends with the words ambiguous "And":

. . . all now merry, contented, nothing amisse;
griefe forsaken, sadness cast off, *Pamphilia* is the
Queene of all content: *Amphilanthus* ioying worthily in her; And
(558)

Carolyn Ruth Swift thinks that Wroth is here implying the continuation of women's endless involvement in the unsatisfactory game of loving inconstant men, which is what actually occurs in the unpublished part, *Urania* Part II. Swift considers that Wroth thus insists women are more constant than men and is stressing the painful and self-destructive aspect of their constancy to unfaithful lovers.[44] Mary Ellen Lamb even finds anger in Wroth's descriptions of women's constancy to their fickle lovers.[45]

Indeed, in *Urania* women quite often express their irritation at being in a position in which they can retain self-respect only through constancy to their inconstant lovers (for instance, 156–61; 190; 251–52; 398; 452–53). However, in view of the historical context of women in early seventeenth-century England, the more important point is that Wroth portrayed her female characters as capable of choosing men to love, not as simply succumbing to men who approached them, and presented this capacity in women as constitutive of their sense of self.

4

To highlight Wroth's emphasis on female subjectivity in the issue of love, we should glance briefly at the representations of women in two works by female writers in late classical and medieval Japanese literature, *The Gossamer Years* (c. 980) and Lady Murasaki's *The Tale of Genji* (c. 1008). The author of *The Gossamer Years* is known only as "The Mother of Michitsuna Fujiwara"; her own name is not known. She was one of several wives of a powerful political figure of the time, Kaneie Fujiwara, who later became the Protector of the Emperor. *The Gossamer Years* is a collection of her memoirs written in the form of a diary, which mostly consists of expressions of her frustrated feelings for her fickle husband. Yet the author consistently denies the position of subject to her heroine. She did not at first welcome marriage with Lord Kaneie, who was strongly attracted by her beauty and poetical talents, but she finally succumbed to his ardent approaches. After a brief description of the arrangements of their marriage, we are immediately told that she was pregnant. After she realized that her husband's love was now directed toward other women, she seems to have tried to maintain her self-respect by writing about the inferior aspects of her rivals and by trying to bring up her son in accordance with the contemporary image of the ideal courtier. Similarly, Lady Murasaki gives none of the ladies who have amorous relationships with Hikaru Genji the subject position in their love. They all become sexually entangled with Genji, not because of their passion for him, but because they are pursued by him and eventually find him irresistible. Utsusemi is an unusual woman in the novel. She defiantly refuses to meet Genji after their first adulterous encounter, but her defiance comes not from her sense of personal integrity, but from her sense of being under obligation to protect her husband's honor. Later her sense of guilt makes her move to a remote country place where her husband, for whom she feels no affection, is in charge, so that Genji has no chance to see her again. The only episode in *The Tale of Genji* that deals with a woman's betrayal of her male lover is the final one, "The Bridge of Dreams." Yet, here again, the heroine, Ukifune, whose name signifies "the lady of the floating boat," and who is deeply loved by Lord Kaoru, supposedly a son of Genji, comes to have a sexual relationship with Lord Niou, a grandson of Genji, as a result of his passionate approaches to her. When her inconstancy is discovered by Kaoru, her sense of guilt causes her to try to drown herself, but after being rescued by a priest, she becomes a nun. Even though she was a woman, Lady Murasaki raised no questions about a situation in which men were allowed to have amorous adventures, whereas women were not.

These differences in the portrayals of women by Japanese writers and by Mary Wroth obviously derive from the differences between the culture of tenth- and eleventh-century Japan and that of early seventeenth-century England, differences particularly related to the religious outlook of Buddhism and Protestantism on womanhood in the respective periods. A full discussion of this complicated but fascinating subject is unfortunately beyond the scope of this essay. However, as Raymond Williams has shown, any culture is constructed through the constant interactions of three modes of ideology, the residual, the dominant and the emergent; [46] and no human being can avoid retaining some elements of the residual and dominant ideologies operating in his or her society. Therefore, although in many ways, both Lady Elizabeth Cary and Lady Mary Wroth maintained the social values of their time, their questioning of the dominant ideologies of womanhood in the English Renaissance contributed to the development of a discourse on female subjectivity in the West; and this achievement becomes even more impressive in comparison to the absence of any sign of such an emergent discourse in the works of Lady Murasaki or "The Mother of Michitsuna Fujiwara." In this respect, unlike the Japanese women writers of the Heian Period, who were more closely tied to the dominant structure of their age, Lady Elizabeth Cary and Lady Mary Wroth were truly among the initiators of a discourse that continues to be of central importance in our post-modern era.

Notes

1. For instance, Barbara Kiefer Lewalski, *Writing Women in Jacobean England* (Cambridge: Harvard University Press, 1993); Elaine V. Beilin, *Redeeming Eve: Women Writers of the English Renaissance* (Princeton: Princeton University Press, 1987); Ann Rosalind Jones, *The Currency of Eros: Women's Love Lyric in Europe, 1540–1620* (Bloomington: Indiana University Press, 1990); Tina Krontiris, *Oppositional Voices: Women as Writers and Translators of Literature in the English Renaissance* (London: Routledge, 1992); Louise Schleiner, *Tudor and Stuart Women Writers* (Bloomington and Indianapolis: Indiana University Press, 1994). *Voicing Women: Gender and Sexuality in Early Modern Writing*, eds. Kate Chedgzoy, Melanie Hansen and Suzanne Trill (Keele: Keele University Press, 1996). Also, the Introductions in the recent editions of female writers in the English Renaissance offer various important perspectives on this issue. See, for instance, Josephine A. Roberts, ed., *The Poems of Lady Mary Wroth* (Baton Rouge: Louisiana State University Press, 1983), 3–81 and *The First Part of The Countess of Montgomery's Urania by Lady Mary Wroth* (Binghamton: Medieval & Renaissance Texts & Studies, 1995), xv–civ; Barry Weller and Margaret W. Ferguson, eds., *The Tragedy of Mariam: The Fair Queen of Jewry* (Berkeley: University of California Press, 1994), 1–59; S.P. Cerasano and Marion Wynne-Davies, eds., *Renaissance Drama By Women: Texts and Documents* (London: Routledge, 1996).

2. For instance, Betty S. Travitsky, *"The Feme Covert* in Elizabeth Cary's *Mariam,"* in *Ambiguous Realities: Women in the Middle Ages and Renaissance,* eds. Carole Levin and Jeanie Watson (Detroit: Wayne State University Press, 1987), 184–96; recently, Schleiner, 175–91.

3. Gary Waller, "Struggling into Discourse: The Emergence of Renaissance Women's Writing," in *Silent But for the Word: Tudor Women as Patrons, Translators, and Writers of Religious Works,* ed. Margaret Patterson Hannay (Kent, Ohio: The Kent State University Press, 1985), 238–56.

4. Elizabeth Cary was also the first Englishwoman to write a full-scale history, *The History of the Life, Reign, and Death of Edward II* (c. 1627, published in 1680). Mary Wroth's prose romance, *Urania,* and her sonnet sequence, *Pamphilia to Amphilanthus,* published together with *Urania,* were the first prose fiction and the first sonnet sequence written by an Englishwoman.

5. *The Lady Falkland: Her Life,* ed. R.(ichard) S.(impson) (London: Catholic Publishing and Bookselling Company, 1861), 8.

6. Lewalski, 190–91; Beilin, 158.

7. *The Lady Falkland.* See also Lady Georgiana Fullerton, *The Life of Elizabeth Lady Falkland 1585–1639* (London: Burns and Oates, 1883).

8. *The Lady Falkland,* 7.

9. *The Lady Falkland,* 7.

10. *The Lady Falkland,* 8–9.

11. *The Lady Falkland,* 14.

12. *The Lady Falkland,* 8.

13. For instance, Travitsky, 184–96; more recently, Schleiner, 175–91.

14. Catherine Belsey, *The Subject of Tragedy: Identity and Difference in Renaissance Drama* (London: Methuen, 1985), 171–75.

15. Lewalski, 190–201; Sandra K. Fischer, "Elizabeth Cary and Tyranny, Domestic and Religious," *Silent But for the Word,* 235–37, also takes this view.

16. Beilin, especially 159–60; Barry Weller and Margaret W. Ferguson, 27.

17. Elizabeth Cary, *The Tragedy of Mariam 1613,* ed. A.C. Dunstan, The Malone Society Reprints (Oxford: Oxford University Press, 1914, reprint, 1992). All quotations from the play in this essay are taken from this edition.

18. Jacques Lacan, *Feminine Sexuality: Jacques Lacan and the École Freudienne,* eds. Juliete Mitchell and Jacqueline Rose, trans. Jacqueline Rose (London: Macmillan, 1982); Michel Foucault, *The Order of Things,* trans. Alan Sheridan-Smith (New York: Pantheon, 1971).

19. Fischer, 235.

20. Dympna Callaghan, "Re-reading Elizabeth Cary's *The Tragedie of Mariam, the Faire Queene of Jewry, Women, "Race," & Writing in the Early Modern Period,* eds. Margo Hendricks and Patricia Parker (London: Routledge, 1994), 163–77.

21. Lewalski, 195.

22. Lawrence Stone, *The Family, Sex, and Marriage in England, 1500–1800* (Oxford, 1977: reprint, London: Weidenfeld and Nicolson, 1979), 37–41.

23. For the divorce case of Frances Howard see, David Lindley, *The Trials of Frances Howard: Fact and Fiction at the Court of King James* (London: Routledge, 1993); Anne Somerset, *Unnatural Murder: Poison at the Court of James I* (London: Weidenfeld & Nicolson, 1997).

24. For King James's order, see John Chamberlain, *The Letters of John Chamberlain,* ed. Norman Egbert McClure, 2 vols. (Philadelphia: American Philosophical Society, 1939), 25 January and 12 February 1620, 2:286–7:289. *Hic Mvlier: Or, The Man-Woman* (London, 1620). For the parallel between Mariam and Salome, see also Weller and Ferguson, 32–5.

25. Belsey, 172–73; Fischer, 234.

26. This analogy, repeatedly asserted by authorities, is based on *Ephesians,* 5:20–30.

27. For instance, Schleiner, 178–79.

28. William Shakespeare, *The Taming of the Shrew,* ed. Ann Thompson, *The New Cambridge Shakespeare* (Cambridge: Cambridge University Press, 1984), act 2, scene 2, 219.

29. Thomas Lodge trans., *The Famovs and Memorable Workes of Josephvs* (London, 1602), 398.

30. Philip Edwards, "Massinger's Men and Women," *Philip Massinger: A Critical Reassessment,* ed. Douglas Howard (Cambridge: Cambridge University Press, 1985), 40–41.

31. Philip Massinger, *The Duke of Milan,* in *The Plays and Poems of Philip Massinger,* eds. Philip Edwards and Colin Gibson, 5 vols. (Oxford; The Clarendon Press, 1976), vol. I.

32. Cary's childhood writing master was the poet, John Davies, who was also well acquainted with Mary Sidney. Fischer, 229, supports the idea that Mary Sidney may have encouraged Cary to write *The Tragedy of Mariam.* See also Mary Ellen Lamb, *Gender and Authorship in the Sidney Circle* (Madison: The University of Wisconsin Press, 1990), 115–41; Weller and Ferguson, 26–30. It is also worth noticing that in *The Duchess of Malfi* John Webster tries to present the Duchess's sense of integrity in a similar way.

33. Waller, 242.

34. Mary Wroth, *Lady Mary Wroth's Loves Victory,* The Penshurst Manuscript, ed. Michael G. Brennan (London: The Roxburghe Club, 1988), act 3, 192. All references to the play in this essay are to this edition.

35. Jones, 121.

36. Jones, 123; see also, 141–42. For the argument of Louis Adrian Montrose, see "'Eliza, Queene of Shepheardes,' and The Pastoral of Power," *ELR* 10 (1980): 153–82; "Of Gentlemen and Shepherds: The Politics of Elizabethan Pastoral Form," *ELH* 50 (1983): 415–59.

37. Ann Rosalind Jones and Peter Stallybrass, "The Politics of *Astrophil and Stella,*" *SEL* 24 (1984): 53–68.

38. Mary Wroth, *The Countesse of Mountgomeries Urania* (London, 1621), 15. All references to the work in this essay are to this edition.

39. Another example is the passage in which Urania turns her gaze on the two youths who have rescued her from a wolf:

> . . . then perceiued she two young men, whose age might bee iudged to bee some seuen-teene yeares; faces of that sweetnesse, as *Venus* loue could but compare with them, their haire which neuer had been cut, hung long, yet longer much it must haue been, had not the daintie naturall curling somewhat shortned it, which as the wind mou'd, the curles so pretily plaid, as the Sunne-beames in the water; their apparrell Goates skinnes cut into no fashion, but made fast about them in that sort, as one might see by their sight they were wild; yet that wilderness was gouern'd by modesty, their skinne most bare, as armes and leggs, and one shoulder, with part of their thighes; but so white was their skinne, as seem'd the Sunn in loue with it, would not hurt, nor the bushes so much as scratch. . . . (16)

40. For the life of Lady Mary Wroth, see Roberts, ed., *the Poems of Lady Mary Wroth,* 3–40; *The First Part of The Countess of Montgomery's Urania,* xc–civ.

41. Michael Montaigne, in *The Essayes of Michael Lord of Montaigne,* trans. John Florio, 3 vols. (London: J.M. Dent and Sons, 1910), in particular in "Upon Some Verses of *Virgil,*" especially 3: 77–95, argues that sexuality is part of human nature and criticizes men for imposing the norm of chastity upon women. It is remarkable how popular Montaigne was among educated women at the time. For instance, the lists of the books possessed by Lady Elizabeth Cary and by Lady Anne Clifford include *The Essayes:* see *The Lady Falkland,* 113; George C. Williamson, *Lady Anne Clifford, Countess of Dorset, Pembroke & Montgomery, 1590–1670: Her Life, Letters, and Work* (Kendal: Tites Wilson and Son, 1922), 341–44. Through the Sidney connection it is most likely that Wroth also read Montaigne. The three books of John Florio's translation of *The Essayes* are all dedicated to the highly educated women at the time: Book I, to Lucy Countess of Bedford and Lady Anne Harrington; Book II, to Elizabeth Countess of Rutland and Lady Penelope Rich; Book III, to Lady Elizabeth Grey and Lady Marie Nevill.

42. Jones, 141.

43. Both Gary Waller, *The Sidney Family Romance: Mary Wroth, William Herbert, and the Early Modern Construction of Gender* (Detroit: Wayne State University Press, 1993), 242–45, and Schleiner, 134–49, describe *Love's Victory* in terms of fantasy. Thus, Waller regards the play as a wish-fulfilling fantasy arising from Wroth's desire for women's autonomy and mutuality, while Schleiner sees its happy ending as a fantasy resolution of the unfulfilled love relationships of her relatives at the Court, namely, Philip Sidney, Mary Sidney, Elizabeth Countess of Rutland and Wroth herself. Although these arguments are stimulating, to look at the play as a representation of wish-fulfilling fantasies, that is, as something

basically unreal, undermines the importance of Wroth's presenting an alternative view of reality to that sponsored by the dominant ideologies of the time.

44. Carolyn Ruth Swift, "Feminine Identity in Lady Mary Wroth's Romance *Urania,*" *ELR* 14 (1984): 328–46; especially 336–37.

45. Lamb, 143.

46. Raymond Williams, *Marxism and Literature* (1977; reprint, Oxford: Oxford University Press, 1990), 121–27.

Fletcher versus "Fletcher"

Shoichiro Kawai

Fletcher versus Beaumont

In *The Pilgrim,* Fletcher's unaided work, the heroine Alinda is disguised as a boy with her face patched (3.3.75) and painted as if "horribly Sunburnt" (4.2.33).[1] Unlike Rosalind—her face smirched with "a kind of umber"—in *As You Like It* (1.3.112), Alinda finds her disguise unsatisfactory.[2] When she meets a man she knows, she pretends to have a pain in her back to make sure that he will not see her face:

> *Severto.* Look up, and be of good cheer.
> *Alinda.* O, I cannot. My back, my back, my back.
>
> > (3.3.40–41)

This is a Fletcherian way of using dramatic conventions. Fletcher buttresses them with a realistic perspective and maintains their traditional effect. In *The Pilgrim,* through the convention of disguise, the heroine's patient love is expressed: "Alinda in disguise" is a theatrical rendition of "Alinda in the struggle of love." She can reveal her love only at the climactic moment when she casts away her disguise and reveals her identity. Her patient love is requited when her lover succeeds in seeing through her disguise:

> *Alinda.* I have been miserable;
> But your most vertuous eyes have cur'd me, *Pedro:*
> Pray ye thinke it no immodesty, I kisse ye.
>
> > (3.7.153–55)

Thus the convention is used to build up a climax, at which a sugary love scene unfolds, with lovers embracing and kissing each other: "I will hang here eternally, kisse ever, / And weep away for joy" (159–60).

Compare this sentimental scene of Fletcher's with Beaumont's satirical love scene. In act 4, scene 5 of *Philaster,* the hero Philaster tries to kill his beloved princess, wrongly suspecting her of infidelity.[3] She gladly places herself before his sword, carried away with the beautiful image of eternal love:

> *Arethusa.*   If my fortune be so good to let me fall
> Upon thy hand, I shall have peace in death.
> Yet tell me this, there will be no slanders,
> No jealousy in the other world, no ill there?
> *Philaster.*   No.
> *Arethusa.*   Show me then the way.
> *Philaster.*   Then guide
> My feeble hand. . .
>
> (4.5.65–70)

At this point, a comical "Country Fellow" intrudes: "Hold, dastard, strike a woman?" With his intrusion, the scene instantaneously loses its heavenly "romantic" atmosphere and becomes a prosaic case of an attempted murder. Degraded from a star-crossed heroine to a mere woman, or a nameless victim of an assault, the princess is enraged: "What ill-bred man art thou, to intrude thyself / Upon our private sports, or recreations?" (4.5.89–90). She is so upset that she speaks out of the character of a tragic heroine and goes so far as to refer to their love affairs as "sports." Thus in an instant the romantic scene is destroyed by laughter. Such deliberate breach of literary decorum is one of Beaumont's favorite jokes, subverting a play world by mingling it with another play world. This technique is pervasive in Beaumont's *The Knight of the Burning Pestle,* in which characters continually speak out of their assigned roles, creating typical "'Beaumont' moments," as Philip J. Finkelpearl calls them.[4]

One may well wonder whether Fletcher and Beaumont are properly understood when some critics regard this typically Beaumontian scene as "a paradigm of Fletcherian dramaturgy,"[5] when Beaumont's pen is confirmed linguistically as well.[6] One of the problems with the recent studies of those fifty-two plays previously called "the Beaumont and Fletcher" plays is that they are now often called "the Fletcher plays," as if all the traits of Massinger, Beaumont, and other collaborators were assimilated in one "Fletcher."[7] This critical practice has continued for more than forty years. In 1952, for example, E. M. Waith uses the adjective "Fletcherian" as "a convenient shorthand term for what pertains to the several authors of the Beaumont and Fletcher plays."[8] This is followed by Clifford Leech's influential book, *The John Fletcher Plays* (1962), which emphasized Fletcher's dominance in the canon to such an extent that it hastily declares that we should use "Fletcher" alone.[9] Leech points out that the term "Beaumont and Fletcher" is inaccurate because Beaumont died early in Fletcher's career. This is true, but when he dismisses "Massinger and Webster and Ford, and others," referring to them as those who "may" have worked along with Fletcher, he is overlooking Massinger's outstanding contribution to the canon. After all, Massinger collaborated with Fletcher in eighteen works, while Beaumont and Fletcher worked in thirteen. Even Joseph W. Donohue Jr., who acutely explicates the significant influence of Fletcher's drama in the seventeenth and eighteenth centuries, unwittingly bases his argument on a loose generalization about the characteristics of "Fletcher."[10] Some critics are conscious of the problem and yet afraid of the danger of treading on the minefield of authorship, assuring themselves that it is futile to distinguish between pens in collaborative works. Although such argument cannot be totally negated, it does not follow that we can attribute the plays to a nonexistent "Fletcher" of multiple personality. This only hinders our appreciation of each dramatist and therefore of the plays.

There is a remarkable difference in Fletcher and Beaumont's dramatic techniques: the sarcastic Beaumont likes to ridicule dramatic conventions and deliberately let them drop to produce comic or satiric effects, while the sentimental Fletcher displays his skills in applying conventions to his drama. In Beaumont's share in *Love's Pilgrimage,* when Leocadia as a boy fears that her father will recognize her, Beaumont makes the hero Philippo comfort her, based on the disguise convention: "He cannot know you in this habit" (5.4.136). But immediately Beaumont smirks at an audience who believes him, making her father no sooner enter than recognize her: "what now? run / Out o' your sex? breech'd?" (5.4.144–45). Again, in Beaumont's act 2, scene 1 of *Beggars' Bush,* when young lord Hubert sees the disguised milkmaid "Minche" for the first time, he readily recognizes the face as his sweetheart Jaqueline's. "Ha? 'tis her face: come hither Maid" (2.1.183), says Hubert. He recognizes Gerrard, too, the protagonist's father, disguised as the beggars' king: "Here was another face too, that I mark'd / O' the old mans" (2.1.203–4).

Contrarily, in act 4, scene 2 of the same play, written by Fletcher, disguise remains a traditional device of obstructing recognition. This time Hubert loses the ease with which he saw through Jaqueline's disguise in Beaumont's scene and has to concentrate very hard to identify her. From his half-uncertain "this wench must be she" (4.2.3), Hubert tries to convince himself that he is seeing

Jaqueline in the milkmaid—"'Tis certaine she" (12), and again, "By heaven 'tis she" (18), until his final exultation, "Heaven curse me else; 'tis she" (37)—in the same manner as Pedro sees through Alinda's disguise in *The Pilgrim* (3.7.145–48). Jaqueline as "Minche" also has to see through Hubert's disguise as a huntsman and to reassure herself in the same manner: "'Tis certaine he" (14) and "'Tis he: it is my deare Love" (24). Effectively employing the traditional disguise convention, Fletcher makes the lovers deliberately delay their recognition and savour its joy in the hopeful mist of uncertainty, just as in the last scene of *Twelfth Night* Shakespeare makes Viola delay her recognition of her brother. In Fletcher, disguise functions not only as an impediment to the lovers' mutual recognition but also as a process through which they gradually reveal and confirm both their identity and their disguised passion. "I never saw ye," says Jaqueline, "But me-thinks ye kisse finely" (16–17). While they role-play as a milkmaid and a huntsman, he kisses her, courts her, and wins her. Through the process of taking off the disguise, they enhance and relive their love, pretending indifference. "How fain she would conceal her selfe? yet shew it" (24), says Hubert. The scene is typically Fletcherian in that it delicately demonstrates both the affectation and the passion of the lovers.

Lois Potter, analyzing disguise devices in the "Beaumont and Fletcher" plays, concludes that "dramatists can pick up or drop a dramatic device as needed."[11] Nevertheless, while Beaumont often drops devices so abruptly that the illusion of play-world is threatened, Fletcher preserves conventions in the same way Shakespeare does. Just as the bearded Falstaff's disguise as a woman miraculously works in *The Merry Wives of Windsor,* so does Tom's in *Monsieur Thomas:* Tom's friend Hylas promises to marry "her" although "her lips are monstrous rugged" because of "her" moustache (5.6.13). Beaumont, on the other hand, is too cynical to adopt such a ludicrous device. In Beaumont's scene in *The Noble Gentleman,* the bearded Jaques as a woman is recognized immediately despite the darkness: "*Jaques,* why *Jaques,* . . . Speake, thou bearded *Venus*" (4.5.66–68).

Perhaps it is also necessary to refer briefly to the dramatic technique of Massinger, Fletcher's most frequent collaborator. Since Robert Boyle and others have succinctly illustrated Massinger's techniques, here it will suffice to mention simply that Massinger is satiric, stagy, descriptive, and hyperbolic.[12] I shall give one example to demonstrate a difference between the conventional Fletcher and the satiric Massinger. In Massinger's share in *The*

Knight of Malta, Gomera the virtuous knight fights against Mount-ferrat the villain. Conventionally a villain is to be defeated even when a good one is old and weak. However, before Gomera triumphs, the villain's strumpet suddenly shoots him with a pistol and ridicules conventional combat with swords as "what these men so long / Stood fooling for" (4.4.21–22). This is very similar to Beaumont's satirical technique. Nevertheless, in recent studies of the "Beaumont and Fletcher" canon, there is little attempt to differentiate between Fletcher and his collaborators.

To distinguish between Fletcher and "Fletcher" is important not only to better understand the canon but also to solve the mystery of why Fletcher enjoyed a tremendous popularity in the seventeenth and the early eighteenth century. If Shakespeare's reputation today is inflated or overblown in any way, so was Fletcher's. Far from being the Bard's inferior collaborator as he is considered to be today, Fletcher was regarded as Shakespeare's equal if not superior.[13] The custom of bracketing of Fletcher's name with Shakespeare's lasted for hundred and fifty years.[14] John Denham says, in a commendatory verse to the first Beaumont and Fletcher Folio, that Fletcher, Jonson and Shakespeare formed a "Triumvirate of wit" (b1ᵛ). When Jonson said, "next himself, only Fletcher and Chapman could make a Mask," he meant Fletcher, not "Fletcher."[15] Today, on the other hand, critics dismiss such aesthetic criteria as if people in the seventeenth century were aesthetically retarded. It is high time, as Sandra Clark recently argues, that we historicize the discrepancy between the evaluation of Fletcher in his time and in ours.[16] In order to do so, it is imperative to reconsider Fletcherian dramaturgy to discover what might have caused such different responses from his time and ours. The remainder of this paper focuses strictly on this point.

Fletcher's Auditory Techniques

Perhaps the most important factor in Fletcher's dramatic techniques that deserves analysis is how he treats his audience. As one of "Ben's sons," Fletcher shares Jonson's attitude; he delights in mystifying and surprising his audience. Nevertheless, while Jonson seeks to fool the audience by concealing the female-page disguise up the last moment in *The Epicoene* (1609) and *The New Inn* (1629), Fletcher always gives out some clues, inducing the audience to suspect tricks in *Philaster* (1609), *The Maid's Tragedy* (c. 1610–11), *The Night Walker* (c. 1611), and *The Loyal Subject* (1618). The joy of Fletcher's drama is at times similar to that of detective stories. William Cartwright praises Fletcher's technique of mystification: "all stand wondring how / The thing will be until it is. . . / The whole designe . . . [is] such / That none can say he shewes or hides too much."[17] It must be added that Fletcher's audience is enticed not only to wonder but also to detect tricks and anticipate the final turn, to appreciate covert dramatic ironies. In other words, the audience enjoys the dramatist's clever manipulation of audience psychology rather than Jonsonian surprise ending.

Misunderstanding Fletcherian drama may occur when we attempt to reconstruct the drama without paying due attention to what is taken for granted in the performance but not fully recorded in the text. Music, for example, is an important element especially in Fletcher. Indeed, songs appear in all fifteen plays that were single-handedly penned by Fletcher. Out of fifty-two plays in the canon, only nine have no songs, but they often include instrumental music as an important part of the drama. Some, such as *The Prophetess* (1622) and *The Island Princess* (1621), are so musical that later they were remade as operatic plays.

Nevertheless, although words for songs are recorded in the text, little is known about how they were performed. As R. W. Ingram argues, "the direction for music on the printed page cannot properly be 'read'."[18] How is music employed in *The Chances,* Fletcher's unaided work? Act 4, scene 3 of the play is written with a special effect of music, but critics have failed to understand it and decided that the scene is flawed.[19] Buckingham and Garrick also missed the point and drastically changed the scene in their adaptations.[20] In fact, it is the most Fletcherian part of the play, the whole scene being a trick set deliberately for the audience. Before the scene in question, there is a preparatory scene in which an enigmatic lady Constantia sings "within" a house. That is to say, the audience hears her sing without seeing her. The audience must listen carefully; on stage servants of the house are suggesting that we should be all ears. "An admirable voice too, harke ye" (2.2.29), says one servant to another. This prepares for the trick in act 4, scene 3, in which again Constantia—or rather a woman who is supposed to be her—is heard to sing "within" a house. This time we have to decide whether it is really Constantia who sings, for she has disappeared and after much ado the characters finally find her hiding place—or so it seems. Now they gather around the house, trying to identify Constantia's voice. To intensify the moment, Fletcher freezes all the actors on stage. This is a crucial moment for the play; nobody moves. "Harke a voice too," says one of them, "Let's not stir yet by any means" (4.3.12–13). The scene is entirely motionless. Nothing visual attracts the audience's attention and naturally they concentrate on the singing voice, as Fletcher shrewdly calculates. It is imperative that the audience listen carefully to the song in order to discriminate between the two very similar singing voices, however alike boy actors' singing soprano may sound.[21] "Was this her own voyce?" asks one character. "Yes sure" answers another; they tempt the audience to misjudge. However, a sharp-eared audience will not be surprised when it turns out later that there are two Constantias—a lady and a strumpet with the same name. Fletcher keeps challenging the audience; immediately after the auditory trick, a visual one follows: on the upper-stage a woman appears wearing the same hood worn by the landlady who vanished with Constantia. If the audience is clever enough to think that this hood is counterfeit too, then it may congratulate itself for not being fooled like the characters in the play. A perceptive audience will not miss John the debauchee's seemingly irrelevant and insignificant aside in which he wonders why the music sexually arouses him—"what bloud have I now?" (4.3.32)—and will understand this joke when it turns out that the second song is sung by a prostitute. Finally it is revealed that "Constantia" in the house is a whore so named, and her bawd happens to wear the same hood as the landlady's. Unlike the reader, the audience bases its own expectation on what it has heard and seen, and by sharing the characters' experience, it understands the drama from their perspective, or even feels some superiority to see the characters on stage completely fooled. The whole point of this scene is lost to a reader, not only because the songs cannot be heard, but also because the hood trick is rendered ineffectual in the text: a stage direction, "*Enter* Bawd *(above)*" (4.3.25), is introduced at the very moment when she must be mistaken for the landlady. The reader is denied the opportunity to be held in suspense both auditorially and visually, which is quintessential in Fletcher's dramaturgy.

Fletcher's Visual Techniques

Much attention has been paid to Fletcher's auditory techniques—actors' declamation (Waith), sound effects (Lawrence), and music (Ingram).[22] They are elements illegible in the text. The same is true of visual effects. A simple direction like "*Enter* De-Gard," when he comes disguised as an eccentric lord in *The Wild-*

Goose Chase (3.1.376), "cannot properly be 'read'" either, for it does not clarify how this lord looks. Unlike the reader who is informed of the identity of the disguised, the audience has to watch as carefully as the characters in the play. Not that the audience is fooled by the disguise, but that, the more convincing the disguise is, the more the audience may enjoy discovering it, delighted at not being fooled by the trick, as in *The Chances* mentioned above. If De-Gard's disguise of the swaggering lord, with his face fully "umber'd, / And mask'd with patches" (3.1.436–37), is so elaborate and impenetrable, we can understand why Fletcher writes a lengthy dialogue between Lugier and Mirabell before De-Gard's entrance. "No Baites? No Fish-hooks, sir? No Gins? No Nooses? / No Pitfals to catch Puppies?" asks Mirabell repeatedly (3.1.364–65). The audience is alerted to a perfect disguise.

In the same play, when Lugier comes disguised in act 3, the Folio directs: "Enter Leverduce, des [i.e. alias] Lugier, Mr. Illiard [i.e. Hilliard Swanston]: (I2ᵛ). The purpose of naming Swanston the actor at this point is to emphasize, as Lawrence points out, "that Swanston was to come on in disguise and speak out of character."[23] Leverduce is not merely "Lugier disguised" but is to be presented as a different character on the stage. Although the direction cannot have been written by Fletcher, for the present text is for the 1632 revival after his death, it shows how acting a disguised part was regarded in 1632.

Unfortunately we can only guess how Swanston performed the disguised part. Like music and visual effects, the actor's characteristics, which were known to the contemporary audience, "cannot properly be 'read'" in the text. When Lylia-Bianca jokes upon the "fat-Fellow" who has "weight enough" in *The Wild-Goose Chase* (3.1.124), or when Lord Aubrey is referred to as "fat" and "corpulent" in *The Bloody Brother (Rollo, Duke of Normandy)* (4.2.235), we have to be reminded that the audience was familiar with the plump John Lowin, who played the parts.[24] Similarly, the popularity of John Shank the comedian, Robert Armin's successor, is taken for granted in *The Wild-Goose Chase*. What G. E. Bentley points out about Shank's role in John Clavell's comedy *The Soddered Citizen* is relevant here: "the audience was sufficiently interested in Shank to tolerate the reminder that the clown on the stage was not Hodge, the countryman of the play, but their old favourite, John Shank, comedian of the King's company."[25] In act 3, scene 1 of *The Wild-Goose Chase,* Shank as Lylia-Bianca's servant rushes in and warns Mirabell of a trick. Thanks to this, Mirabell is not tricked and instead ridicules those who tried to trick him.[26] For the reader, this turn of events may seem quite arbitrary; it looks as if the servant is introduced in the play merely as a plot mechanism. However, we should imagine how Shank played the part. He entered, holding his head and shouting to someone off-stage: "Nay, if I bear your blowes, and keep your councel, / You have good luck, Sir; I'll teach ye to strike lighter" (3.1.419–20). Too brief and insufficient though they may seem to the reader, these lines no doubt allowed the comedian to create a very funny scene, that of a servant beaten by his master and cursing him. Unlike the reader, the audience, amused by their favorite comedian, probably found it natural that the ruse be revealed to Mirabell in order only to dissipate Shank's—not the servant's—spleen. Because now it is impossible to appreciate the virtuosity of the original actors after three centuries and half, Taylor and Lowin's compliments to the reader in the Folio of *The Wild-Goose Chase* (1652) may sound a bit sarcastic: "Onely we wish, that you may have the same *kind Joy* in *Perusing* of it, as we had in the *Acting*" ([A]2ʳ).

The Conventional and Sentimental Fletcher

Fletcher's array of conventional devices is so stunning that his mastery of stage effects is often misconstrued as the main aim of his drama.[27] However, his rapid display of devices is only an expedient for building up dramatic tension to produce climactic moments. That Fletcher is actually indifferent to his various devices can be confirmed by the fact that the same devices are repeatedly adopted in various plays. For instance, a type of comic steward who worries about his prodigal master recurs again and again in Jaques in *The Noble Gentleman*, Pedro in *The Woman's Prize*, Savill in *The Scornful Lady*, and Lance in *Wit without Money*. The trick of Clorin's feigning wantonness to deceive a wooer in *The Faithful Shepherdess* is repeated by Honora in *The Loyal Subject*, Isabella in *Women Pleased*, and Florimel in *The Maid in the Mill*. Fletcher's devices such as supposed corpses jumping out of coffins and feigned invalids in bed are no more than clichés also found in other dramatists' plays. He casually snatches any conventional materials in order to create a new drama. In other words, Fletcher does not care which materials he uses; it is how these fabrics are woven into a play that counts. It is not surprising, therefore, that *The Wild-Goose Chase* is a remake of his own *The Woman's Prize, or The Tamer Tamed*, which itself is a sequel to Shakespeare's *The Taming of the Shrew*. Neither does it matter that *Wit without*

Money uses the same love intrigue as *Much Ado about Nothing.* In *Wit without Money,* Vallentine and the widow are tricked into marriage by others who spread false rumours that they love each other, just as Benedick and Beatrice are deceived in *Much Ado.* The widow's response—"they seeme grave fellowes, / They should not come to flout" (5.1.78–79)—reminds us of Benedick's speech: "I should think this a gull, but that the white-bearded fellow speaks it" (*Ado* 2.3.118–19). Vallentine's line—"In pitty, and in spite Ile marry thee" (5.4.73)—resembles Benedick's "I take thee for pity" (*Ado* 5.4.93). Fletcher is repeating these sequences in order to bring the play to the very moment he wants to make—the moment when the widow proposes to marry Vallentine under the pretence of accusing him: "Have not you married me, / And for this maine cause, now as you report it, / To be your Nurse?" (5.4.36–38). While Shakespeare's lovers admit their love openly in public, Fletcher's lovers never discard coy pretence till the end. "I must confesse I did a little favour you," the widow allures him, "And with some labour, might have beene perswaded" (5.4.40–41). This is Fletcherian play of love—always coy and pretentious. In brief, the tremendous display of dramatic devices is there, not simply because it is entertaining but also because it functions as a foil to sentimental climactic moments.

The Fletcherian war of the sexes *is* sentimental, notwithstanding Wallis's argument to the contrary.[28] In *The Scornful Lady,* the lady is overwhelmed by "griefe" (3.1.200) when she believes the news of her lover's death. Similarly, in *Monsieur Thomas,* when Thomas falls out of the window, Maria dashes out of the house and shows her love in spite of herself. Before they confess their true feelings, however, they swiftly resume their affected contempt when they realize that they have been tricked; immediately another sequence of tricks begins and all sentiments are obscured behind it. In the case of *The Wild-Goose Chase,* the heroine Oriana is not, as Appleton assumes, a "high-mettled" woman;[29] she is shy and reticent and her lines count less than one third of Lylia-Bianca's. Just as the maudlin Livia in *The Women's Prize* is helped by her friends, so Oriana, who weeps (2.1; 4.3), is guided by her friends. It is because of this helplessness of hers that both the audience and Mirabell feel pity and are almost deceived by her feigned sickness in bed.

> *Mirabell.* Oh fair teares; how ye take me.
> *Oriana.* Do you weep too? you have not lost your Lover?
>
> (4.3.76–77)

The couple weep. The renowned Joseph Taylor as Mirabell must have been able to shed a tear or two. If Taylor acted Mirabell's remorse convincingly, the audience might have suspected that the play was not a comedy after all but a tragi-comedy. As Marco Mincoff argues, "the essential effect of seventeenth-century tragi-comedy is pity, a sentimental pity that turns to rejoicing."[30] Apparently Fletcher intends the scene to be emotional, for he gives a warning similar to that against perfect disguises. "Take great heed," exclaims Bellure to Mirabell, "shee'll cheate thee" (4.3.107–9). But Mirabell, perfectly deceived by the trick, confesses his "repentant Love" (line 112). By this brief, sentimental moment, the audience can confirm that there is true affection concealed behind the characters' affectation.

Fletcher's Language

Fletcher is misconstrued in literary criticism when his language is considered to be the only component of his drama. His language may suffer from "the absence of essential poetry" and may be compared to "cut and slightly withered flowers stuck in the sand," as T. S. Eliot once said,[31] but the soul of his drama lies not in such "flowers"—gathered from the garden of the conventional art of rhetoric—but in his dramatic art of arranging those flowers. As is often pointed out, Eliot speaks about verses from a poet's perspective, and his influence has led critics to devaluate Beaumont and Fletcher's language, ignoring the range of their theatrical achievement. Some critics, however, accurately understand the significance of their theatrical language. Waith, among others, perceptively explains the characteristics of heroic speeches in Fletcherian tragedy: "The exact content of the speeches becomes less important the more the general intention is taken for granted, until only intensity of feeling counts."[32] In short, the virtue of their language lies in its ability to elevate passions rather than humanistic veracity. That is to say, the strength, the cadence, and the rhythm of the language are more important than its meanings. Fletcher's words are akin to melodies—each note has little meaning in itself, but taken together they express deep feelings. It is natural, therefore, that silence—set in deliberate contrast to rich language—has a deeply dramatic significance.

In act 2, scene 2 of *The Two Noble Kinsmen,* Fletcher deliberately repeats trite remarks on friendship over a hundred lines to prepare for a dramatic moment when the loquacious Palamon suddenly holds his tongue and looks away from Arcite. Arcite repeatedly asks Palamon to continue talking about friendship—"Speake on Sir" (2.2.117), "Pray forward" (line 122), and "Will ye goe forward Cosen?" (line 126)—but Palamon is frozen. There is a calculated dramatic irony here: in spite of their talk about friendship, they become rivals in love, and it begins with this silent moment when Palamon sees Emilia and is dazzled by her beauty. The mute Palamon keeps looking away from his 'friend' until the bewitching spell is temporarily broken:

> *Arcite.* Cosen, Cosen, how doe you Sir? *Why Palamon?*
> *Palamon.* Never till now I was in prison *Arcite.*
>
> (2.2.131-32)

the dramatic moment lies in his enchantment, contrasted by his seemingly eloquent lecture on friendship. We have to read between the lines and fill in the silent moment.

Throughout this paper I have emphasized that there are many elements that cannot properly be "read" in Fletcher. The same thing can be said of any dramatist, but in Fletcher's case, the drama is as pretentious and dissimulating as his characters are. We are requested to immerse ourselves in his calculated sophistication, to appreciate covert dramatic ironies. Thus Fletcher—less symbolic than Shakespeare, less satirical than Beaumont and Jonson, and less stagy than Massinger—composes his drama with pose, style, wit and *savoir-faire*. Fletcher's worth lies in his delineation of affected ladies and gentlemen and their love intrigues. In the age when theater aspired to imitate "Actions, such as might / And have been reall, and in such a phrase, / As men should speak in,"[33] it is natural that Fletcher was considered a champion.

Notes

1. Unless otherwise noted, quotations from the "Beaumont and Fletcher" canon refer to *The Dramatic Works in the Beaumont and Fletcher Canon*, gen. ed. Fredson Bowers, 10 vols. (Cambridge: Cambridge University Press, 1966–96).

2. Quotations from Shakespeare are from *The Riverside Shakespeare*, gen. ed. G. Blakemore Evans (Boston: Mifflin, 1974).

3. For this "famous moment in *Philaster*," see Nicholas F. Radel, "'Then thus I turne my language on you': The Transformation of Theatrical Language in *Philaster*," *Medieval & Renaissance Drama in England* 3 (1986): 129–47.

4. Philip J. Finkelpearl, "Beaumont, Fletcher, and 'Beaumont and Fletcher': Some Distinctions," *English Literary Renaissance* 1 (1971): 163. See also Finkelpearl, *Court and Country Politics in the Plays of Beaumont and Fletcher* (Princeton: Princeton University Press, 1990), 157–60.

5. Arthur Kirsch, "*Cymbeline* and Coterie Dramaturgy," *ELH* 34 (1967): 288–89.

6. The dramatists' shares in the "Beaumont and Fletcher" canon are based on Cyrus Hoy, "The Shares of Fletcher and His Collaborators in the Beaumont and Fletcher Canon (I)–(VII)," *Studies in Bibiography* 8 (1956): 129–46; 9 (1957): 143–55; 11 (1958): 85–99; 12 (1959): 91–116; 13 (1960): 77–108; 14 (1961): 45–68; 15 (1962): 71–90; and Bertha Hensman, *The Shares of Fletcher, Field and Massinger in Twelve Plays of the Beaumont and Fletcher Canon*, 2 vols., Jacobean Drama Studies, vol. 6 (Salzburg: Universität Salzburg, 1974). These works supersede E. H. C. Oliphant's *The Plays of Beaumont and Fletcher: An Attempt to Determine Their Respective Shares and the Shares of Others* (New Haven: Yale University Press, 1927).

7. The fifty-two plays refer to those fifty-two plays in the 1679 Folio plus *Henry VIII, Sir John van Olden Barnabelt*, and *A Very Woman*, minus Beaumont's *The Knight of the Burning Pestle*, Ford's *The Laws of Candy*, and Shirley's *The Coronation*.

8. Eugene M. Waith, *The Pattern of Tragicomedy in Beaumont and Fletcher* (New Haven: Yale University Press, 1952), 2.

9. Clifford Leech, *The John Fletcher Plays* (London: Chatto & Windus, 1962), 1–3.

10. Joseph W. Donohue, Jr., *Dramatic Character in the English Romantic Age* (Princeton: Princeton University Press, 1970), 24.

11. Lois Potter, "The Plays and the Playwrights: 1641–60" in *The Revels History of Drama in English*, 8 vols. (London: Methuen, 1975–83), 4: 282.

12. Robert Boyle, "Beaumont, Fletcher, and Massinger," *New Shakespeare Society's Transactions* 8 (1886): 585. See also Henri Jacob Makkink, *Philip Massinger and John Fletcher: A Comparison* (Rotterdam: Nijgh & Van Ditmar's Uitgevers-Mij, 1927); Baldwin Maxwell, *Studies in Beaumont, Fletcher, and Massinger* (Chapel Hill: The University of North Carolina Press, 1939); Frederick S. Boas, *An Introduction to Stuart Drama* (London: Oxford University Press, 1946); Henry W. Wells, *Elizabethan and Jacobean Playwrights*, 2nd ed. (Port Washington, New York: Kennikat Press, 1964).

13. William Cartwright declares that Shakespeare is "dull" compared to Fletcher in his commendatory verse in the First Folio (d2^v).

14. Some began to criticize the bracketing of Fletcher with Shakespeare around 1750. See Peter Whalley, *An Enquiry into the Learning of Shakespeare* (1748; reprinted, New York: AMS, 1970), 11; William Dodd, *The Beauties of Shakespear: Regularly Selected from each Play with a General Index Digesting them under Proper Heads*, 2 vols. (1752), reprinted in *Eighteenth Century Shakespeare*, gen. ed. Arthur Freeman, nos. 8 and 9 (London: Frank Cass, 1971), 8: xix.

15. Quoted from "Ben Jonson's Conversations with William Drummond of Hawthornden," in C. H. Herford and Percy and Evelyn Simpson eds., *Ben Jonson*, 11 vols. (Oxford: Clarendon, 1925–53), 1: 133.

16. Sandra Clark, *The Plays of Beaumont and Fletcher: Sexual Themes and Dramatic Representation* (London: Harvester, 1994), 2–10.

17. The First Folio, d2^r. See also James Shirley and Thomas Palmer's eulogies (A4^v and f2^v).

18. R. W. Ingram, "Patterns of Music and Action in Fletcherian Drama," in *Music in English Renaissance Drama*, ed. John H. Long (Lexington: University of Kentucky Press, 1968), 94.

19. See Arthur Colby Sprague, *Beaumont and Fletcher on the Restoration Stage* (Cambridge: Harvard University Press, 1926; reprint, New York: Benjamin Blom, 1965), 222 and John Harold Wilson, *The Influence of Beaumont and Fletcher on Restoration Drama* (Columbus: The Ohio State University Press, 1928), 48.

20. George Villiers Second Duke of Buckingham, *The Chances* (London, 1667); David Garrick, *The Chances* (1754), in *The Plays of David Garrick,* 7 vols. (Carbondale: Southern Illinois University Press, 1980–82), vol. 6.

21. There is a possibility that the second song is sung by the same boy actor who played Constantia to fool the audience completely, but this is very unlikely for Fletcher, who constantly gives clues to the audience and challenges it to discern them.

22. Waith, 86–98; William J. Lawrence, *Pre-Restoration Stage Studies* (Cambridge: Harvard University Press, 1927), 204–5, 211–19. As for music, see also Edwin S. Lindsey, "The Music of the Songs in Fletcher's Plays," *Studies in Philology* 21 (1924): 325–55.

23. Lawrence, 391.

24. *The Bloody Brother: A Tragedy by John Fletcher and Nathan Field (circa 1616–17) and Refurbished by Philip Massinger (circa 1630) as "Rollo, Duke of Normandy,"* ed. Bertha Hensman (New York: Vantage, 1991).

25. G. E. Bentley, *The Jacobean and Caroline Stage,* 7 vols. (Oxford: Clarendon, 1941–68), 2: 563–64.

26. Shank played Lylia-Bianca's servant in the 1632 revival of *The Wild-Goose Chase,* which was, in all probability, his part in the first production. Shank is wrongly assigned to the role of Petella in T. W. Baldwin, *The Organization and Personnel of the Shakespearean Company* (Princeton: Princeton University Press, 1927), 176 and Bentley 2: 562–63. See Bowers's "Textual Notes" to his edition, 6: 336.

27. See L. C. Knights, *Drama and Society in the Age of Jonson* (London: Chatto and Windus, 1937), 297; Kathleen M. Lynch, *The Social Mode of Restoration Comedy* (New York: Macmillan, 1926), 20; G. C. Macaulay, "Beaumont and Fletcher" in *Cambridge History of English Literature,* eds. A. W. Ward and A. R. Waller, 15 vols. (Cambridge: Cambridge University Press, 1907–27), 6: 121.

28. Lawrence B. Wallis, *Fletcher, Beaumont & Company: Entertainers to the Jacobean Gentry* (New York: King's Crown Press, 1947), 29.

29. William W. Appleton, *Beaumont and Fletcher: A Critical Study* (London: George Allen & Unwin, 1956), 105.

30. Marco Mincoff, "*The Faithful Shepherdess:* A Fletcherian Experiment," *Renaissance Drama* 9 (1966): 174.

31. T. S. Eliot, *Selected Essays* (London: Faber, 1932), 155.

32. Waith, 128. Waith's argument is based on Moody Prior's that Beaumont and Fletcher's language "becomes largely the instrument for the expression of passion." See Prior, *The Language of Tragedy* (New York: Columbia University Press, 1947), 100.

33. Henry Glapthrone, *The Ladies Privilege* (1637), A3[v].

The Primacy of the Sense of the Body over the Sense of the Line: David Garrick's Acting of Shakespeare

MANABU NODA

Introduction

SIMON McBurney, the artistic director of a British theater company named *Theatre de Complicité,* talked about the modern perception of time during a post-performance talk to a mainly Japanese audience.[1] Although his talk was not recorded, I will summarize the part of his talk which is relevant to this essay, since I worked as his interpreter not only during his talk but throughout the five-day workshop he conducted with Japanese actors and actresses between performances. One of the points he made was this: in this highly capitalistic, highly consumerist age, our consciousness is mainly focused either on the near past or the near future. An object of desire belongs to the near future insofar as we see it only as a commodity to be purchased, whereas the process of labor to earn the required amount of money is immediately sent off by our consciousness to the realm of the near past, since our main concern is whether we have earned enough money for the target commodity. The purchased commodity, again, is quickly thrown into the near past when something else draws our attention. What is obviously lacking in this short cycle of desiring, earning, and buying is a sense of the "here and now." TV and cinema are suitable for this mode of temporal perception, because the narrative structure dominant in the two genres is designed to keep the viewer in suspense, making him incessantly inquire what will happen next. Therefore, the main concern of *Theatre de Complicité* is, as the company's name suggests, to reinstate theater as a privileged medium for evoking a sense of immediacy and recreating the audience's desire for the present by negotiating a sense of complicity between the viewers and the actors.

180

Before continuing, we should note that the simplicity of McBurney's argument is deceiving. McBurney is not the kind of optimist who believes in the discourse-free sharing of any given experience. In answering a question from a member of the audience (the question was whether Paul Claudel was as "universal" as Kabuki), he acknowledged the problematic nature of the concept of universality. He tentatively suggested, however, that, after essentialization through efforts to uncover the layers of cultural and ideological contexts, there remains something for which the word "universal" appears to be the only possible description. This, I think, is a totally viable working hypothesis for any artist who tries to reach as many people as possible who are culturally and ideologically diverse. Far from acquiescing in the exploitation of relations to impose Eurocentered cultural imperialism on the audience, McBurney did not pretend to hide the element of *bricolage* inherent in the process of creating their shows—they make use of whatever is at hand to establish an effective rapport between the stage and the audience. Hence complicity: it is inevitably provisional in nature. The working out of this hypothesis, as he is fully aware, requires the act of *bricolage* on the part of every accomplice in the theatre. The notion of complicity itself implies a shared act of *bricolage*.

Any form of cultural or social appropriation of the past has an element of bricolage, and Garrick's "contemporization" of Shakespeare is not an exception. The eighteenth century saw in Garrick's acting a perfect way to explain a discourse which was widely shared in the period—the primacy of the body over the mind. The agent of the act of *bricolage* here is not Garrick so much as his contemporaries. Garrick served as a point of endorsement for so many assumptions of the period concerning human nature, the mode of the ideal human behavior, and the structure and functions of the human body. How those premises found their "proofs" in Garrick's acting, how in people's eyes Garrick appeared to epitomize them, is the question this essay attempts to answer. While the eighteenth century saw the rise of character criticism in the field of Shakespeare studies, that character and its psychology were discussed very much in terms of the body. We would miss this physical and physiological aspect if we saw the eighteenth-century criticism on Shakespeare only as a preliminary process for the Romantic psychologizing of Shakespeare, the best example of which perhaps is Samuel Taylor Coleridge. Garrick's acting and its perception by his contemporaries were much more physical. Garrick not only made Shakespeare a contemporary to his audi-

ence, but he also "con-temporized" the audience through Shakespeare in the sense that they physically shared the sense of
McBurney's "here and now" which the character played by Garrick was undergoing.

The Sense of the Present Meeting the Sense of Physical Presence

McBurney's talk helps clarify the two levels of the idea of contemporaneity with regard to David Garrick's acting and the way it
was perceived by his audience. The first level of contemporaneity is
that of cultural appropriation which occurred when Garrick made
Shakespeare contemporary to his audience through his acting.
Praise for Garrick proliferated in private correspondence as well
as in the public press. He was thought to be the champion of Shakespeare, shedding new light upon the obscure parts of the Bard's
texts. Through him the past emerged in the present in a more
intelligible form. His acting was thought to be a much better commentary on Shakespeare than any editor or critic could give.[2] It
would be impossible, however, to gauge the importance of Garrick's acting if we concentrated only on the revolutionary nature
of his acting. What is more important is that Garrick's rise attests
to the existence of the body-over-mind discourse which he drew
on, and which also served as the receptacle for the audience's
perception of his acting. Garrick contemporized Shakespeare in
that he epitomized that discourse of the period through Shakespeare, his acting, and his body. It was a premise which the audience rediscovered and reconfirmed through observing his acting.
In France the association between sensibility and morality was
even greater. Sensibility was regarded as tantamount to the ethical
capacity in the eighteenth century. According to Arthur Wilson,
the century was "two ages in one": it was "more obviously, at least
to text-book writers, the Age of Reason but no less, the Age of
Sensibility":

> "The language of the heart is universal", said La Rochefoucauld. "One
> needs only sensibility to understand and speak it." The Eighteenth
> century at first neglected to listen; but in the latter half of the century
> it made amends, until, at last, only the dulcet accent of emotion, for
> which sensibility was the interpreter, was esteemed.[3]

In this scene, Garrick's body provided an arena where an act of
discursive complicity between the actor and the audience was es-

tablished. In his body people not only found "proofs" for the premises they upheld; they also found in it a good opportunity to prove
their moral capacities.

This level of contemporaneity will reveal itself more as we examine the second level of Garrick's acting—the level concerning the
sense of the present shared by the audience. In the course of the
eighteenth century, there was a shift of emphasis in dramaturgy.
Joseph W. Donohue, Jr. argues that from Fletcherian drama on
there was a tendency to move away "from the objective presentation of actions on the stage toward a more subjective presentation
of their antecedents." That is to say that, in the revelation of dramatic character, the point of emphasis shifted gradually from action
to reaction:

> Plays of this sort have a structure based on a series of circumstances
> and events unconnected by a strict logic of causality (or Aristotelian
> "action"); their situations are deliberately brought out of the blue for
> the purpose of displaying human reactions to extreme and unexpected
> occurrences. In these plays the intelligible unit is not the thematic part,
> placed within a coherent series of other parts, but . . . the scene, which
> exists in effect for its own sake.[4]

This fading away of the Aristotelian "strict logic of causality" was
embedded in the skeptic empiricism of the eighteenth century. One
of its implications is that man is surrounded by an unpredictable
world which ultimately resists objective recognition. This skeptical
attitude, if pushed to the extreme, clearly shows its connection
with the dramaturgical structure. It exploits the theatricality of
scenes at the risk of disjoining the logical coherence of dramatic
action, since the structure tends towards a series of unconnected
incidents, each of them made as sensational as possible. Writing
on what he regarded as a deplorable state of the theatre, Oliver
Goldsmith makes one player in *The Vicar of Wakefield* criticize
the state of the stage: "It is not the composition of the piece, but
the number of starts and attitudes that may be introduced into it
that elicits applause."[5] The protagonist of his age had every reason
to exhibit starts and "attitudes," which means a frozen posture
expressive of strong emotion. To the eyes of the protagonist, the
world he is thrown into—the world of unpredictable incidents unconnected to each other—appears quite inscrutable. Consequently,
he cannot but entertain a feeling that he is always living in the
eternal present which is disconnected from the past and the future.
Where moments are not connected but only conjoined, it is impossible to enjoy a linear concept of time, in which the present neatly

sinks into the past as the future comes in—the future, rather, barges in. This view of the structure of time strongly recalls Hume, according to whom causation is not actually a purely logical matter but rather a geographical one: "whatever objects are consider'd as causes or effects, are contiguous."[6] There is no consistent time line here.

When the sense of the line is so violated, the immediate sense of the body prevails. The thrill and sensation that this eternal present causes enable the actor and the audience to share a strong sense of the present. The present is singled out of the time line, and the character is forced to live the present by letting his sensibility control his *ex tempore* (re)action. The sharing of temporal perception involved sharing a strong sense of the present time—McBurney's "here and now." The sense of the present here also implies the sense of physical presence. The audience saw in Garrick the ideal body-machine at work; his body epitomized the physiological notion of sensibility. Almost all the acting and elocution handbooks of the period endorsed the importance of sensibility as the source of good acting. It was broadly believed that, as a comprehensive faculty which governs the whole process of stimulus reception and its expression, sensibility enables the actor to feel the passions of the role, enter into it, and finally display it on stage with utmost truthfulness and sincerity.[7] Therefore, a good actor's body, being extremely sensitive to the stimuli from the exterior world, should respond quickly and forcefully. With his quick turns and agile transitions from one passion to another, Garrick showed how the dramatic body—the body of sensibility—performs its functions in the world of empirical skepticism.

The supremacy of sensibility in acting was embedded in philosophical and physiological debates from Descartes on. Descartes not only established *cogito* as the starting point of the modern mind; he also presented the image of a mechanized body which could eclipse the superiority of the mind. Descartes' machine-soul dualism was so influential that it provided a model for those physiologists and philosophers who followed to work on after the Restoration and throughout the eighteenth century:

> Though the concept of animal spirits has ancient roots, Descartes divested it of its magical properties and integrated it into a physical system of force and matter. He deflected subsequent practitioners by radically streamlining the model of the relation of mind and body.[8]

One of the "deflected" was Thomas Willis, an anatomist who identified the soul with the brain. Willis thought of the brain as being totally dependent for its functions on the working of the nerves. John Locke, who was himself a physician after studying under Willis in Oxford, incorporated Willis's theory into the science of man by publishing *An Essay concerning Human Understanding* (1689). Therefore, Locke's philosophy and the eighteenth-century empiricism which followed inevitably have mechanistic, and even materialistic implications. Neurology, with all its mechanistic tones, was vulgarized and appropriated during this period, becoming by Garrick's time a "national, even European or universal, common knowledge."[9]

In accordance with the dramaturgical shift from action to reaction, the style of acting in the eighteenth century came to emphasize the exhibition of desperate responses to assaulting stimuli. The grandiose declamation of pre-Garrick actors such as Colley Cibber or James Quin was too slow to cope with the dramaturgy full of unforeseen incidents and *ex tempore* reactions from the protagonist. Hence the shift from declamation to gesture, for which Garrick was greatly responsible.[10] Garrick's self-esteem as the flagbearer of theatrical innovation is obvious when he writes to the Countess of Burlington that the "Notions of Acting" are so different between him and the Cibbers that "If he is right I am, & ever shall be in yᵉ wrong road."[11] Compared with the declamatory style of the Cibbers, Garrick's style put much heavier emphasis on the physical. In its affective power, the physical was much stronger than the verbal. Georg Christoph Lichtenberg's description of Garrick's "Hamlet start" at the appearance of Father Hamlet's ghost is not only a good account of Garrick's physical style of acting; it also attests to the immense affective power of his acting:

> Garrick turns sharply and at the same moment staggers back two or three paces with his knees giving way under him; his hat falls to the ground and both his arms, especially the left, are stretched out nearly to their full length, with the hands as high as his head, the right arm more bent and the hand lower, and the fingers apart; his mouth is open; thus he stands rooted to the spot, with the legs apart, but no loss of dignity . . . His whole demeanour is so expressive of terror that it made my flesh creep even before he began to speak. The almost terror-struck silence of the audience, which preceded this appearance and filled one with a sense of insecurity, probably did much to enhance this effect.[12]

For Lichtenberg, who was Professor of Experimental Physics at the University of Göttingen, Garrick's acting was a perfect example of how the body should react in the moment of strong shock and terror, so much so that he was physically shaken, like the rest of the audience, by Garrick's acting. This physical delineation affected the audience physically, since the well-wrought representation of passions was thought to affect the hearts of those who saw it: "if the passions were eloquent, the just images of passions in art were hardly less so . . . any true imitation of a passion was by definition 'pathetical'."[13] It would naturally follow that the sense of the passionate present which was expressed through Garrick's body was physically shared by the audience. It appeared very much like a congregation of a Nonconformist church:

> Whitefield's oratorical "pathos," his ability to get his congregation sobbing, was admired by Garrick. Implementing very similar techniques in the theatre now aiming to reform its audience by making them weep, Garrick invoked similar responses.[14]

Just as the sight of audience physically shaken by the sermons of George Whitefield not only proved his oratorical power and the measure of his audience's devotion, so the sight of sobbing audience in Garrick's Drury Lane Theatre was the ideal mode of audience response. It is also important to note that to be able to freely display emotions was highly appreciated. Those who believed that they were endowed with exquisite sensibility untiringly boasted of this gift, thus incorporating the idea of sensibility in the debate on taste. Good taste here is a faculty which makes it possible not so much to judge as to feel beauty. Taste was not so much mental as physical. In *Letters concerning Taste* (1755), John Gilbert Cooper describes good taste:

> A *good* TASTE is that instantaneous Glow of Pleasure which thrills thro' our whole Frame, and seizes upon the Applause of the Heart, before the intellectual Power, Reason, can descend from the Throne of the mind to ratify it's Approbation, either when we receive into the Soul beautiful Images thro' the Organs of bodily Senses; or the Decorum of an amiable Character thro' the Faculties of moral Perception; or when we recall, by the imitative Arts, both of them thro' the intermediate Power of the Imagination.[15]

Since the efficacy of sensibility was basically determined by the make-up of the body, people tried hard to display their emotions openly in order to show that they were physically gifted, because in terms of sensibility, to be physically gifted also meant being morally advanced. The lack of sensibility meant moral deficiency due to a lack of sympathy. Therefore, to see a just delineation of passions on the stage and still remain unmoved was regarded as something to be ashamed of. If there was any element of complicity, whether intentional or unintentional, in the theater of Garrick, this social discourse played a great part of forming it.

The Sense of the Body Overriding the Sense of the Line

As the front runner of modernization in the mid-eighteenth-century theater, not only in London but also in Europe as a whole, David Garrick received his share of criticism. One criticism was that he ignored the grammatical construction of his lines in speaking them. The best known instance of this criticism appears in Sterne's *Tristram Shandy:*

And how did *Garrick* speak the soliloquy last night?—Oh, against all rule, my Lord,—most ungrammatically! betwixt the substantive and the adjective, which should agree together in *number, case* and *gender,* he made a breach thus,—stopping, as if the point wanted settling;— and betwixt the normative case, which your lordship knows should govern the verb, he suspended his voice in the epilogue a dozen times, three seconds and three fifths by a stop-watch, my Lord, each time.— Admirable grammarian![16]

This criticism was a far cry from that of the old guard, the admirers of the old declamatory style of acting. However, Sterne himself was not on the side of the old guard. In the manner which best suited this astute satirist of the age, he lost no time in rebuking the critic. Being asked whether, in suspending his voice, Garrick made any "expression of attitude or countenance to fill up the chasm," the critic confessed to his rather quaint way of enjoying a performance: "I look'd only at the stop-watch, my Lord."[17]

Garrick's acting did not make sense unless it was watched. In Sterne's eyes Garrick's acting was "some magick" released "feel-ingly," with the vibrations of "every Fibre about your heart."[18] With this almost excessive power of gestural representation, Gar-rick's emotional appeal "was also linked to a subversion of lan-guage and a diminution of the deepest of traditional aesthetic standards, characteristics of sentimental fiction and of cognate evangelical theology."[19]

Garrick was fully aware of this sort of criticism. In one of his letters he frankly admitted, "I have been frequently abus'd by ye Gentlemen of ye Pen for false Stops."[20] When he wrote this he had in mind Thomas Fitzpatrick, whose *An Enquiry into the Real Merit of a Certain Popular Performer* (1760) recorded twenty alleged inaccuracies which Garrick was accused of making. On occasion his attempts at justification appear in his correspondence. Of the letters of this prolific correspondent only a small portion is extant, but it is indeed only in these letters that Garrick, who was never keen to theorize his method, bothered to explain and defend his acting. In one letter he justifies the way he spoke Hamlet's line:

> *I think it was to See—my Mother's Wedding.* I certainly never *stop* there, (that is, close yᵉ Sense) but I as certainly, *Suspend* my Voice, by which Your Ear must know, that yᵉ Sense is suspended too, for Hamlet's Grief causes yᵉ break & with a Sigh, he finishes yᵉ Sentence— *my Mother's Wedding.*[21]

It was a common practice to defend the theatrical pause as being a suspension, not a stop, and Garrick here is only following that line. The use of suspension, a well established concept in rhetoric and elocution of the period, is allowed only when the effect overrides the harm done by grammatical violation. Thomas Sheridan, the father of Richard Brinsley Sheridan, was a very influential elocutionist in eighteenth-century Britain. Garrick is on the subscription list of Sheridan's *A Course of Lectures on Elocution* (1762). The passage in this book concerning the effective use of pauses specifies that rhetorical pauses be employed cautiously because they are an irregular means of impressing the audience. Where grammatical construction does not seem to admit the insertion of a pause, the "liberty is to be used with great caution" because "pauses of this sort put the mind into a state of suspense, which is ever attended with an uneasy sensation." The tone should be carefully chosen so that "the hearer will have notice that the sentence is not closed, and his attention is only suspended, without perplexing his understanding."[22]

However, further in the letter where he justifies his delivery in the role of Hamlet, it becomes evident that the actor is trying to explain this suspension in terms of his corporeal mechanism rather than in elocutionary terms: "I really could not from my feelings act it otherwise; & were I to have ye Pleasure of talking this Matter over with You, I flatter myself, that I could make You, by various Examples, feel the truth of my Position."[23] The workings of his body-machine cause the pause in this line. Insofar as the make-up of the body is determined by nature, to follow the workings of his body, i.e. to follow his sensibility, is a totally justifiable act of sincerity. He is, then, just following nature. The sense of the body, therefore, overrides the sense of the line he utters.

Garrick himself would choose to show rather than to tell if it were possible. The artist Francis Hayman asked for Garrick's opinion on his plates which eventually appeared in Sir Thomas Hanmer's *Shakespeare's Works* in six volumes, second edition (1771).[24] In a letter addressed to Hayman, Garrick described what he thought to be the most appropriate postures and facial expressions for his friend's plates. The scene to be engraved was the discovery of Iago's calumnious plot (*Othello,* act 5, scene 2). Garrick's delineation of corporeal expressions is interesting in itself, but much more so is the fact that Garrick twice promised Hayman to give a better delineation by physical demonstration:

> Othello (y[e] Principal) upon y[e] right hand (I believe) must be thunder struck with Horror, his Whole figure extended, wth his Eyes turn'd up to Heav'n & his Frame sinking, as it were at Emilia's Discovery. I shall better make you conceive My Notion of this Attitude & Expression when I see You. . . . Iago on y[e] left hand should express the greatest perturbation of Mind, I should Shrink up his Body, at y[e] opening of his Villany, with his eyes looking askance (as Milton terms it) on Othello, & gnawing his Lip in anger at his Wife; but this likewise will be describ'd better by giving you the Expression when I see You.[25]

Obviously, the simplest explication for this is that, between an actor and a painter/engraver, pictorial demonstration is a much more convenient means of communication than language. It is also important to note, however, that the physical features given in this letter are clearly made to correspond with specific passions. eighteenth-century Neoclassicism viewed gestural representation as articulate as language. The idea of the unity of appearance as a variant of the norm of decorum requires the coherence of corporeal signs—the body and the voice—to language. Passions were the referents according to which lines were to be articulated. It was a corollary of the age that the main task of the stage was to represent passion. Therefore, if corporeal signs should be concordant with linguistic signs, the posture and movement of the body, as well as vocal tone, should be articulated. The more the body articulates, the more closely it approaches the state of language. It was just another form of *ut pictura poesis:* "The art of the actor here stands midway between the plastic arts and poetry," said none other than Lessing.[26]

The way Garrick saw his own acting was shared by the audience. The physiological aspect came before the individualization of the

character, since that aspect was supposed to be basically the same
with all human beings though it might vary in its efficacy. One
good example can be seen in Roger Pickering's analysis of Garrick's Richard III in the tent scene:

> that Monster in Blood and excessive Villany, wakes in all the Terrors
> of an Imagination distracted by conscious Guilt.
>   *Rich.*   Give me a Horse—bind up my Wounds!
> *[the mark of a pause] Have Mercy, Heav'n![27]

It is interesting that soon after this comment, Pickering gives a
physiological explanation to the pause before he goes on to the
appropriateness of Garrick's acting in terms of the individual character of Richard III:

> A man, awaken'd in *Surprize,* requires *Time* to recover himself for
> coherent Speech: One, awaken'd in *Terror,* more; because Terror re-
> tards the Motion of the Blood, and the Flow of Animal Spirits is
> check'd, in Proportion. Were it for no other Reasons, a PAUSE at the
> End of the first Line is *necessary,* according to the *usual* Affection of
> Nature upon *such* Occasion.
>   But, to bring a remorseless Wretch to Feeling, and from *Feeling*
> to *Pray,* requires a PAUSE *indeed.* Exquisitely just and beautiful is
> SHAKESPEARE'S *Expression;* exquisitely just and beautiful is GAR-
> RICK'S *Action,* in so small a *Compass*![28]

Richard III as a specimen of human beings in general comes before
the Richard III as an individual, although it is arguable that this
individuality ("a remorseless Wretch") is a product of somewhat
crude generic thinking. Pickering believed that, just as Garrick felt
when he played Hamlet, Richard III could not "from his feelings"
act otherwise. The pause which Garrick inserted was believed to
be explicable, it for no other reason, as a natural consequence of
the actor with sufficient sensibility and power of emotional identi-
fication following the dictates of his body. Pickering was talking in
physical terms just as Garrick did.

The highly stylized representation of passions in the eighteenth
century must be viewed in the context which was shared both by
actors and viewers. At bottom is the general idea of man: an ideal-
ized human body which has a proper anatomical structure with all
the "natural" functions. Individual variation comes only after this.
This context explains the broad reception of the painter Charles
Le Brun's iconography of passions in his *Conférence . . . sur l'expression générale et particulière* (Paris and Amsterdam: 1698),[29]

which heavily draws upon Descartes's formulation of passions in *Les Passions de l'âme* (The Passions of the Soul) (1649). In the introduction, Le Brun explains passion, "a Motion of the Soul," according to the Cartesian physiology of machine-soul dualism. The "extremities of the Nerves" receive stimuli from outside, after which the sensation is transmitted by "a certain subtil air or spirit" to the brain through "the nerves" which have "Channels, or Pipes" for the spirit to go through. Then the process travels back to the muscles to form facial expressions.[30] The powerful influence which Le Brun's formulation exerted on the theories of acting—a pedagogical version in English was published as late as 1863—would be unintelligible without a broad understanding in the period that Le Brun's iconography was based upon "human nature," i.e., the physiological structure and workings of the human body.[31]

There is another context that worked in tandem with this physiological thinking of the period in putting the body before language. As a system of signs, language, with its arbitrariness and articulation, was deemed to be the remotest from the object to be represented, while gestural representation, being visual rather than verbal, was thought to be more immediate to passions.[32] One thing that we should always bear in mind when considering the representation of passion in the eighteenth century is that passion, as an object of representation, does not have a visual quality. Hume admits that "we can never pretend to know body otherwise than by those external properties, which discover themselves to the senses."[33] It lends itself to perception only when it is represented either visually or verbally. Joseph Addison employed visual resemblance as the fundamental means by which to measure the distance between the signifier and the signified, but it does not apply to the representation of passions.[34] As long as it remains in the domain of the visual, resemblance cannot be applied to the representation of passions as a measure of fidelity of the representation to the represented. In the physiological context of the eighteenth century, passions are ultimately the motion inside the body, or different modes of vibrations in the nerves.[35] It is nonsensical to compare a certain mode of nerve vibration with its representation, whether it is visual or verbal, and say the representation visually resembles the original object. Consequently, the boundary between passions and their physical representations became more and more blurred. If muscles move due to the functions of the nerves, and if passions are only the result of nerve vibration inside the body, there is only a small step to the point where one can say that passions are nothing other than the way the body reacts. The movement of bodily organs, therefore, can affect the mind and create passions. Pretension can turn into real passion. This possibility came to be suggested more and more often in the latter half of the century until at the beginning of the nineteenth century it saw a clearer form in the words of Charles Bell:

> It is a fundamental law of our nature that the mind shall have its powers developed through the influence of the body; that the organs of the body shall be the links in the certain chain of relation between it and the material world, through which the immaterial principle within shall be effected.[36]

Considering the closeness—even possible overlap—between passions and the body, it is no wonder that the body should express passions before words. Hume says that as far as violent passions are concerned, "Actions are, indeed, better indications of a character than words."[37] The immediacy of gesture before language is reflected in the way the verbal follows the visual in the representation of passions. Linguistic signification is arbitrary, whereas the physical signification is built into the body and is, therefore, universal. Louis de Cahusac, an eminent playwright and opera librettist, makes clear the primacy and universality of gesture as part of the corporeal, primitive means of expression at the beginning of his article "Geste" in Diderot-D'Alembert's *Encyclopédie*. The movement of the body and the countenance, according to his explanation, is "one of the primary expressions of sentiment, the expressions given to man by nature." Therefore, "gesture is and will always be the language of all the nations." Then he gives a piece of advice on acting, which is that gesture should always precede speech, because "gesture is much more prompt": speech needs some moments to take form and to strike the ear; gesture which sensibility makes quick, always starts at the very moment when the soul experiences the emotion.[38]

By foregrounding gesture, Garrick's new style of acting gave scope to a more agile expression of passions. His delineation of passions was regarded as true to life precisely because it was quick. The pauses which he inserted in his lines occurred at moments when his body took over his mind. And with his super-quick turns and transitions, he acted out the picture of the man who desperately responds to stimuli from the outside world which ultimately refuses any attempts at objective comprehension.

Garrick's Body: Where Fashionable Ideas Meet

In his *An Essay on Acting* (1744), Garrick half-jokingly gives his own definition of acting:

> ACTING is an *Entertainment of the Stage*, which by calling in the Aid and Assistance of *Articulation, Corporeal* Motion, and *Occular Expression, imitates, assumes,* or *puts on* the various *mental* and *bodily Emotions* arising from the various Humours, Virtues and Vices, incident to human Nature.[39]

This tongue-in-cheek passage still manages to convey Garrick's view of his own profession. "Occular Expression" suggests that Garrick himself was confident in the expressiveness of his eyes, while "bodily Emotion" clearly reflects the mechanistic view of the body which was prevalent in his era. Later in his *Essay,* where Garrick stresses the importance of close observation, he equates human nature with the internal workings of the human body:

> THE only Way to arrive at *great Excellency* in *Character* of *Humour,* is to be very conversant with *Human Nature,* that is the noblest and best Study, by this Way you will more accurately discover the *Workings of Spirit* (or what other Physical Term you please to call it) upon the different *Modifications* of *Matter.*[40]

Garrick, like any of his contemporaries, was quick to appropriate dominant social, cultural, and scientific discourses into his own vocabulary. His famous letter to Sturz in 1769, in which he criticizes the French actress Clairon, is also a good example of how he includes the then fashionable concepts in his formulation of ideas:

> But then I fear . . . the Heart has none of those instantaneous feelings, that Life blood, that keen Sensibility, that bursts at once from Genius, and like Electrical fire shoots thro' the Veins, Marrow, Bones and all, of every Spectator.—Mad^m *Clairon* is so conscious and certain of what she can do, that she never (I believe) had the feelings of the instant come upon her unexpectedly.[41]

All the key words of his era are there: sensibility, genius, anatomical terms, and the intense sense of the present: "the feelings of the instant come upon her unexpectedly." It is at those intense moments when the genius actor's body-machine starts to operate with full force. The twenty-five years which passed between his *Essay* and this letter to Sturz is reflected in the disappearance of "humours" and the introduction of the then fashionable concept of "electricity." Garrick's body was the meeting point of those important ideas of his age. Not only did his audience note those ideas in his acting but Garrick himself fully exploited those ideas in formulating the image of his own profession. He picked those fashionable ideas, though in vulgarized forms, to assess the image of himself as an actor who was fully aware that he somehow was the embodiment of sensibility.

This is an act of *bricolage*, because Garrick is trying to choose from whatever is at hand to get things done, that is, to form a workable image of his body in the world he lives in "here and now." This act of *bricolage* is around the perception of the body. And the perception of the body is here simultaneously extroverted and introverted. It is extroverted when we take the body to be the agent of perception. In this case, we have the body with its built-in sensibility, open and often vulnerable to the sensation caused by unforeseen stimuli coming from without. In the case of the introverted body, we interpret it as the object of perception. This will eventually lead to questioning representability of even gestural language. For if passions are nothing but vibrations within the body, and if the nerves which transmit as well as retain those vibrations resonate, what will become of the predictability of human nature? Won't there be a danger of resonation going out of control? Can we still get the identifiable images of passions after we know that some very complex interactions are going on between the neural fibers within our body? Like the chaos theory of our age, will we able to see an island of order in the sea of confusion and unpredictability? These are the questions that Romanticism had to face after Garrick. The physiological discourse as epitomized in Garrick embraces within itself an element which foreshadows the shift from Neoclassicism to Romanticism, which may roughly be rephrased as the process of internalization.

Notes

1. The talk was given on 1 October 1995 in the Globe Tokyo.
2. See George Winchester Stone, Jr., "David Garrick's Significance in the History of Shakespearean Criticism: A Study of the Impact of the Actor upon the Change of Critical Focus during the Eighteenth Century," *PMLA* 65 (1950), 183–97 (184).
3. Arthur M. Wilson, "Sensibility in France in the Eighteenth Century: A Study in Word History," *French Quarterly* 13 (1931): 35–46.

4. Joseph W. Donohue, Jr., *Dramatic Character in the English Romantic Age* (Princeton: Princeton University Press, 1970), 27–28.

5. Oliver Goldsmith, *The Vicar of Wakefield* (1766), in *Collected Works of Oliver Goldsmith,* ed. Arthur Friedman, 5 vols. (Oxford: Clarendon, 1966), 4: 96.

6. David Hume, *A Treatise of Human Nature* (1739–40), ed. L. A. Selby-Bigge (1888); 2nd ed. P. H. Nidditch (Oxford: Oxford University Press, 1978), 75 (1.3.2).

7. For the importance of sensibility in acting as was propounded in the eighteenth century, and some theoretical problems this view caused, see Joseph R. Roach, *The Player's Passion: Studies in the Science of Acting* (Newark, Del.: University of Delaware Press, 1985), 98–115.

8. Roach, *The Player's Passion,* 65. Also see Aram Vartanian, *Diderot and Descartes: A Study of Scientific Naturalism in the Enlightenment* (Princeton: Princeton University Press, 1953) 203–88 (Chap. 4, "From Cartesian Mechanistic Biology to the Man-Machine and Evolutionary Materialism").

9. George S. Rousseau, "Science," in *The Context of English Literature: The Eighteenth Century,* ed. Pat Rogers (London: Methuen, 1978), 153–207. For the role Willis played not only in providing Locke with the physiological basis for his *Essay* but also in establishing the scientific paradigm (regardless of its veracity) for the eighteenth-century thinking in general, see Rousseau, "Nerves, Spirits, and Fibres: Towards Defining the Origins of Sensibility," *Blue Guitar* 2 (1976), 125–53.

10. See Alan S. Downer, "Nature to Advantage Dressed: Eighteenth-Century Acting," *PMLA* 58 (1943), 1002–37.

11. To the Countess of Burlington, 18 October 1750, *The Letters of David Garrick,* eds. David M. Little and George M. Kahrl, 3 vols. (London: Oxford University Press, 1963), 1: 158–59.

12. Georg Christoph Lichtenberg, *Lichtenberg's Visits to England as Described in His Letters and Diaries,* trans. and eds. Margaret L. Mare and W. H. Quarrell (Oxford: Clarendon Press, 1938), 10.

13. Brewster Rogerson, "The Art of Painting the Passions," *Journal of the History of Ideas* 14:1 (January 1953), 68.

14. G. J. Barker-Benfield, *The Culture of Sensibility: Sex and Society in Eighteenth-Century Britain* (Chicago: University of Chicago Press, 1992), 72.

15. John Gilbert Cooper, *Letters concerning Taste* (London: R. and J. Dodsley, 1755), 3.

16. Laurence Sterne, *The Life and Opinions of Tristram Shandy, Gentleman* (1759–67), ed. Ian Campbell Ross (Oxford: Clarendon, 1983), 143.

17. *Tristram Shandy,* 144.

18. *Letters of Laurence Sterne,* ed. L. P. Curtis (Oxford, 1935), 236 (to Garrick, 1765), and 157 (to Garrick, March 1762); also see John Mullen, *Sentiment and Sociability: The Language of Feeling in the Eighteenth Century* (Oxford: Clarendon Press, 1988), 175.

19. Barker-Benfield, *The Culture of Sensibility,* 298.

20. To Hall Hartson? 24 January 1762, *The Letters of David Garrick,* 1: 350.

21. *The Letters of David Garrick,* 1: 350. The scene referred to corresponds to *Hamlet,* 1.2.177, in *William Shakespeare: The Complete Works,* eds. Stanley Wells and Gary Taylor (Oxford: Clarendon, 1988).

22. Thomas Sheridan, *A Course of Lectures on Elocution: Together with Two Dissertations on Language; and Some Other Tracts Relative to Those Subjects,* new ed. (London: 1798), 137–39 (the edition referred to in this essay.)

23. *The Letters of David Garrick,* 1:350–51.

24. See George Winchester Stone, Jr. and George M. Kahrl, *David Garrick: A Critical Biography* (Carbondale: Southern Illinois University Press, 1979), 455.

25. Garrick to Francis Hayman, 18 August 1746, *The Letters of David Garrick,* 1: 82–83.

26. Gotthold Ephraim Lessing, *Hamburg Dramaturgy* (1767), trans. Helen Zimmerman (New York: Dover, 1962), 19.

27. Roger Pickering, *Reflections upon Theatrical Expression in Tragedy* (London: W. Johnston, 1755), 50.

28. Pickering, *Reflections,* 51.

29. The English translation was titled *The Conference of Monsieur Le Brun, chief Painter to the French King, Chancellor and Director of the Academy of Painting and Sculpture, upon Expression, General and Particular* (London: 1701).

30. See *Conference of Monsieur Le Brun,* 3–4.

31. *Lebrun's Passions Delineated in a Series of Nineteen Studies, Admirably Adapted for Students, and All Who Wish to Read the Various Expressions of the Human Face* (London: William Tegg, 1863).

32. See W. J. T. Mitchell, *Iconology: Image, Text, Ideology* (Chicago: University of Chicago Press, 1986), 7–46.

33. Hume, *Treatise,* 64 (1.2.5).

34. See "The Pleasures of the Imagination," *Spectator,* 411–421 (1712). For Addison's videocentrism, see for example Walter John Hipple, Jr., *The Beautiful, the Sublime and the Picturesque in Eighteenth-Century British Aesthetic Theory* (Carbondale: Southern Illinois University Press, 1957), 13–24.

35. How the Cartesian premise of the animal spirit developed into the theory of nerve vibration is concisely explained by Roach. See *The Player's Passion,* 104–9.

36. Charles Bell, *The Anatomy and Philosophy of Expression as Connected with the Fine Arts* (1804), 3rd ed. (London: John Murry, 1844), 83.

37. Hume, *Treatise,* 575 (3.3.1).

38. Louis de Cahusac, "Geste," in *Encyclopédie, ou Dictionnaire raisonnée des sciences, des arts et des métiers,* eds. Denis Diderot and Jean Le Rond D'Alembert, 17 vols. (Paris: Briasson, 1751–65), 7: 651–52 (1757). My translation.

39. David Garrick, *An Essay on Acting: In which will be consider'd the Mimical Behaviour of a Certain Fashionable Faulty Actor, and the Laudableness of Such Unmannerly, as Well as Inhuman Proceedings. To Which will be Added, A Short Criticism of his Acting Macbeth* (London: W. Bickerton, 1744), 5.

40. *An Essay on Acting,* 9–10.

41. To Helfrich Peter Sturz, 3 January 1769, *The Letters of David Garrick,* 2: 635.

Individuality in Johnson's Shakespeare Criticism

NORIYUKI HARADA

1

KENNETH Burke propounds his conception of "circumference" in *A Grammar of Motives* as an effective method of understanding the "dramatism" of human behavior and thought. According to his explanation, "circumferences" are the "contexts of varying scope," with which one can place a subject in a certain position for definition or interpretation. He says that one should be always on the alert for "relationships between the circumference and the 'circumfered'," because "one must implicitly or explicitly select a circumference" and the choice of circumference "will have a corresponding effect upon the interpretation of the act itself."[1]

Conceptions of individuality and universality in literature are inseparably connected with the difference of the circumference which authors provide for their subject matter in order to realize their literary ideal. When a writer conceives the wide circumference which covers the whole society or universe and intends to describe an individual person as a part of the whole, the dichotomy of individuality and universality, or rather the priority of universality over individuality, is observable in the work. However, for the writer who emphasizes the inner world within an individual person and narrows the circumference from the whole universe to an individual, universality is merged into individuality and the psychology of an individual person becomes significant.

The change of author's view from universality to individuality, or reduction of the circumference, may account for the transition from neoclassicism to romanticism in the second half of the eighteenth century and the early nineteenth century. When authors consider human nature to be intrinsically fixed and limited within tradition and organization and choose the wide circumference, universal regularity surrounding individual persons and their society is preserved and their works are generally called classical. In contrast with this, when authors believe in the infinite possibilities of man and pay intense attention to an individual within the narrow circumference, tradition and organization are merged into individuality and the authors' achievements are classified as romanticism.[2] And thus, as a possible explanation, one may say that a motivating force of the transition is the authors' inclination to reduce their circumference from universality to individuality.

This might be applied to the variation in relative importance of individual characters in Shakespearean criticism at the time. On the one hand, when a critic holds the wide, neoclassical circumference and comprehensively appreciates the world described by Shakespeare, his attention to the characters' individuality recedes behind universality. On the other hand, when a romantic critic narrows the focus to individual characters, he seeks universality within each character's individuality; the external world is reduced to the reflected image of each character's mind. If, as D. Nichol Smith precisely states, "the third quarter of the eighteenth century" is "the true period of transition in Shakespearean criticism,"[3] the transition is undoubtedly due to the new critical attention to Shakespeare's characters and their individuality.

Attention to Shakespeare's individual characters does appear before the period. As early as 1679, John Dryden, touching on Shakespeare's character sketch in his "Containing the Grounds of Criticism in Tragedy," says that "no man ever drew so many characters, or generally distinguished 'em better from one another."[4] In 1725, Alexander Pope, praising Shakespeare's description of nature, refers to his character sketch in the preface to his edition of The Works of Shakespear. "His [Shakespeare's] *Characters*," he says, "are so much Nature her self," and so "every single character in *Shakespear* . . . is as much as Individual as those in Life itself; it is as impossible to find any two alike: and such as from their relation or affinity in any respect appear most to be Twins, will upon comparison be found remarkably distinct." He goes so far as to say that "had all the Speeches been printed without the very names of the Persons, I believe one might have apply'd them with certainty to every speaker."[5]

However, it is certain that the new critical attitude reaches full strength in "the third quarter of the eighteenth century." In 1753, Joseph Warton in an essay in The Adventurer discusses Shakespeare's plays and reduces the "characteristical excellencies" to the three qualities: "his lively creative imagination; his strokes of nature and passion; and his preservation of the consistency of his characters."[6] George Lyttelton, focusing his attention on Shakespeare's distinctive character sketch, says in his *Dialogues of the Dead* (1760) that Shakespeare "painted all characters . . . with equal truth and equal force" and "if human nature were destroyed, and no monument were left of it except his works, other beings might know *what man was* from those writings."[7] In his *Elements of Criticism* (1762), Lord Kames asserts the importance of the character sketch and points out Shakespeare's excellence in this respect: "To draw a character is the master-stroke of description. . . . [Shakespeare] exceeds Tacitus in the sprightliness of his figures: some characteristical circumstance is generally invented or laid hold of, which paints more to the life than many words."[8] Although his essays cannot escape blame for "unsubtlety of much of their analysis,"[9] William Richardson early offers a psychological explanation for some remarkable characters from Shakespeare's plays.[10] Following this, we have Maurice Morgann's *Essay on Dramatic Character of Sir John Falstaff* (1777), one of the most excellent criticisms of a Shakespearean character. Thomas Whately's *Remarks on Some of the Characters of Shakespeare* was published in 1785; in it he strongly states the importance of examining the characters in Shakespearean criticism: "there is, within the colder provinces of judgment and knowledge, a subject for criticism, more worthy of attention than the common topics of discussion: I mean the distinction and preservation of *character*."[11] Of course, each critic's focus, method or strain differs. Richardson, employing the concept of "ruling passion," aims to explicate humanity of inhuman characters in the tragedies, while Morgann, with his deep insight into Falstaff's psychology, asserts Falstaff to be a man of "natural courage," instead of sharing the popular view of his cowardice. As noted earlier, Warton comments on the "consistency" of Shakespeare's character as one of the three "characteristical excellencies," while Whately firmly regards Shakespeare's character sketch as the only subject "more worthy of attention than the common topic of discussion." But it is obvious that critical attention to Shakespeare's individual characters and their individuality, as a whole, increases in magnitude during the period and after.

However, one cannot neglect the dominant critic at the time, whose critical principle has been regarded as the former neoclassical doctrine of regularity and universality and, therefore, as the most antagonistic critic to the new tendency. Samuel Johnson had a lifelong interest in Shakespeare and published remarkable works including his 1765 edition of Shakespeare, but, considering the tendency, it is quite natural that his generalization of Shakespeare's characters "excited much clamour against him."[12] In particular, his remarks in the preface to his edition were notorious. "In the writings of other poets," he asserts, "a character is too often an individual; in those of Shakespeare it is commonly a species."[13] This comment, which seems to the condense neoclassical view of limited individuality, immediately drew protests from his contemporaries. William Guthrie, for instance, contributed an essay to the *Critical Review* and complained, "Can any of Shakespeare's successful characters . . . be termed a species? or rather, do they not please by being oddities, or, if Mr. Johnson pleases, individuals?"[14] David Garrick, a former pupil of Johnson, was also "to the highest degree exasperated with Johnson," concerning the comment in the preface.[15]

More acrimonious criticism on Johnson's inclination to anti-individuality was brought out by the romantic critics after Johnson. Concurring with A. W. Schlegel's principle in *Lectures on Dramatic Art and Literature,* Samuel Taylor Coleridge devoted several lectures on Shakespeare to an attack on Johnson's "strangely overrated contradictory & most illogical Preface."[16] In the twelfth lecture at the London Philosophical Society, he, discussing the character sketch of Hamlet, asserted that "Dr. Johnson did not understand the character of Hamlet."[17] William Hazlitt also strongly opposed Johnson's view of the character's generality. In the preface to his *Characters of Shakespear's Plays,* he wrote:

> Thus he [Johnson] says of Shakespear's characters, in contradiction to what Pope had observed, and to what every one else feels, that each character is a species, instead of being an individual. He in fact found the general species or *didactic* form in Shakespear's characters, which was all he sought or cared for; he did not find the individual traits, or the *dramatic* distinctions which Shakespear has engrafted on this general nature, because he felt no interest in them.[18]

"Each individual," he says in another essay on Shakespeare, "is a world to himself. . . . I can, therefore, make no inference from one individual to another; nor can my habitual sentiments, with respect to any individual, extend beyond himself to others."[19] In contrast to Johnson's concept of "a species," Hazlitt never permits readers and critics of Shakespeare to generalize the characters, and pays his absolute attention to each character's individuality. In his view, one who reads Shakespeare must identify himself with the characters. In this he shares Charles Lamb's view that, "we see not Lear, but we are Lear."[20] We may say that absolute attention to individuality, or antagonism to Johnson, reaches the peak at this point.

However, admitting the romantic inclination to see a character's individuality, a reader of Shakespeare is still himself and not a character. We can see Lear and sympathize with Lear, but we cannot be Lear; we are our own individual selves. This deadlock seems to be inherent in romanticism itself and I shall return to the question later. But first, what has to be noticed is that, contrary to his antagonists' assertion, Johnson, in reality, never does ignore the individual characters, nor generalize them recklessly. If one reads Johnson's Shakespeare criticisms—not only the preface but also the others—carefully, he will certainly discover Johnson's pendulum between each character's individuality and the universal regularity surrounding the individuals. In particular, as Arthur Sherbo already mentioned, the importance of his notes to the edition should not be overlooked, although, as Edward Tomarken recently pointed out, even today there is "little work that does not either ignore the *Notes* or subordinate selected remarks from them to the *Preface*."[21] Thus, in the next section, I will begin by casting light on Johnson's unique attention to the individual characters, examining his notes and other writings. Then, taking the literary tendency at the time into consideration, I will clarify what is the true difference between Johnson and his antagonists, and what is not. If what took place between Johnson and his antagonists is regarded not as a sort of improvement but as a mere change of scope, and the later romantic attention to individuality has limitations as well as the former neoclassical one, it is time to correct the distorted image of Johnson reflected on the romantic mirror and, as G. F. Parker says, "taking Johnson seriously" again is an important task.[22]

2

For this analysis of Johnson's criticism, two helpful points will be offered. The first concerns his historical sense, which plays an important role in his Shakespeare criticism as well as other writings; the second concerns his special remarks on the personages and his psychological description of them, which is nourished by his numerous biographical writings.

Johnson's historical sense has characteristic origins.[23] Throughout his life, he was sensitive to the antiquities and familiar with some antiquarians: Thomas Percy, Thomas Astle and John Nichols. It is true that he was always critical of pedantic antiquarianism, but, undoubtedly, he was always interested in tangible objects and individual facts which told history vividly. With respect to these objects and facts, he did not always force himself to abstract universality from them. He had an eye for historic facts as they were. In addition, he had another experience of confirming history tactually before he began editing Shakespeare: the experience of making the catalogue of the Harleian Library from 1743 to 1744. Cataloguing the collection, he had an opportunity to verify some medieval and early modern records and stories from their originals, in which some of the important sources of Shakespeare's plays were included.

He did not have any ambition to be a scholarly historian or antiquarian, however. What he aimed to be was a writer who could draw universality from individual facts and people in the past in order to appeal to the common reader. Making the catalogue of the Library was certainly a great task; however, it was a job for scholarly historians or antiquarians and far from his purpose. Editing and criticizing Shakespeare, on the other hand, appeared to be a reasonable way to realize his own literary ideal, because he thought that individual facts, events, and people in history were excellently unified in Shakespeare's plays and their universality was successfully expressed. Thus, he stopped the task of cataloguing at the halfway point in 1744 and shifted his attention to editing and criticizing Shakespeare in 1745. Although the 1745 edition was abandoned because of troubles over the copyright, this principle was preserved. Johnson was not satisfied with a pedantic and oversubtle explanation of history, nor with erroneous generalization of individual facts and people. What he wished to do was to show his contemporary readers true universality drawn from exact individuality.

Of course, it is true that his knowledge is limited and his historical investigation is insufficient. But his critical framework based on his historical sense should be noted; he is eager in making Elizabethan circumstances clear and, from the Elizabethan context, he tries to discuss the plays. In other words, he, examines the individuality of the Elizabethan age itself as observed in the plays and then goes on to explain the source or historical validity. This is why he makes an effort to give readers a proper historical knowledge of the age and distinguish what is common to every human society from what was peculiar to the age.

In fact, he often exercises this sort of historical sense in the notes to his edition of Shakespeare. For instance, in the long explanatory note to *Macbeth*, 1.1, he earnestly shows the appropriateness of Shakespeare's using supernatural witches, which are uncommon even to the eighteenth-century readers. He says:

> In order to make a true estimate of the abilities and merit of a writer, it is always necessary to examine the genius of his age, and the opinions of his contemporaries. . . . [A] survey of the notions that prevailed at the time when this play was written, will prove that Shakespeare was in no danger of such censures, since he only turned the system that was then universally admitted to his advantage, and was far from over-burthening the credulity of his audience.[24]

He then comments on Shakespeare's historical validity in demonocracy, referring to Photius's *Bibliotheca,* St. Chrysostom's *De Sacerdotio* and King James's *Daemonologie.* Finally he mentions:

> Upon this general infatuation Shakespeare might be easily allowed to found a play, especially since he has followed with great exactness such histories as were then thought true; nor can it be doubted that the scenes of enchantment, however they may now be ridiculed, were both by himself and his audience thought awful and affection.[25]

The note to *Macbeth,* 4.1, the infernal scene, is also expository:

> As this is the chief scene of inchantment in the play, it is proper in this place to observe, with how much judgment Shakespeare has selected all the circumstances of his infernal ceremonies, and how exactly he has conformed to common opinions and traditions.[26]

Johnson's interpretation that Shakespeare did not make a display of his eccentricity far from the real history can be found in the other notes as well. It is safe to say that, by placing Shakespeare's plays in the Elizabethan context, he tries to examine the meaning of the individual characters and events.

As a general rule, this objective distance from the historical point of view is weak in its romantic attention to the individual characters. Romantic critics are always eager to identify themselves with the characters regardless of the distance. Thus, in some cases, their excessive appreciation of the characters may fail to understand the real meaning of the description in the Elizabethan context. For instance, in the note to *Hamlet,* 3.3, in which Hamlet spares the king because he finds the king at prayer and thus safe from damnation,[27] Coleridge, strongly opposing Johnson's comment on the scene, points out, "Dr. Johnson's mistaking of the marks of reluctance and procrastination for impetuous, horror-striking fiendish-

ness!"[28] And then, as mentioned above, he asserts that "Dr.
Johnson did not understand the character of Hamlet." On the other
hand, Johnson's note to this scene reads as follows: "[Hamlet's]
speech, in which Hamlet, represented as virtuous character, is not
content with taking blood for blood, but contrives damnation for
the man that he would punish, is too horrible to be read or to be
uttered."[29] On the face of it, Johnson's comment shows his lack of
insight into Hamlet's psychology and fails to catch the sentiment
of the character. However, taking his historical knowledge of the
Elizabethan audience's common response to the scene into consideration, one finds that the reverse is the case. For, as Elmer Edgar
Stoll points out, "Dr Johnson is nearer to the Elizabethans on this
point than Coleridge, who did not have the general knowledge of
Elizabethan literature which was necessary to support historical
criticism, though he preached the historical point of view."[30] In this
sense, one may go so far as to say that Johnson tries to understand
Shakespeare's uniqueness or even eccentricity as the first step
toward judging the plays properly, whether he is in favor of it or
not, while Coleridge blindly admires the reality of Shakespeare's
character sketch without ascertaining what is unique and what
is bombastic in the Elizabethan circumstances. This means that
Coleridge might risk the danger of mistaking his own interpretation
for Shakespeare's original design.

In general, the difference of purpose between Johnson and the
romantic critics including Coleridge—the difference between an
inclination to the universality of the plays and particular attention
to the individual characters—is caused by the difference in their
points of view. However, if, through worship of Shakespeare, the
romantic critics tend to identify themselves with the individual
characters so excessively that they do not always base their criticism on enough consideration of the Elizabethan atmosphere, their
attention to the characters is open to the criticism of being fictitious
or self-complacent. At least, one can say that, though Johnson laid
stress on universality rather than individuality, this does not mean
he was ignorant of the individuality of each character. Instead, it is
the result of his acute awareness of the historical distance between
Shakespeare and the eighteenth century reader.

As to this distance, Johnson's historical sense is interwoven with
his view of life writing and character sketch. He never forgets the
distance between an author and a character. Or rather, as a critic
of Shakespeare, he was always aware of the two kinds of distance:
the one is between each character and Shakespeare, the other is
between Shakespeare's description and Johnson himself. When

one who reads Shakespeare identifies himself with a character, he, having worshiped the omnipotent author, merges into the plays and the characters. However, Johnson does not approve of this "passive capability." Instead, he strictly tries to focus his attention on the merits and the demerits of Shakespeare's character sketch and draw from it the universality which had wide application to eighteenth-century readers. He persists in being not an admirer, but a critic.

This sense of distance can be clearly observed in his preface. He recognizes that the drama is not a real world, but "a just picture of a real original," which represents "to the auditor what he would himself feel, if he were to do or suffer what is there feigned to be suffered or to be done."[31] Holding on to this objective distance, he says:

> The reflection that strikes the heart is not, that the evils before us are real evils, but that they are evils to which we ourselves may be exposed. If there be any fallacy, it is not that we fancy the players, but that we fancy ourselves unhappy for a moment; but we rather lament the possibility than suppose the presence of misery, as a mother weeps over her babe, when she remembers that death may take it from her.[32]

Then he approves of Shakespeare's rejection of the unities of time and place, which "arise evidently from false assumptions,"[33] because "the spectators are always in their senses, and know, from the first act to the last, that the stage is only a stage, and that the players are only players."[34] Johnson never does blindly adhere to classical laws and regularity; instead, he has the freedom to appreciate Shakespeare's uniqueness in character sketch and dramaturgy by preserving the objective distance.

This may account for his perceptive comments even on some characters whom the romantic critics hardly have interest in or entirely ignore. Even if a critic feels no sympathy with a character, or he cannot recognize "poetic language" in the character's speech, the critic should take the character's existence in the play into account, because it has the possibility of providing a clue to the secret of the dramaturgy or of the author's scope in writing. Although the comments based on this attitude often seem to be dull or trivial, Johnson dares not delete them from his notes. For instance, contrary to Coleridge whose reference to Falstaff is strangely weak and unsympathetic, Johnson's comment on the character is worth regarding.[35] And also any reference to such minor characters as Lennox and "another Lord" in *Macbeth*, for whom Johnson has regard in the note to his edition, cannot be seen in Coleridge's criticism, nor in Hazlitt's.[36]

Concerning Johnson's attention to the characters, what has to be noticed first is the objective distance observed in his critical mind. However, this does not mean he is indifferent to the psychological description of the characters. Instead, he has an eye for it, insofar as it is a "just picture of a real original."

In fact, his insight into the psychology of a character or a person, connected with his biographical writings, was cultivated early in his career. In *Life of Savage,* which was published just before he started preparing the 1745 edition of Shakespeare, he, examining Savage's psychology, intended to describe his own personality which appealed to the common readers. This principle is often referred to in the *Rambler* essays and later in *Rasselas.* "The business of a poet," he says in *Rasselas,* "is to examine, not the individual, but the species; to remark general properties and large appearances" and "exhibit in his portraits of nature such prominent and striking features, as recall the original to every mind." And then he goes on to say that an author "must neglect the minuter discriminations, which one may have remarked, and another have neglected, for those characteristicks which are alike obvious to vigilance and carelessness."[37]

This statement, as well as the one in the preface mentioned previously, should not be regarded as the expression of Johnson's ignorance of the individuality of the characters. It is because, when Johnson says in the preface that Shakespeare "holds up to his readers a faithful mirror of manners and of life,"[38] Johnson should perceive Shakespeare observes the variation and mutability of manners and life in detail and draws universality from individual matters in order to hold up "a faithful mirror." As a critic, Johnson certainly pays attention to the life and manner of an individual character as a basis for the universality which he aims for. Thus, attention to each character's psychology is indispensable for Johnson as well as the romantic critics.

For instance, in the note to *Macbeth,* 1. 7, in which Lady Macbeth persuades her husband to murder Duncan and take the throne for himself, Johnson penetrates both characters' psychology and describes what common readers can apply to their own lines:

> She urges the excellence and dignity of courage, a glittering idea which has dazzled mankind from age to age, and animated sometimes the housebreaker, and sometimes the conqueror; but this sophism Macbeth

has for ever destroyed by distinguishing true from false fortitude, in a line and a half. . . .

> I dare do all that may become a man,
> Who dares do more is none.

This topic . . . is used in this scene with peculiar propriety, to a soldier by a woman. Courage is the distinguishing virtue of a soldier, and the reproach of cowardice cannot be borne by any man from a woman, without great impatience.

She then urges the oaths by which he had bound himself to murder Duncan, another art of sophistry by which men have sometimes deluded their consciences, and persuaded themselves that what would be criminal in others is virtuous in them. . . .[39]

Johnson likens his reading to Shakespeare's own observation of human nature and mentions at the beginning of the note: "The arguments [of Lady Macbeth and Macbeth] . . . afford a proof of Shakespeare's knowledge of human nature."[40] Similarly, in the note to *Macbeth*, 2.1, which refers to Macbeth's soliloquy just before murdering Duncan, Johnson comments:

Macbeth has . . . disturbed his imagination by enumerating all the terrors of the night. . . . As he is going to say of what, he discovers the absurdity of his suspicion, and pauses, but is again overwhelmed by his guilt, and concludes, that such are the horrors of the present night, that the stones may be expected to cry out against him. . . .

He observes . . . that on such occasions "stones have been known to move." It is now a very just and strong picture of a man about to commit a deliberate murder under the strongest convictions of the wickedness of his design.[41]

Instead of scholarly annotation, Johnson intends to penetrate Macbeth's psychology and show "human nature" which is in common with the readers. As far as the emphasis on a character's inner world is concerned, this attitude is similar to the romantic one. But Johnson is strictly analytical and independent of a character, while the romantic faith in the character sketch often leads to sympathy for a character and worship of Shakespeare. If the romantic critics need "passive capability" to understand the psychology of a character, Johnson's criticism refuses it and requires "active capability" instead.

3

From the above analysis of Johnson's historical sense and his closeness to the character's psychology, one can naturally find that

Johnson does not always think lightly of the character's individuality. On the other hand, one can also conclude that the romantic
critics' absolute attention to individuality, or their worship of
Shakespeare's character sketch, does not always catch the essence
of individuality. For Johnson, it is only through minute observation
of individual facts and people that an author can draw universality,
and, therefore, he cannot but pay enough attention to individuality
as well as universality. Johnson's antagonists assert first the importance of individuality, but, because of their excessive sympathy
with their favorite characters or their blind admiration for Shakespeare, they sometimes overlook the Elizabethan context and
sometimes cannot escape partiality in the study of a character's
individuality.

As a satisfactory explanation for this difference, one can say
that Johnson and his antagonists differ in respect to the sense of
the distance between the critic himself and Shakespeare's plays.
Johnson always tries to observe the plays from a distance and
explain them as objects of criticism, while his antagonists, especially the romantic critics, intend to reduce the distance and identify themselves with a character, relying on the omnipotent author.
In romantic criticism, the circumference is narrowed to the individuality of a character, and even the critic's self becomes imma-
nent in the character. In his criticism he moves with the characters
as if he himself were one of them. In this sense, individuality means
both the character's and the critic's.

Two questions now arise. One is about the universality Johnson
conceives. As a matter of course, the universality Johnson conceives is, after all, Johnson's, and not another's. Fundamentally,
universality should be applied equally to everything and everyone,
but, as far as it is a creation of an individual person, it is doubtful
whether such universality is really possible. Johnson's answer to
this problem is not necessarily theoretical; he often leaves the final
judgment on his writing and criticism to time. In the preface to his
Dictionary, he confesses that "whether I shall add any thing by
my own writings to the reputation of English literature must be
left to time."[42] This attitude can be observed in his criticism of
Shakespeare. "To works . . . of which the excellence is not absolute and definite, but gradual and comparative; to works not raised
upon principles demonstrative and scientifick, but appealing
wholly to observation and experience," he says in the preface to his
edition of Shakespeare, "no other test can be applied than length of
duration and continuance of esteem."[43] As to this attitude and his
characteristic consciousness of time, there is room for argument.

But to inquire further into this matter would undoubtedly obscure the outline of our argument.

For the present, it may be more useful to look at the second question: the problem of universality which is merged into individuality. As mentioned above, we can see Lear and sympathize with Lear, but we cannot be Lear insofar as we have our own individual selves. Thus, if one respects his own individuality, he cannot perfectly identify himself with a character because he is, of course, different from the character. And if the romantic critics wish to transcend this deadlock, their belief in individuality should be universalized beyond the framework of an individual. Concerning this problem, the romantic critics seem to have made a compromise, as Walter Jackson Bate already remarked. Referring to Coleridge's theory of imagination and his Shakespeare criticism, he explains the "compromising spirit" of English romanticism: "Through a brilliant eclecticism, he [Coleridge] tried to establish at least a theoretical mutual dependence between particular and universal by maintaining the vital ferment of potentiality inherent in the former and its organic transmutaion into the latter."[44] Thus, for Coleridge, Shakespeare "did not merely abstract generalizations from his knowledge of specific individuals: rather, in addition to this secondary and merely assisting process, he grasped the living force, the law and active thread of connection, which binds the specific with the general."[45] This compromising spirit which preserves the "precarious and at bottom loosely empirical balance between the ideal and the concrete,"[46] is susprisingly similar to Johnson's pendulum between individuality and universality. The only difference is the starting point; Coleridge, as well as the other romantic critics, starts from an individual, while Johnson conceives the dichotomy from the first. And it should not be overlooked that to start from an individual often means to start from an explication of the critic's own imagination about the characters, not from an examination of them.

Needless to say, the accomplishments of the romantic critics should be greatly appreciated. It is especially important to bear in mind that, internalizing universality which was rather abstractly argued in the neoclassical period, they base their criteria on their own individuality and on individual characters in literary works. But, as the resulting compromise shows, the advisability of their circumference remains a matter for debate. The universality which Johnson conceives is certainly Johnson's own; nevertheless, a glimpse of true universality, which cannot be observed in the romantic view, is still read in his works.

I do not approve of T. E. Hulme's discussion and prediction, in which he, referring to a vital difference between romanticism and classicism, mentions that "a romantic movement must have an end."[47] But, after the prosperous period of romantic Shakespeare criticism which lasted until the early twentieth century, it is time to reexamine the difference between Johnson and his antagonists carefully, because something that the romantic critics set aside or purposely ignored may be concealed therein. In particular, Johnson's characteristic treatment of individuals—his objective distance from Shakespeare and the characters, and his universality drawn from individual characters—will certainly give readers a key to a new perspective on Shakespeare.

Notes

1. Kenneth Burke, *A Grammar of Motives* (California: University of California Press, 1969), 77–78.

2. As to this view of neoclassicism and romanticism, T. E. Hulme's "Romanticism and Classicism" provided an insight, although my argument in this paper is entirely different from his. See T. E. Hulme, *The Collected Writings of T. E. Hulme*, ed. Karen Csengeri (Oxford: Clarendon Press, 1994), 59–73.

3. D. Nichol Smith, Introduction to *Eighteenth Century Essays on Shakespeare*, ed. D. Nichol Smith (Oxford: Clarendon Press, 1963), xxxii.

4. John Dryden, "The Grounds of Criticism in Tragedy" in the Preface to *Troilus and Cressida, The Works of John Dryden*, 20 vols. (Berkeley: University of California Press, 1956–89), 8 : 239.

5. Alexander Pope, Preface to *The Works of Shakespeare*, ed. Alexander Pope (London: printed for Jacob Tonson, 1725), 1 : 2–3.

6. Joseph Warton's essay, "On Shakespeare's Characterization," in *Adventurer*, 25 September 1753. See *The Adventurer*, 2 vols. (London: Payne, 1754; reprint, New York : AMS, 1968), 1 : 134.

7. George Lyttelton's *Dialogues of the Dead* is quoted in *Shakespeare: The Critical Heritage*, ed. Brian Vickers, 6 vols. (London: Routledge, 1973–81), 4 : 411.

8. Henry Home, Lord Kames, *Elements of Criticism*, 3 vols. (Edinburgh: Miller, 1762), 3 : 182.

9. G. F. Parker, *Johnson's Shakespeare* (Oxford: Clarendon Press, 1989), 181.

10. William Richardson's essays on Shakespeare, including *Philosophical Analysis and Illustration of Some of the Characters of Shakespeare*, are quoted in *Shakespeare: The Critical Heritage*, 6: 118–24, 208–11, 351–70, 490–99, 627–28.

11. Thomas Whately, *Remarks on Some of the Characters of Shakespeare*, 2nd ed. (Oxford: Parker, 1808), 2.

12. James Boswell, *The Life of Samuel Johnson, LL. D.*, ed. George Birkbeck Hill, rev. L. F. Powell (Oxford: Clarendon Press, 1934–64), 1 : 499.

13. Samuel Johnson, Preface to the 1765 edition, *Johnson on Shakespeare*, ed. Arthur Sherbo, Yale Edition of the *Works of Samuel Johnson*, vol. 7, 8 (New Haven: Yale University Press, 1968), 7: 62.

14. Guthrie's criticism is quoted in *Shakespeare: The Critical Heritage*, 5: 214.

15. John Hawkins, *The Life of Dr. Samuel Johnson,* ed. Bertram H. Davis (London: Cape, 1962), 442.

16. E. L. Griggs, ed., *Collected Letters of S. T. Coleridge,* 6 vols. (Oxford: Clarendon Press, 1956–71), 4: 642.

17. Samuel Taylor Coleridge, *Shakespearean Criticism,* ed. Thomas Middleton Raysor, 2 vols. (London: Dent, 1960), 2: 153.

18. William Hazlitt, *The Complete Works of William Hazlitt,* ed. P. P. Howe, 21 vols., Centenary Edition (London: Cass, 1967), 4: 176. It is obvious from this comment that Pope's criticism on Shakespeare's characters has an influence on the romantic critics, although some important differences between Pope and the later critics should not be neglected. In a sense, the reception of Pope is a romantic transformation of his key words and ideas. For instance, when he says that Shakespeare's "characters are so much Nature her self," he implies by the word "Nature" the whole unity, or "Nature methodiz'd," but this implication is ignored in the romantic critics. See his "An Essay on Criticism" in *Pope: Poetical Works,* ed. Herbert Davis (Oxford: Oxford University Press, 1966), line 89.

19. Hazlitt, *Complete Works,* 4: 19.

20. Charles Lamb, *The Works of Charles and Mary Lamb,* ed. E. V. Lucas, 7 vols. (London: Methuen, 1903–5), 1: 107.

21. Edward Tomarken, *Samuel Johnson on Shakespeare: The Discipline of Criticism* (Athens: University of Georgia Press, 1991), 6. See also Arthur Sherbo, *Samuel Johnson, Editor of Shakespeare* (Urbana: University of Illinois Press, 1956), 62.

22. G. F. Parker, *Johnson's Shakespeare,* 1.

23. As to Johnson's sense of history throughout his career, see John A. Vance, *Samuel Johnson and the Sense of History* (Athens: University of Georgia Press, 1984).

24. Johnson, *Johnson on Shakespeare,* 8: 752. As far as Johnson's notes to *Macbeth* are concerned, specific circumstances should be considered, because, apart from some revisions in the later editions, there is a distinct version: the notes to the abandoned 1745 edition, published as *Miscellaneous Observations on the Tragedy of Macbeth.* But, all the references to the text of the notes in this paper are taken from the notes to the 1765 edition which have not been altered since the 1745 edition. See also *Johnson on Shakespeare,* 7: 3–45.

25. Johnson, *Johnson on Shakespeare,* 8: 755.

26. Ibid., 8: 783.

27. In the original, Hamlet says: "Then trip him, that his [Claudius'] heels may kick at heaven / And that his soul may be as damn'd and black / As hell, whereto it goes" (3.3.93–95). The text quoted is from William Shakespeare, *The Arden Shakespeare: Hamlet,* ed. Harold Jenkins (London: Methuen, 1982), 318.

28. Coleridge, *Shakespearean Criticism,* 1: 29–30.

29. Johnson, *Johnson on Shakespeare,* 8: 990.

30. Stoll's comment is quoted in the note to Coleridge's "Notes on the Tragedies of Shakespeare" in *Shakespearean Criticism,* 1: 30. See also Elmer Edgar Stoll, "Hamlet: An Historical and Comparative Study," *University of Minnesota Studies in Language and Literature* 7 (Minneapolis: University of Minnesota Press, 1919).

31. Johnson, *Johnson on Shakespeare,* 7: 78.

32. Ibid., 7: 78.

33. Ibid., 7: 79.

34. Ibid., 7: 77.

35. G. F. Parker, comparing Coleridge's comment on Falstaff with Johnson's, states that "Johnson's Falstaff is so dangerous because we cannot help but warm to him even while we see him for what he is; Coleridge, by contrast, can and does refrain from such dangerous sympathy." See G. F. Parker, *Johnson's Shakespeare*, 87. Coleridge's response to Falstaff is also distinct from Schlegel's and Hazlitt's sympathetic explanation. So, from this topic, one may point out any distinction between Coleridge and the other romantic critics. But, because the distinction is inseparably connected with the variety of romanticism itself, the fuller study of it lies outside the scope of this paper, and I would prefer to leave the details to another occasion.

36. In the note to *Macbeth*, 3. 6, Johnson, taking effective dramaturgy into consideration, points out the excess of the personages. See Johnson, *Johnson on Shakespeare*, 8: 783. He certainly pays enough attention even to such minor characters. A possible explanation for Johnson's minute attention may be that he was acutely aware of Shakespeare's dramaturgy as a model of his own dramatic writing, at least in his early career. But after the failure of *Irene*, his only dramatic work published and performed in 1749, he becomes reticent concerning this awareness of dramaturgy as a dramatist, although subtle traces can be still observed in his Shakespeare criticisms in his middle and late years.

37. Johnson, *Rasselas and Other Tales*, ed. Gwin J. Kolb, Yale Edition of the *Works of Samuel Johnson*, vol. 16 (New Haven: Yale University Press, 1990), 43–44.

38. Johnson, *Johnson on Shakespeare*, 7: 62.

39. Ibid., 8: 767.

40. Ibid., 8: 767.

41. Ibid., 8: 771–72.

42. Johnson, Preface to *A Dictionary of the English Dictionary* (London: printed by W. Strahan for J. and P. Knapton, et al., 1755), n. p.

43. Johnson, *Johnson on Shakespeare*, 7: 59–60.

44. Walter Jackson Bate, *From Classic to Romantic: Premises of Taste in Eighteenth–Century England* (Cambridge, Mass.: Harvard University Press, 1949), 184.

45. Ibid., 185.

46. Ibid., 184.

47. T. E. Hulme, "Romanticism and Classicism," *The Collected Writings of T. E. Hulme*, 72.

Contributors

NORIYUKI HARADA is Associate Professor at Kyorin University in Tokyo. His primary interest is Dr. Johnson and his works.

MARIKO ICHIKAWA is Associate Professor at Ibaraki University in Mito. She is studying the Shakespearean stage.

ARATA IDE is Associate Professor at Toyo Eiwa College in Yokohama and teaches Renaissance drama.

SOJI IWASAKI is Professor of English at Nanzan University in Nagoya. He is the author of *The Sword and the Word: Shakespeare's Tragic Sense of Time* (1973) and *Shakespeare and Iconology* (1994).

YOSHIKO KAWACHI is Professor of English at Kyorin University in Tokyo. She is the author of *Calendar of English Renaissance Drama: 1558–1642* (1986) and *Shakespeare and Cultural Exchange* (1995), and the editor of *Shakespeare Worldwide: Translation and Adaptation.*

SHOICHIRO KAWAI is Associate Professor at the University of Tokyo. He is working on a study of costuming in Shakespearean plays.

AKIKO KUSUNOKI is Professor of English at Tokyo Women's Christian University and the author of *Rebellious Women in English Renaissance Drama and Society* (forthcoming). She is writing a book on women writers in the English Renaissance.

TED MOTOHASHI is Associate Professor at Tokyo Metropolitan University and teaches English literature. He is currently doing research into post-colonialism, the discourse of cannibalism, and the formation of modern Japanese nationhood.

MANABU NODA teaches English at Tokyo Medical and Dental University. He is working on a study of the eighteenth-century British theater.

MIKI SUEHIRO teaches English literature at Tokyo Metropolitan University. He is completing research into Renaissance drama and contemporary literary history.

YUKARI YOSHIHARA teaches English language and literature at Chikushi Jogakuen Junior College for Women in Fukuoka. She is studying on Shakespearean texts and Japanese adaptations.

Index

215